Sex differences in human communication

Sex differences in human communication

Barbara Westbrook Eakins
   The Ohio State University

R. Gene Eakins
   Wright State University

Houghton Mifflin Company   Boston
      Dallas   Geneva, Ill.   Hopewell, N.J.
      Palo Alto   London

Printed in the U.S.A.

Library of Congress Catalog Card Number: 77-77660
ISBN: 0-395-25510-4

Illustrations by Nancy Lawton

Contents

3 Why can't a woman be more like a man? communication between the sexes 57

4 Sex patterns in sound 82

5 When words speak louder than people: the language of gender 111

6 Silent sounds and secret messages 147

Preface

A marriage of purposes

This book is a result of our mutual interest in the subject of communication and the sexes and of our personal enjoyment in doing things together, both on a private and professional level. Being married has not made the project any easier; but neither has it, we suspect, added more difficulties. What it has done is to give us together a more balanced view than we might have had individually. In writing and working through our materials we have become more acutely aware of ourselves, both as sexual and as androgynous beings. At times it has been disconcerting or amusing to see distillations of ourselves in the research findings—disconcerting when it has been oneself, amusing when it has been one's mate.

We do not pretend to have the last word on questions of sex differences in communication. Certainly there are many individual differences in communication; neither all women nor all men are alike, nor can their communication characteristics be categorized in terms of sex alone. But research has uncovered some interesting trends in differences between the sexes, and many of those differences appear to have little basis in biology or innate sex differences.

An important assumption of this book is that human communication skills and abilities can be described and codified. If they can be described and codified, they can be taught. And if they can be taught, human communication behavior can be modified. Undoubtedly there is no one perfect model of communication interaction that needs only to be discovered and applied without fear of failure. The models we use will differ with our personalities, as well as with our culture and our times. We are, however, working under the assumption that all of us, male and female, will do a better job of managing our communication habits after we have examined the verbal and nonverbal behaviors that compose them.

Once we have familiarized ourselves with (1) the different ways our language deals with the sexes, (2) the different ways some females and males use words, (3) differences in verbal interaction among the sexes, and (4) some nonverbal communication differences, we can better appreciate the elements underlying some of the problems in our relationships. Perhaps then we shall be better prepared to work through the difficulties that human communication differences inevitably produce. With more insight into our own communication behavior, we may be able to devise new and better ways of relating to one another in our ever changing world.

We believe that this textbook can be used as an enrichment to a variety of different courses in human communication, whether it be a basic course or a course in male-female communication. Instructors in women's studies should find this book a particularly appropriate text.

What this project has done for us, we hope it will do for our readers: raise doubts about everyday communication behaviors and beliefs that we take for granted. Socrates said, "An unexamined life is not worth living." It is our ambition that the material in the succeeding chapters will make an examination of ourselves and of our interactions with others meaningful, stimulating, and challenging.

B.W.E.
R.G.E.

Acknowledgments

We wish to thank the following people for their encouragement and helpful criticism in preparing the manuscript: John Baird, University of Michigan; Larry Coleman, University of Texas; Joyce Frost, University of Montana; Bonnie Johnson, Pennsylvania State University; Jo Sprague, California State University at San Jose; and Linda St. Clair, State University of New York at Albany.

We also wish to acknowledge the help of our six children, Alan, Gene, Diane, Dawn, Faith, and Keith Eakins, who supplied some of our most colorful examples and who were among our severest critics. A special note of thanks goes to Dawn, who supplied some of the preliminary artwork.

To the many colleagues and friends from whom we got ideas, encouragement, and help during the formative stages of this project, we say "Thank you." These include Nancy Henley, Cheris Kramer, Robin Lakoff, Bonnie Ritter-Patton, Robert Pruett, William E. Arnold, and Eugene Cantelupe.

We especially want to thank the administration and staff of Arizona State University for their whole-hearted cooperation and support.

Finally, we wish to express our gratitude to the two secretaries, Cledith Johnson and Patty Norris, who cheerfully prepared the numerous drafts of the manuscript.

Sex differences in human communication

1 The sexes: discriminations without differences and differences that discriminate

You are woman. I am man.
You are smaller, so I can be taller than.
You are softer to the touch.
It's a feeling I like feeling very much.
—Bob Merrill and Jule Styne[1]

These lyrics from a song Omar Sharif sang to Barbra Streisand in the movie *Funny Girl* say something about our feelings about being a man or a woman in today's society. Although Barbra Streisand does not respond by singing a lyrical analogue from the woman's point of view, the viewer senses her acceptance of the two differing gender profiles.

What does it mean to be a woman or a man in our society? Often it does indeed mean a physical difference in height, in girth, in weight, and in firmness of muscle tissue. Sometimes, however, the female may have the advantage in size and strength, and the male may be smaller, lighter, and softer to the touch. But being female or male can have a significance that carries beyond physical features. It can mean, as we shall read later:

- A man curses; a woman uses euphemisms such as *fudge*.
- A man shouts in anger; a woman counts to 10 or weeps.
- A man argues before the group; a woman listens.
- A man wows them with his party jokes; a woman laughs appreciatively.
- A man sits, sprawled relaxedly, legs apart, at a social gathering; a woman sits up straight, knees together.

Some of the questions we shall consider include the following: Is the stereotype of the "strong silent male" and the "chatty female" close to the fact? What are some of the differences in the way language labels, describes, and circumscribes women and men? What are some differences in the types of words either sex uses? Who uses the most words? Are there differences in the types of utterances either sex uses? Is either sex more verbally polite than the other? What differences in style of communication exist between the sexes? What about the use of

Sometimes it is the female who has the advantage in size and strength.

humor? Is either sex more adept? Who uses humor more? What does it mean for a woman or a man to have a sense of humor? What are the most frequent topics of conversation among women and among men? Who interrupts whom most in dialogue or in group interaction? Who takes more turns in conversation? What are some of the differences among males and females in nonverbal communication? Who touches whom more? Which sex is apt to give way when meeting on the street? Who smiles more? What paralinguistic differences have been found to exist?

It is our intention to explore this world of mixed communication. To attempt to isolate the communication of women from that of men and study either as a discrete variable would be fruitless. Certainly the evolution of the Women's Liberation movement into the Feminist movement has highlighted every facet of the existence of women. Our purpose is not to wield another cudgel in the polemic struggle for women's emancipation. Instead, we hope to cast new light on the relatively unexplored phenomenon of communication as it is practiced by women and by men.

We believe that in a good society men and women should not insist on or take for granted certain talents, qualities, roles, and functions for each other. An attempt to discourage or suppress some qualities or characteristics in either sex is an attempt to suppress humanity itself. We anticipate that any illumination cast or insights gained will serve to better the condition of all. It is our firm conviction that both sexes will thrive if a value system emerges that stresses maximum growth and human liberation.

As a steppingstone to this goal, however, we would insist that we first need to know many of the key differences in female-male communication. We need to be aware of the disparate expectations and behaviors that may unnaturally limit the sexes and unfairly erode our potential for expressing ourselves as complete human beings.

The full use and development of its human resources is one mark of a healthy society. It must guard against social conditioning that stunts or prevents full participation by its members. We hope that such a society can avoid anything approaching the extremes of the female underachieving and the male overachieving dichotomy. There is a tragic flaw in a culture when a small boy who is asked what he would be when he grew up if he were a girl replies, as one child did, "Oh, I guess I would grow up to be nothing." Even the most casual observer of the human condition must note with a degree of compassion the plight of the American woman in the television interview who admits apologetically that she is "only a housewife." On the other hand, we view the tragic example of the young boy who hangs himself from remorse at his poor performance in the high-pressure competition of a Little League baseball contest, where failure is not tolerated and overachieving is the name of the game.

This, then, is the task that we have set for ourselves—to compare and contrast the communicative modes of women and men and to suggest means of improving these interactions. Our first step will be to investigate the genetic and cultural differences that influence communication.

Genetic differences

Human biology seems to recognize the unity of human beings before it recognizes their sexual differences. In each fertilized egg 44 of the 46 chromosomes go to make up a human being and have nothing to do with sex. Two are added to differentiate the organism as female, XX chromosomes, or as male, XY chromosomes. Or in some cases females may have an X or XXX pattern and males an XXY or XYY pattern.

Hormonally, the sexes are not opposites. Everyone has a share of all three sex hormones, estrogen, androgen, and progestin. The sexes fall along a continuum, with most males having a preponderance of androgen at one end and most females a preponderance of estrogen at the other.

In the past it has been supposed that raging hormonal imbalances plague women, making them prey to their emotions and thus unstable and unfit for positions of responsibility. However, scientists are discovering that men as well as women have monthly cycles of physical, emotional, and intellectual highs and lows that are biologically determined. Furthermore, men as well as women go through a menopausal period when hormonal readjustment takes place.[2]

The appearance of secondary sex characteristics varies widely among individuals. Due to differences in hormonal balance and individual body structure, there is considerable overlapping between and among the sexes. For example, some women have considerable facial hair and some men have little or none. Some men have noticeable breast development, and some women are essentially flat-chested.

There is a broad spectrum of general physical differences between the sexes, but males seem to have a greater proportion of muscle to fat tissue than females. Females tend to have a lower center of gravity and a different pelvic structure for childbearing, and on the average, the male skeleton is taller and larger.

And yet some of these differences are not greater than differences that may exist between peoples of different ethnic mix, environment, or lifestyle. For example, among different tribes, the average Tutsi male is six feet one, but the average Mbuti pygmy man is four feet six. Such a variance in size renders the comparison of women and men within the same tribe inconsequential.[3]

Some experts distinguish sex characteristics at three different levels:

1 primary sex characteristics, which have to do with reproduction, hormonic differences, and the production of spermatozoa or ova
2 secondary sex characteristics, which are anatomical in nature and include distribution of body hair, differential bone structure, and size
3 sexual characteristics, which are social-behavioral in nature, are related to culture, and include learned, patterned communication behaviors such as posture, facial expression, leg position, and the like[4]

On the basis of these categories, an argument can be made for a distinction between the terms *sex* and *gender*. *Sex* can refer to the biological differences between females and males—differences in the genitals and reproductive functions. *Gender* can be considered a cultural term referring to the social classifications of "masculine" and "feminine." Sex, femaleness or maleness, can be determined on the basis of biological evidence. Gender, masculinity or femininity, may vary with the culture, the time, and the place.[5]

Gender distinctions are at the heart of the old joke about the two young children peeping through the hole of a fence at a summer nudist colony. The boy whispers, "Who are those people? Women or men?" "I can't tell," replies the girl. "They haven't got any clothes on!"

Cultural differences

Recognizing that genetic differences account for a part of the difference in the way people view each other, we are still confronted with a host of cultural variables that influence strongly our behavior. What we wear, consume, and enjoy as entertainment is influenced by biases based on gender expectation. Our religious, educational, and political institutions promulgate attitudes along sexist biases.

Yet our cultural accouterments may include, not only the clothing or material accessories we wear, but the very facial expressions we assume and the tonal qualities we add to our voices: a "sweet, feminine smile" rather than a "determined male frown"; or "the loud, commanding voice of a man" in contrast to "the soft, gentle voice of a woman." These are patterned behaviors from our unwritten but ever present cultural files of "what females do" and "what males do." Almost from the moment we are born, we begin assimilating certain "appropriate" behaviors from the words, actions, and discerned attitudes of those around us.

To analyze in detail the behaviors that are unconsciously patterned by society does not seem fruitful except in cases in which we suspect socialization or automatic shaping of our behaviors may block our development as useful, productive, balanced human beings. One of the most harmful beliefs we acquire through social programming is that female characteristics are not only different from male characteristics, but are opposite. That is, we have the idea that whatever is feminine is not masculine and vice versa. If one carries this reasoning further, suitable activities and work for men will include no women, and those appropriate for women will include no men. Yet common sense would lead us to expect that abilities and traits, along with their "opposites," would be distributed among *both* sexes. To expect gentleness and sensitivity only from women and action and ambition only from men overlooks the qualities one would hope to find in any mature *person*.[6]

A group of psychologists, psychiatrists, and social workers were asked to check off on a list of bipolar traits, terms (such as *ambitious–not ambitious, dependent–not dependent*) that characterized mature, socially competent people. One group assigned traits to mature, healthy females; another to mature healthy males; and another to mature healthy adults.[7] The terms checked for healthy males tended to be chosen for healthy adults, whereas those for healthy females were significantly different from those selected for healthy adults. The implication seemed to be that women were not healthy adults. As Estelle Ramey quipped, "A woman has a choice. She can be a normal woman or a mature adult!"[8]

Concepts of self and of others

Stereotypes are commonly accepted overgeneralizations about women and men. The force and directness of sex stereotypes can shock us when they are brought to our attention. As our own consciousness is raised, our words and actions reflect back to us our biases in brilliant clarity.

There are various popular beliefs about what women and men do and don't do. Such beliefs are stereotypes or overgeneralizations about the sexes. Certain qualities, behaviors, rights, and so forth seem to belong to an individual because the person fits a particular category.[9] For example, in a study of college students' stereotyped beliefs about the qualities and behaviors that supposedly characterize each sex, it was found that certain adjectives were used more often for one gender than for another.[10] Females were characterized by both sexes in terms such as *sophisticated, poised, well mannered, tactful, pleasant, sociable, modest, gentle, affectionate, kind, sentimental,* and *lovable.* Females were perceived as possessing social skills and grace and were expected to project warmth and emotional support. The unfavorable characteristics of the women's stereotype seemed to be distorted versions of the favorable ones: social excesses—for example, *snobbish, formal, submissive, vain*— and unreasonable emotionality—for example, *touchy, fearful, moody, temperamental.*

The stereotype of males held by both sexes involved a straightforward uninhibited social style, rational competence, and vigorous action. Modifiers included such terms as *easygoing, informal, frank, humorous, witty, thorough, deliberate, steady, logical, ambitious, courageous, aggressive,* and *dominant.* Unfavorable characteristics of males as viewed by both males and females seemed to be mild exaggerations of their supposedly positive qualities of being direct, competent, and active. Terms to describe their negative attributes included *boastful, outspoken, stubborn,* and *hardheaded.*

Men were seen as "frank and straightforward in social relations, intellectually rational and competent, and bold and effective in dealing with the environment." Women were viewed as possessing the "social amenities, emotional warmth, and a concern for affairs beside the material."

Not only do the sexes agree about what the different characteristics of women and men are, but they are very certain about which characteristics are more socially desirable for adults of either sex. A study of college women and men showed that both sexes viewed more of the typical male traits as socially desirable, whereas fewer of the typical female traits were rated as valuable for an adult individual.[11] The positively valued masculine traits in themselves did not have higher socially desirable scores than positively valued feminine traits. It was just that more so-called male traits than female traits were positively valued.

When the self-concepts of the college students were examined,

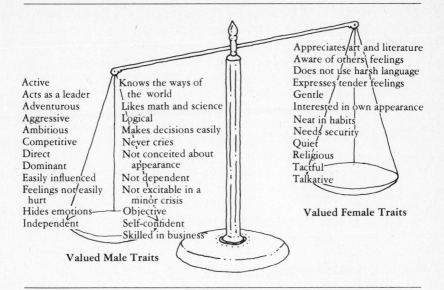

Valued Male Traits		Valued Female Traits
Active	Knows the ways of	Appreciates art and literature
Acts as a leader	the world	Aware of others' feelings
Adventurous	Likes math and science	Does not use harsh language
Aggressive	Logical	Expresses tender feelings
Ambitious	Makes decisions easily	Gentle
Competitive	Never cries	Interested in own appearance
Direct	Not conceited about	Neat in habits
Dominant	appearance	Needs security
Easily influenced	Not dependent	Quiet
Feelings not easily	Not excitable in a	Religious
hurt	minor crisis	Tactful
Hides emotions	Objective	Talkative
Independent	Self-confident	
	Skilled in business	

Masculine traits are considered more desirable than feminine traits.
Based on results reported by Paul Rosenkrantz et al., "Sex-Role Stereotypes and Self-Concepts in College Students," *Journal of Consulting and Clinical Psychology* 32, no. 3 (1968): 291. Copyright 1968 by the American Psychological Association. Reprinted by permission.

their personal ratings correlated with the stereotypes for their sex. The women and men saw themselves as falling into the stereotypic sex categories. However, the self-concepts of the women and men in the study were less extreme—that is, less feminine or less masculine—than the general pattern they described for their sex as a whole.

There seems to be a difference in the value placed on male and female stereotypes. The male stereotype is more socially desirable than the female stereotype. Since the self-assessment of the individuals tended to follow the general beliefs about their sex, we may infer that the women viewed themselves as having less worth in relation to the men. There is no reason to project such a result, since the women were highly capable college students on an equal intellectual footing with the men in the sample.

When one considers the time, money, and effort expended to prompt us to recognize and want to purchase a particular brand of aspirin, it is awesome to contemplate the factors that must be responsible for such marked sex stereotypes. Such factors are powerful enough to etch a behavioral profile, along with a negative self-valuation, into the self-concept of females.

We must note that the previously mentioned studies included only college students, who represent a small segment of the general population in age, status, and economic level. It is possible that subjects with different education, age, social, and occupational levels would yield different patterns. However, there is evidence to suggest that people hold stereotypes across the boundary lines of age, marital status, religion, and education[12] and therefore reason to believe that this is generalizable at least to the white American population.

Feminists have been complaining for some time that society views the so-called male characteristics as being superior to the female ones. Furthermore, some studies show that at some time about 4 out of 5 girls want to be boys, whereas less than 1 out of 2 boys wish they could be girls. It has also been found that 80 percent of the women wanting to have babies prefer to have males. Commenting on this preference by potential mothers, Sheila Tobias says regretfully that it is "as if to reproduce themselves would be a less noble and less significant undertaking."[13]

Most of us accept sex stereotypes as a matter of course. We've all heard, haven't we, "That's just like a man," or "That's the way women are!" Why is that the "way" a woman or man is? "Because they're born that way" is usually the implied or explicit answer.

Stereotyping constrains not only females; males too can be limited by cultural expectations. One researcher used word scales in a semantic differential technique to measure people's concepts of what is typical femininity and typical masculinity and what is ideal femininity and ideal masculinity. By the use of factor analysis, researchers identified two main factors that accounted for the major portion of the feminine and masculine concepts. They were potency and social behavior. Potency measures physical and emotional strength, and social behavior measures the ability to get along with others.

The scores from both female and male raters seemed to indicate that they viewed the ideal male as possessing tenderness, kindness, and consideration. Both sexes preferred males to be "strong but very tender."[14] Their concept of ideal masculinity entailed greater ability to get along with others than the male stereotype prescribed, and their concept of ideal femininity called for greater emotional and physical strength than the female stereotype called for. Unconscious behavior patterning according to the stereotypes society presents seems to prevent men, as well as women, from realizing what both sexes see as their ideal potential.

Our behavior is often controlled by the approval or disapproval we discern in others. And it is probably true that we receive approval from others—are seen as "good"—to the extent that our behavior is in line with our culture's norms for typical femininity or typical masculinity.[15] The problem is that society's norms for either sex seem to be deficient, in that they do not provide a profile of a complete human being.

Social constraints

Clare Daniels, chairwoman of the Michigan Commission on Women, dramatically pinpoints the stifling power of our stereotypes and the

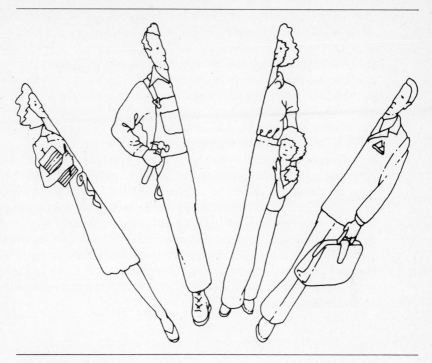

Sex-role profiles are incomplete.

problem within ourselves that results from our social programming when she speaks of the enemy in the field of management: "We have met the enemy, and it is us." The female manager's enemy is both women and men, or "mainly the society that formed both—men in psychological patterns suitable for the corporate world and women in patterns that conflict with its aims and methods." Dr. Anne Jardim, a management program director at an Eastern college, believes women and men feel differently about aggression, self-confidence, planning, risk-taking, and strategy. It is a fact of life that business organizations fit the male experience. She thinks that in order to succeed in leadership positions, women must resocialize themselves. Social conditioning may prevent many capable women from working effectively as executives and may keep many men and women from fully accepting women in these positions.[16]

The same forces can thwart males in work situations—a male nurse or male secretary, for example. The way men perform in tra-ditionally female occupations and the way their associates view them is all too often hampered by their biases. About a year ago, during a period of high unemployment, an Arizona newspaper ran a feature story about a man who was unable to get a job doing housework. He felt that the simple fact of his being male prevented him from getting hired. Apparently most of us so thoroughly associate cooking, cleaning, and caring for a home with being female that we cannot allow men such skills as baking a cake, laundering clothes, or cleaning a floor.

Our stereotypes affect our evaluations in unexpected ways. In one study the same lecture was delivered to two groups of students. One group heard the lecture from a male; another heard the lecture, word for word the same, from a female. Listeners received the lecture differently depending on whether it was delivered by a man or a woman. The words from the male were accepted as much more authoritative, while those from the woman were viewed as less credible.[17]

The same principles may apply to the printed page. Identical sociology papers were presented to groups of college students.[18] In one case, the paper was said to be authored by Joan T. McKay. In the other case, it was said to be authored by John T. McKay. When the readers, female college students, thought its author was a woman, they tended to view the paper as presenting careless data and unsound arguments, portending a less than positive professional future for its writer. When they thought the author was a man, they viewed the paper in a much more positive light, and rosier prospects were predicted for its supposedly male author.

A consequence of cultural differences: struggling to fit the stereotypes

Awareness is not always easy to come by. Often our very involvement in our culture blinds us to certain observations or perspectives. Some behaviors are so much a part of our lives we cannot perceive them. It is something like standing too close to a mirror with, perhaps, just the tip of the nose touching the glass. We can't see our image—just blobs and blurs. In the case of some stereotypes or social learning, we wonder, "Are we ever able to stand back far enough?" It is certain we must try.

Although many listeners view "Mary Hartman, Mary Hartman" primarily as a soap opera spoof, it has proved interesting for its focus on our overgeneralized but underexamined beliefs about the characteristics of women and men. Through the comic devices of exaggeration and incongruity, the program examines how women and men try to live up to and achieve some kind of identity through their "appropriate" sex-role stereotypes and yet constantly fall short of their goal.

We recognize a certain tragicomic truth in the character of Tom Hartman, Mary's husband. The same societal pressures and stereotypes that relegate his wife to the kitchen trap him in his work on the assembly line. At times Tom seems unable to cope with his situation and is reduced to tears. He resents this so-called weakness, since in our society tenderness and open display of emotions are not condoned for males.

Plagued by anxieties concerning his sexual performance, Tom has an affair with a female payroll clerk and develops venereal disease. After some vacillation, he turns again to Mary. Tom's inability to live

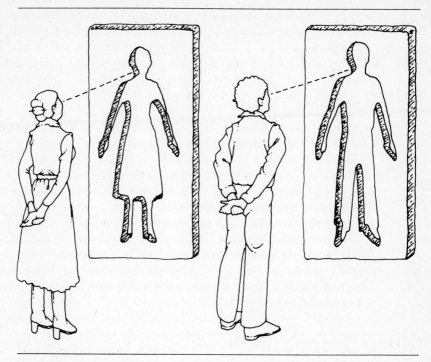

Stereotypes limit choices.

up to the male stereotype is apparently behind some of his unhappiness
and frustration. But he can ill face this problem, let alone recognize it.[19]
Unable to identify the source of his own problems, Tom is, of course,
powerless to help Mary solve hers. He cannot muster the necessary
wisdom of an all-knowing Father Knows Best to aid her. Nor can he
protect Mary from the outside world as a Matt Dillon or John Wayne
character would do.

Similarly, although the characterization of Mary Hartman is distorted and comic, it effectively pinpoints the power of social conditioning and the ways women can be victims of it. Mary is a comic paradigm
of the ultimate consumer and "compleat" wife and mother. She
"genuinely feels inadequate because the bugs aren't frightened into
running away by the insect spray, or because she can't see her reflection
in the plastic dish detergent container." She "buys all the right prod-
ucts, cleans and scrubs her home on a rigid schedule, takes out library
books to try to be a more interesting sex partner, works at being a good
wife and mother by the policies set out by Dr. Joyce Brothers, and
waits for happiness to find her."[20]

The program seems to demonstrate, in a humorous vein, that both
women and men suffer when their socialization closes off their options.
They can be deprived of originality and initiative if they are limited to

certain behaviors so that they may conform to platitudes or bromides concerning women's or men's "natural" roles. We will see this later in relation to differences in communication behavior.

Changes in sex roles

We all know that women and men are different. We accept many differences with a conventional wisdom that intuits without evidence. But the kind and extent of these differences is open to a wide spectrum of interpretation. We seem particularly concerned at present with the issues of how the sexes are different and to what extent these differences are due to biological or cultural factors.

We are living in a time of changing relationships between the sexes. But the changes have been continuous and not unforeseen. Modern technology is having an homogenizing effect on women and men. In much of today's work, sex and physical characteristics make little difference. A 98-pound woman or a 250-pound man can with equal ease punch a computer card, keep financial records, work on an assembly line, run a laboratory test, or counsel a client. The jobs requiring physical strength that gave men an advantage in the past have diminished in number.

With homogenization of the sexes, the woman's world/man's world dichotomy has been breaking down. Less often are male and female relationships organized on two separate and parallel tracks. This is especially true since smaller families and shortened childbearing years have meant that motherhood absorbs less of women's time, and the ease of contraception makes it possible for some women to choose not to have children at all. "The mystique of the great, powerful fighting male is one of the casualties of modern technology. So, too, is the mystique of the great earth mother, the 'nestling' subsex who found fulfillment only in motherhood."[21] That so many seemingly outmoded sex stereotypes continue to exist may be due to cultural lag. Presumably as men's and women's work and interests continue to converge, many of the sterotypes of this decade will break down and become blurred.

But change comes slowly. Although we recognize that stereotypes and unquestioned, automatically accepted beliefs can unfairly pigeonhole either sex, we generally assume that stereotypes make life harder for young women than for young men. This may be less true today. In fact a good case may be made for the opposite view—that women may be better off than men. Matina Horner, President of Radcliffe College, insists that it may be young men who are in for trouble. In studies on the ability of women and men to cooperate, she found that in test situations calling for cooperation in work projects and relay races, the women could work well with both sexes. The males, however, "either developed total feelings of powerlessness or they became completely authoritarian." Furthermore, she felt that "the men

We are moving from a dual-world to a single-world society.

were surprised by cooperative conditions in which nobody wins or loses, and they simply didn't know how to integrate them into their experience. For the men, it raised all sorts of concerns about loss of power." Horner maintains that even males who give lip service to the evils of competition actually perform very differently when put in a situation calling for cooperation. "They were simply never taught cooperation."[22]

Some scholars predict that the values of our technical, urbanized society of the future will center on cooperativeness with a considerable de-emphasis on competitiveness. This may mean that young men with a macho-competitive socialization are ill-suited for such a new value system. Typically the male's sense of self-worth has come from arenas of combat, where he has struggled on the job ladder, competed in sports, vied in entertainment, or fought in politics. If cooperation becomes more desirable than competition, then the male's main source of esteem will have been undermined. Inevitably there must come a sense of displacement or bewilderment, something like the frustrated character in the television situation comedy who lamented the loss of "his day," wailing: "But that's the way it *used* to be. And now that it's my turn, they've changed the rules!" For many women, because of the way they were socialized, these have been their "rules" all along.

Estimates from the Department of Labor predict that only 20 percent of the jobs existing in the next decade will require a college education. When we think of the increasing numbers of youths attending college now and in the future, this projection dramatizes the gloomy prospects of a future with women and men ruthlessly pitted against each other for a limited number of jobs. Regardless of one's admiration for the old pioneer spirit of competitiveness, a rational solution to such a future would seem to be "a more sane and balanced sense of cooperativeness."[23]

We seem now to be emerging from the old dual-world structure into a one-world setting in which women and men are working together. But the new model of companionate, social relationships calls for more interaction and greater psychological interdependence between the sexes. Because there is more interaction on the person–human being plane and less on the man's world/woman's world parallel pattern, there is more chance for differences to create friction. Now more than ever there is a need to understand and reconcile differences and to build more satisfying relationships. It is doubtful that we could eliminate all differences even if we wanted to. But we will be far ahead in our efforts to build better relationships if we can at least understand some of the differences and appreciate the nature of the interactions between and within the sexes.

Sex and communication

Our interest in this book lies specifically in communication variables, verbal and nonverbal, and their relation to the sexes. For some time, communication has been studied in connection with such categories as race, class, religion, political setting, and economic background, but little attention has been given to sex as a variable. In some research, male speech has been assumed to be the norm and so the researcher used male subjects only, without bothering to include any females.[24] The problem is that often results have been reported as if the findings apply to *both* sexes, when they may not in fact. Sheila Tobias, with mixed amusement and irritation, told of one researcher who was having some difficulty with a study and finally threw out the material gathered from female subjects because it "skewed his data"![25]

Sex cannot be so easily dismissed when we consider that it is one of the primary indexing factors we use when we interact with people or think about them. In our society a person's gender matters very much, for to a great extent it determines how others act and react.

We shall imagine ourselves in the ordinary situation of driving down the street.[26] We glance at a figure strolling down the sidewalk, wearing blue jeans, sandals, a casual shirt, and shoulder-length hair. From these clues alone, it is not readily apparent which sex the person is. So we turn around and crane our necks, managing the wheel between looks. We get additional sex clues by more careful inspection of the person's visible anatomical characteristics, noting the manner of walk, scrutinizing the facial features, or looking for the presence or absence of cosmetics. The point is that somehow it seems very important to us to know whether the person walking along is female or male. Why? Why is it so important to determine the sex of a person? In most cases, it tells us how to respond to that person.

Our thirteen-year-old son goes to school with a girl who has a relatively low-pitched voice. She is sometimes mistaken for a boy over the phone. When others in our family answered her phone call and mistook her for a boy, they responded differently in verbal style, tone of voice, and even in the way they recorded her phone message than they did when they learned she was female.

The consequences of sex can be awesome to contemplate. Physician Estelle Ramey tells the poignant story of a set of identical male twins.[27] A short while after their birth, they were being routinely circumcised when the penis of one of the children was accidentally destroyed in the operation. After much professional conferring among physicians and psychiatrists, the decision was made to surgically convert the injured young boy into a female. Ramey told of the decidedly different ways these two identical twins were treated and responded to in the years following the operation. The boy, as we would expect, was rough-housed, indulged in noisy play; given mechanical toys, play trucks, cars, and building sets; and in general, tumbled about in good-natured physical activity. The other, in contrast, was dealt with delicately; given dolls, tea sets, and play ovens; admonished not to get dirty; and, in general, restricted more in physical activity. By the time she was 10, the "girl" was baking cookies. Commented Ramey with irony, "She doesn't even have the genes for cookies!" Ramey lamented that no one would ever advise *her* to aspire to be President.

Not the least of the areas in which sex has consequences is that of communication. We need to gain insight into communication patterns as they vary according to sex. This knowledge can help us become aware of conditioned behaviors that we may wish to correct in ourselves and can aid us in understanding or adjusting to differences in others, particularly those of the opposite sex.

Causes of sex differences in communication

Our aim is to examine sex differences in communication. But merely cataloguing differential behaviors may profit us little, unless we attempt to speculate on what is behind the differences and what relation some of the sex differences bear to other variables.

What are some possible explanations for sex differences in communication? To our way of thinking there are probably six main ways to
account for such differences.

Innate differences One possible explanation is that the differences we
note are inborn. Since men and women have different reproductive
functions and different anatomical structures, perhaps it is natural that
their communication patterns might also be different.[28] This explanation, however, would seem more likely to account for nonverbal differences, such as manner of moving, sitting, and gesturing, than for verbal
dissimilarities.

Physical differences in males and females have not been judged
sufficient to account for the distinctive nonverbal behaviors displayed
by each sex. Anthropologist Ray Birdwhistell, who has spent many
years researching patterns of nonverbal behavior, believes that sex differences in body language are culturally determined.[29]

Personality A variation on the theme of innate differences is the suggestion that women and men may differ innately in personality. The sexes
differ in hormones and in chemical make-up of the body. Whether the
differences result in special personality traits characteristic of each sex,
however, we cannot be sure. If we could find an absolutely free and
open society, we could observe people's natural development, but it is
generally assumed that no society exists which is informally structured
so that differences can rise to the surface naturally. Cultural stereotypes
and social pressures on the sexes probably override real differences and
create artificial ones.[30]

It has been suggested that if there are inborn personality differences between the sexes, analyses of these differences in a free environment would probably produce overlapping bell curves, without large
enough variation to differentiate the traits by sex. Viewed graphically
they would appear like this: ⟋⟍⟋⟍

We suggest that there are a number of possible explanations for
sex differences. However, we personally do not accept these first two
theories—innate differences and personality—as among the best explanations for most of the sex differences we discuss in forthcoming chapters. The remaining four explanations seem to us to be more tenable,
taken individually or together.

Cultural elaboration A number of sex differences may be due to cultural
elaboration of gender. Birdwhistell has concluded that many sex differences in body movement, posture, gesture, facial expression, and the
like are culturally learned. Compared to many animals, human males
and females do not differ greatly in secondary sexual characteristics;
they are "weakly sexually dimorphic." Whereas the males and females
of some animals differ so greatly in physical characteristics that they do
not even appear to belong to the same species, human beings of both

sexes are very much alike. Birdwhistell suggests that because of our relative unimorphism—the relative sameness of males and females—human beings have gradually developed an elaborate system of gender display. They have worked out certain rituals and patterns of verbal and nonverbal behavior that belong distinctively to and mark each sex. In other words, humans somehow experience the need to develop a detailed system of gender display in order to emphasize and display differences that are not great to begin with.[31]

The establishment of class differences serves as a useful analogy to clarify the gender-display theory that sex differences can be created where none exist.[32] Class differences can be created by the houses and neighborhoods we live in, the cars we drive, the clothing we wear, even the way we groom ourselves. Such artifacts can serve to differentiate a privileged class from a nonprivileged class. Clothing worn by wealthy people, for example, does not keep them any warmer as a rule. It does serve to exhibit class differences and to keep the distinctions straight. In the same way, according to the theory, some sex differences are created that do not exist naturally. They serve to exhibit, mark, and emphasize sex distinctions. On the other hand, differences that exist naturally could conceivably be minimized by social needs and pressures.

An added facet of the cultural-elaboration explanation is the argument that females and males are socialized to different stereotyped personality patterns in our society. Females are supposedly brought up to be passive, docile, self-effacing, and self-deprecating. Their verbal and nonverbal gestures follow from a personality patterned, elaborated, and embellished by society. In the same way, males are socialized to another pattern, and therefore their communication follows from that personality.

A retelling of the old story about the experiment with short- and long-whiskered rats makes this point quite well.[33] Short-whiskered rats were put in a conditioning box where they learned to respond only to red lights. Long-whiskered rats were put in a box and taught to respond to blue lights. After the rats were conditioned, the researcher wrote up the experiment as if the rats' responses resulted from a difference in whisker length. It is possible that, just like the different conditioning boxes, the varied social environments for the sexes are creating the differences.

Division of labor by sex   A fourth explanation is that sex communication differences are related to the division of labor in our society. Our society relegates certain work, activities, responsibilities, and privileges to people on the basis of sex. Even with women's recent political and economic progress and the new attitudinal climates encouraged by the women's movement, the belief persists that childcare and home-related tasks are solely "woman's work," despite the fact that the number of working women has climbed to a new high. Over 45 percent of all women, married or single, work, and nearly 1 in 4 households is headed by a woman.[34] There are, of course, some specialized duties around the house—car repair, outside home maintenance, and carpentry tasks—relegated to males. These specializations according to sex probably carry over into many aspects of communication.

Outside the home there is probably more lip service than hand, foot, salary, or hiring service paid to the equal employment opportunity ideals of the nation, for there is still a good deal of sex typecasting in jobs. Engineering, medicine, industrial management, and the clergy, for example, have relatively few females in their ranks. On the other hand, there are few males in secretarial work, nursing, elementary school teaching, food service, and domestic work. A number of communication differences may be linked to these sex differences in occupation. The allocation of different activities, duties, roles, and work environments according to sex can contribute to disparate conversational topics, dissimilar styles of talk, distinctive vocabularies, divergent nonverbal communication patterns, and other sex-typed language variables.

Male dominance   A fifth possible explanation for sex differences in communication involves what some refer to as the factor of male control. According to this theory, communication takes place in the cultural context of male dominance—dominance that is built into the familial, economic, political, religious, and legal structures of society. This power structure and the relationship of superior to subordinate can be seen in our communication as well. Patterns of nonverbal communication such as touching, smiling, and staring, as well as verbal mechanisms including use of expletives, forms of address, explanation, commands, and requests, all supposedly function to reflect, establish, or maintain power relationships.[35]

A corollary of this is that patterns of dominance and submission, or of superior/subordinate relationships, follow an asymmetric pattern, and this asymmetry is reflected in communication. Between equals there is a mutual exchange of behavior. For example, two persons call each other by the first name: "Hello, Jill." "Hi there, Jenny." Or Jon thumps Gerry on the back, and Gerry claps Jon on the shoulder. This is reciprocal and balanced behavior.

But the subordinate at the office probably does not "first-name" the boss, although the boss may address her or him by first name. And the college student rarely thumps the professor on the back, although the reverse may often occur. Between nonequals there is an asymmetry, a nonmutuality, of behavior. One person has a privilege that the other does not. The theory is that this power asymmetry applies to the sexes and manifests itself in differences in staring, smiling, touching, interrupting, use of expletives, use of names, and so on.

Differing value systems   A sixth possible explanation for sex differences in communication is that individuals' value systems may differ according to sex. Although this apparently relates to socialization and cultural elaboration, the idea merits separate discussion. Two value systems are generally believed to exist in American society. One, the dominant orientation, is supposedly appropriate for those of higher rank, such as American males. The other is an alternate, or variant, system said to be the perspective of females and other persons of lower status.

The dominant value system is characterized by an emphasis on individual achievement, independence, external evaluation, instrumental behavior to overcome obstacles, and future time orientation. This system is prescribed for males or persons of higher rank.

The variant, or alternate, theme appropriate for females and persons of lower status contrasts with the instrumental-active orientation. It stresses group identity (duty, loyalty to kin), the importance of existence and self-realization, harmony with the world, and a present time orientation.

In the variant orientation the goals and welfare of the group are foremost; whereas in the dominant value system the goals and welfare of the individual are primary. The variant system stresses existence; the dominant system stresses action. Finally, in the variant system there is a concern for what the individual is; the dominant system is concerned more for what the individual can accomplish.[36]

The differing value systems may account for behavioral differences between the sexes. Males have been shown to be more aggressive and domineering, to view the world as a hostile environment from which one must forcibly grasp success and reward. Females supposedly have a more social orientation. They are more concerned with developing their interpersonal skills, more people-oriented, more concerned with harmonious interpersonal relations. They manifest greater dependency and emphasize caring for and relating to others. They supposedly see the world as benevolent and view success as obtainable through love and good fortune, without independent effort.[37]

In our society the male tends to have an active and instrumental attitude that relates to his view of the world as something requiring conquest or manipulation through competitive skills and resources. The female, on the other hand, has a passive affective attitude that is related to her view of the world as something requiring placation and cultivation through nurturance and cooperation.

These differing orientations may manifest themselves in relations between the sexes. The male initiates activity, is usually deferred to, puts his interests first, and acts directly to further them. The female keeps herself responsive to the male, is sensitive to his needs, puts her own interests second, and uses indirection in gaining her own ends.[38]

One dramatic example of the active and instrumental attitude of the male of the species is described by Jessie Bernard. She calls it the "cichlid effect" and provides a provocative elaboration of the general theme of male dominance/female submissiveness. The cichlid effect derives its name from a particular kind of fish, the cichlid, a peculiar creature. The two sexes of the cichlid have no identifying signs to differentiate them, and in the past it was difficult for biologists to distinguish one from the other. In fact, it was considered a scientific accomplishment when Oehlert, a biologist, finally solved the mystery.[39]

Color, size, shape, or a combination of these things is of no help in telling the cichlid sexes apart. Furthermore, male and female are alike in their movement patterns, when they are performing the sex act and fertilizing and laying eggs. To make matters even more difficult, both female and male cichlids are capable of aggression, of fear, and of similar sexual responses. The key is that the three kinds of behavior are related differently for the two sexes. Sexual behavior is coupled with aggressive behavior in the male; in the female, sexual behavior is related to fear. The strange phenomenon manifests itself in this way: fear and sexuality cannot exist in the male at the same time. If the male has the slightest fear of his partner, his sexuality is curbed. Conversely, if the female has so little fear or awe of her partner that her aggression is not suppressed, she does not react sexually to him. The result is that a male can mate only with an awe-inspired and therefore submissive female, and a female can mate only with an awe-inspiring and therefore dominant male. The sexuality of the male cichlid depends on the female's awe. She must defer to him, or his masculinity is extinguished. He must be dominant, or he literally ceases to be a male, and the female will not conceive. "The aggressive cichlid is, indeed, a 'castrating female.'"[40]

One can draw a parallel between human beings and cichlids. Human male sexuality, like the cichlid's, may be vulnerable to female aggression and diminished by lack of female subservience or awe. It is often dependent on deference. Even though male sexuality can endure cultural restraints and physical mistreatment, it may not be able to withstand the cichlid effect. This vulnerability of male sexuality is apparently social and based on relationships with women.

Sexual initiative is to be distinguished from sexual aggression. Either women or men can take the initiative sexually, for example, and signal preliminary interest in the other. But only men can be aggressive sexually. The reverse is not true: "Female initiative is successful only when the male is willing. . . . He can take her; [but] she must excite or incite him. If he does not become aroused, she cannot have him sexually." Of course, this presents difficulties to males; it puts them to the test. For while a female can be unaroused sexually and still participate, can pretend, a male's success or failure—particularly his failure—is highly visible.[41]

This view raises the question: If women are incapable of being sexually aggressive against men, does it follow they must be incapable of using other forms of aggression outside the bedroom? Is it necessary for women to be conciliating, nurturing, and stroking in other areas of life too? Why not men as well? Does the cichlid effect have to infiltrate all relationships between the sexes?

We have reviewed some possible explanations for sex differences in communication. We hope they provide fruitful ways of viewing and trying to account for some of the research findings we discuss in the chapters ahead. Whatever the case, we would add our voices to the chorus that sings the decisive song of Bernard Shaw in regard to womankind and mankind: "Woman [is] the female of the human species and not a different kind of animal."[42]

Communication and social change

There are those who would pass over communication and linguistic matters as insignificant. What can such considerations do to change society and its firmly entrenched stereotypes and inequities? It is easy to agree that language reflects society; that is, social change creates language change. It is not so easy to see how the reverse might be so: that language can affect society. Some linguists such as Robin Lakoff reluctantly acknowledge that language can at best influence attitudes slowly and indirectly. Even these changes in attitudes will not result in social change "unless society is receptive already."[43]

Yet we would argue that it is difficult to separate language and society. Language does not so much *reflect* society as it makes up a part of social process.[44] Communication is a form of behavior. To use a certain label in speech, for example, *fag*, and cause a listener to categorize someone in a specific evaluative way is a form of action. The same holds for the communicative act of interrupting, which in effect exercises a form of control over another's speech. Using a vocal rise in pitch at the end of utterances to seemingly ask approval or defer to another is no less a social act.

These communication acts, verbal and nonverbal, are all part of the micropolitical structure that undergirds the larger political-economic structure of our lives. They help establish, maintain, and convey the various signals of control, compliance, defiance, and dependence that influence us and those around us.[45]

Suggested activities

1 Examine character descriptions of females and males in some modern novels or in magazine fiction.

    a. Analyze differences and similarities in the ways the characters are described and record your findings. Describe and quote passages as examples and support for your conclusions.

    b. Catalogue key descriptive words that you think are significant for either sex.

2 Anthropologist Lionel Tiger, in his book *Men in Groups* (New York: Random House, 1969), discusses the theory of male bonding. Tiger

thinks male grouping today could be viewed as a "reflex" arising from the habits inculcated in the species ages ago when primitive males hunted together in packs and women stayed behind. The women had no need to develop techniques of cooperation and working together, since they did their separate jobs, caring for individual living sites. In practically all cultures men are seen to be in control of the major institutions. Tiger suggests it is male bonding that enables men to work together in industry, politics, religion, the military. This, he theorizes, is why women find it so hard to be accepted as members of these power groups. They feel out of place, just as they do in the traditional bonding activities of males such as hunting, fishing, and other all-male outings.

a. Compare and contrast the interaction of all-female and all-male groups. Since it is difficult to be privy to opposite-sex groups, get a friend of the opposite sex to offer her/his observations. Do the talkers relate to one another in the same way in all-female and in all-male groups, in your opinion? How or how not?

b. Do you believe there is really such a thing as male bonding?

c. Do you believe there is such a thing as female bonding? Give verbal examples and accounts. Quote conversation to support your views.

3 Differences in the way women and men communicate may be only reflections of the relative positions they hold in our society.

a. Poll your friends, neighbors, and relatives to see how many of them agree with this view.

b. Catalogue the various reasons given for agreement or disagreement.

c. What conclusions do you draw about how those around you view sex and communication?

4 Social change is believed by some to create language change. Can you provide any support for the reverse argument that language change can influence attitudes and create social change? Provide narrative accounts, incidents, or hypothetical examples to support your view. Draw upon the wisdom of others as well as your own.

2 Power, sex, and talk

Much of what has been written about communication focuses on emotional dimensions and affiliative relationships such as attraction, liking, and intimacy. Apparently it has been assumed that communication is taking place between equals in status or power. Little attention has been paid to power relationships. Some theorists maintain that power is the strongest organizing concept by which to explain some sex differences in conversation. Female and male behaviors are seen as paralleling the differences between superior and subordinate relationships. Asymmetry, or imbalance in communication behavior, is viewed as a sign of difference in status. Symmetry, or reciprocal behavior, is seen as signifying affiliation and equal status.

Henley[1] takes the structure of the use of terms of address as a model for theorizing about communication. Simply stated, the paradigm of terms of address is as follows: status is characterized by asymmetry of address. Subordinates address superiors by title and last name ("Miss Flores," "Dr. Sommer," "Major Weldon"), but superiors can take more liberty and address subordinates by more familiar forms, such as first name or nicknames ("Rose," "Debbie," "Honey"). Affiliation or solidarity is indicated by symmetric, or balanced, use of familiar, or close, terms and polite, or distant, terms. So two lovers may address each other as "Darling" and "Dearest," respectively; two company managers with offices opposite one another may use the familiar "Carol" and "Barbara"; and two professors in different departments in a large university may use the more polite and distant "Dr. Nichols" and "Dr. Lawrence."

Furthermore, as a general formula, if a certain form of address is used by superiors to subordinates, it is also used between intimates—for example, first names; if a certain form is used by subordinates to superiors, it is also used between strangers—for example, title and last names. If there is a difference in status between two people, then the right of changing to more familiar forms of relationship belongs to the superior—for example, Dr. Abbott may decide to call the lab assistant "Carl."[2] See Table 2.1.

Table 2.1 Asymmetry and symmetry in address

	Uses terms	Right to initiate change in relationship
Asymmetry		
Superior	Familiar-close	Yes
Subordinate	Polite-distant	No
Symmetry		
Equal	Familiar-close or polite-distant	Yes
Equal	Familiar-close or polite-distant	Yes
Intimate	Familiar-close	Yes
Intimate	Familiar-close	Yes
Stranger	Polite-distant	Yes
Stranger	Polite-distant	Yes

We can use this model to look at other verbal matters and see that asymmetry, or imbalance, signifies a status or power difference. We would probably not hesitate to assign each of the following behaviors to a superior's or subordinate's role:

Superior	Subordinate
Orders or commands	Complies
Asks or requests	Acquiesces
Interrogates	Replies
Declares	Agrees
Interrupts	Allows interruption; stops talking

Some interesting studies on self-disclosure pinpoint further the notion of asymmetry of behavior between status unequals. It has been found that subordinates in work situations tend to disclose or reveal more personal information about themselves to their superiors than their superiors reveal to them.[3] The head of the chemistry department may inquire about the health of the building maintenance man's wife, but the maintenance man, although assuming a friendly air, generally does not take the familarity of asking about the professor's spouse. The doctor elicits personal information from the patient, but for the patient to question the doctor so would be considered an affront. The same holds true for client and psychiatrist, job seeker and prospective employer, client and social worker, pupil and teacher, and so on.[4]

There is an asymmetry or nonmutuality in amount of personal or self information given between nonequals. More personal information flows toward greater status or power. Less personal information flows toward lesser status or power. Those in positions of power can remain aloof and detached, giving very little information about themselves.

Those with little power, such as poor people, minorities, those receiving unemployment compensation, and children, must reveal more about themselves. Providing information about ourselves, especially in situations of inequality, gives the receiver power over us. The receiver has information about us; we in turn do not have access to such information about that person. This gives the receiver a resource we do not have.

The "cool" that some persons display has aptly been described in terms of minimal self-disclosure:

"Cool" is nothing more than the withholding of information, that is, refusing to disclose one's thoughts and emotions, and the value it gives to street people, poker players, and psychiatrists is of the same sort. People in positions of power do not have to reveal information about themselves, perhaps the ultimate exemplars of this principle being Howard Hughes and the fictional Big Brother. Closer to home, we have the example of psychiatrists (usually male) to whom much is disclosed (by their predominantly female clientele), but who classically maintain a reserved and detached attitude, revealing nothing of themselves.[5]

Some patterns of asymmetry have been observed in some areas of communication involving the sexes. More familiar terms of address tend to be used for women than for men, for example.[6] The point is that the model of asymmetry or nonmutuality that was set forth for nonequals in status is a useful structure in which to view some of the female and male differences throughout the entire book. If we apply the model to various outputs, exchanges, and strategies, we may gain added insight into some distinct elements that seem to have little relationship to anatomical differences.

Outputs

Among the common beliefs about women and men threaded through our culture are those concerning the way females and males talk. An example from our own family comes immediately to mind. We were returning from a two-hour automobile trip with our daughters and sons, and although space and refreshments may have been in short supply, words were not. As talk centered increasingly on the foibles and eccentricities of various school instructors, one teenage son at length addressed two of his sisters with mild irritation: "You remind me of a bunch of little old ladies." "What do you mean?" his seventeen-year-old sister snapped back. "Why not a bunch of little old men?" "Oh, c'mon now," he said. "Men don't gab that way."

Quantitative differences between the sexes

Rather than contentedly nurturing these common beliefs, suppositions, and myths, we need to investigate speech behavior to see what differences in amount of talk actually exist between females and males. We decided to look at verbal exchanges in university faculty meetings as one way of getting at the variables of talk.[7] We audiotaped and transcribed seven faculty meetings at a university during the academic year, with the knowledge of participants. Using a stop watch, we timed speaker turns, counting the total length of the turn from beginning to end. Internal silences or pauses within a turn were not tabulated. With one exception, the males surpassed the females in number of verbal turns taken. The woman with the fewest turns averaged 5.5 a meeting. The man with fewest turns not only had over twice as many as she, but he exceeded all the other women except one in number of turns.

An interesting pattern emerged when the scores of the same sexes were grouped together. Except for the department chairman, who often could be present for only a portion of the meetings, the number of turns follow a hierarchy of power or status, according to rank, importance, or length of time in the department. The person with more power tended to take more turns. Of course, it could be argued that the more talkative person achieves more status and acquires more power in the group situation. The males, without exception, spoke longer per turn. The longest average turn for a male was 17.07 seconds. The longest average turn for a female was 10 seconds. But it was not quite so long as the average *shortest* turn for a male, 10.66 seconds. Shortest average turn time for a female was 3 seconds.

A similar pattern of greater talkativeness of males has been found in other research. Wood studied the spontaneous speech of females and males asked to describe photographs.[8] Eighteen males and 18 females each spoke to two listeners, a female and a male, one at a time. Speaker and listener sat back to back so that they could hear but not see each other. The investigator sought answers to the following questions:

1 Do women and men differ in the length of their talk?
2 Does the length of talk differ according to whether the subjects talk to the same sex or the opposite sex?
3 Do women and men differ in some ways when speaking with the same sex and with the opposite sex?
4 Do women and men differ in how they react to success or failure in talking to the same or to the opposite sex?

Wood showed 12 photographs of a man's face, one at a time, to each subject. Only the expression changed from picture to picture. Speakers were to describe each picture so that the hearer would be able to pick it out from a set of 25 pictures. The speaker was informed whether the listener chose the correct picture or not.

The results were secretly fixed in advance. False feedback was given so that the speaker would succeed and fail in a predetermined order to test the response of the talker to success or failure in communicating. Trials were in groups of four. One group of trials might be programmed to be reported as successful (S), another as failures (F), and another as alternating (A) success and failure in getting the listener to select the correct picture. The false reports were ordered differently for different subjects. There were three arranged feedback series:

(S)   (A)   (F)
(F)   (S)   (A)
(A)   (F)   (S)

Wood found that male conversation groups used significantly more words per utterance than females. An utterance was the stretch of talk used to describe any particular picture. Males talked more whether they conversed with the same or the opposite sex and no matter which of the three orders of feedback they received.

There were interesting differences in the responses of the sexes to the false feedback. Females did not noticeably change the length of their talk under the three orders of success or failure. But there was a significant difference in the males' talkativeness according to the feedback series used. Males talked longer in the (A) (F) (S) sequence. That is, male speakers used more words when they went through a supposed series of alternating failure and success (A), and then a series of failed trials (F), before success (S) in the final series. When they met failure at the beginning and middle of their test, they produced more words through their total performance than the male speakers who got success feedback at the start. There was only a slight tendency for this to be the case for females, and the difference was not significant.

So males seem to be more sensitive to success or failure of communication than females. Our culture may put more of a premium on successful speech for males than for females. Feeling more pressure to speak well, a male may be more sensitive to success or lack of it in getting his message across. If females accept the folk view that women's speech is unorganized or illogical and confused, they may view communication failure casually with a so-what-else-is-new attitude of resignation.

In another investigation, subjects were seated before a tape recorder and asked to describe paintings and engravings. They could take as much time as they needed and were told to be as thorough as possible and try to leave nothing out.[9] Females took considerably less time in their descriptions than the males. The average time for females for all descriptions was 3.17 minutes, while the average time for males was 13 minutes. The investigator noted that in the case of three male talkers, they "simply talked until the tape ran out." She then let them continue another 5 minutes each and "then tactfully terminated the interviews," adding, "There is really no way of determining how long they might have continued." When given as much time as they thought necessary to describe a picture, men talked considerably longer than women. There was no significant difference in the speed of talk for either sex. Women averaged 113 words per minute and men, 107.9.

Qualitative differences between the sexes

Description versus interpretation Concerning the style or quality of some female and male talk, several interesting discoveries have been made. Males have been found to have a more empirical style of speech in some cases. In the photograph study, men's speech contained more objective descriptions and accounts of the pictures' observable features. Females' speech tended to be creative in style. Physical features of the photographs were *interpreted* by the females rather than described. They became emotionally involved in the situation expressed by the picture, so that "a reaction rather than physical entity was described."[10]

Particular words used by several representative females and males in the study were examined. A list was made of words used exclusively by the males, those used exclusively by the females, and those common to both sexes. Two-thirds of the words used exclusively by the males were nouns such as *background, centimeter, dots, fraction,* and *v-shape.* Verbs used by the males only included such words as *intersect, joins, parallels, protruded,* and *tapers off.* Modifiers such as *black, closer, elliptical, oblique,* and *right-triangular* also were used only by males. These words seem to relate to observable features of the pictures. They do not appear to convey judgment, interpretation, or emotion. They describe. Only one-third of the words used exclusively by females were of this type.

The list of words used exclusively by women included nouns such as *bird, cheese, death, family,* and *spinach.* Verbs included *enjoying, gotten up, might be posing, might have just put,* and *has been surprised.* Modifiers used included *confused, distasteful, peek-a-boo, questioning,* and *skeptical.* These words seem to be related to the photographs more indirectly than straight factual description. They are used to form impressions and make interpretations or comparisons of what is seen. Such words create a style very different from an objective description. Compare the following passages. The first uses the so-called male words:

The eyebrows intersect to form a v-shape in the center. The eyes are narrowed and elliptical. The mouth droops a centimenter at each corner and parallels a shadow line on the face.

In the next passage, the so-called female words seem to result in an interpretive style:

He has a distasteful look, and he might be posing as skeptical of what he hears.

The fact that more words were used in the empirical style and fewer words in the creative or interpretive style does not seem surprising on second thought. Compare "His mouth is set in disappointment and he just looks defeated," an interpretive approach, with an empirical description of the height of the eyebrows, number of forehead wrinkles, or angle of mouth. The second approach will require more words generally.

It could be argued that eventually the interpretive-emotive style might lead to longer utterances. An ambiguous "He just looks defeated" might not convey the idea of defeated as clearly as a detailed explanation. A better measure might be to calculate the number of words it takes to successfully communicate an idea, rather than the number of words spoken in giving a preliminary description. At any rate, it appears that an objective style may require more words than a subjective approach, at least in beginning explanations. There is also a suggestion that the males' utterances may have been longer because the men in the study had a tendency to repeat.

Numerous times in university classes we have used an exercise in which a speaker with her/his back to the group instructs members of the group how to draw an arrangement of squares. No gestures are used, no questions are allowed, and the exercise is timed.[11] In by far the majority of cases, the males have spoken longer than the females. And yet, overall, there seemed little difference between the sexes in the number of persons correctly drawing the arrangement of squares from their oral directions.

Although we did not tape record and transcribe the descriptions, we observed several tendencies: females did not seem to repeat their instructions as often as males, and they seemed more casual in their approach. For example, some women would describe one portion of the arrangement as "a box standing on its end touching in the middle of the box below it." Males tended to repeat themselves more. Most were more literal and analytic, as in specifying, "The left side of the square intersects the midpoint of the top side of the square below it at about a 45 degree angle."

In the study on descriptions of paintings, males used more numerals in their descriptions than women and they used them differently.[12] Men tended to count while giving their descriptions. In describing a bookshelf, for example, one man said, "There are one, two, three, four, five, six books on. . . ." Nowhere was this counting behavior displayed by the females. The sexes also differed in handling numbers. Women preceded half their numerals with indicators of approximation, such as "*about* six books," "six *or* seven books," or "*around* five *or* six books." Perhaps this reflects some culture-induced "math phobia" in females noted by some educators.

There was a difference in the sexes' use of topic-shift markers. Certain words were used to mark a change of topic in the descriptions. Perhaps the speaker had described one part of the picture, for example the foreground, and had prepared to move on. Generally he or she used some marker to show a topic change. Topic-shift markers included pauses; interjections, such as "OK!" "All right!" "Now!"; conjunctions *and, or,* or *but;* or a combination of these devices.

Women used significantly more conjunctions, such as *and,* than did men. Men used interjections, "OK!" for example, as markers for topic shift: "There's a small shelf with some books piled up on it. OK! Now the man is wearing. . . ."

These and other distinctions may indicate, as the researcher declared, that "Men and women simply do not speak English in the same way."

"Women's language" Robin Lakoff strongly agrees that English is spoken differently by women and men. She believes that each sex learns special styles of speech through socialization. By introspection, she examined the speech of herself, those around her, and in some instances the media and identified a special women's language that she believes is used by and about women. Some of her observations parallel several comments linguist Otto Jespersen made some years ago.[13]

One characteristic of women's language involves color distinctions. Women supposedly make more precise discriminations in naming colors than men do. For example, show someone a drapery or rug that is a brilliant bluish-red. If the speaker is a woman, she might say, "That's fuchsia." A man might say, shrugging, "It's red," or even, "It's purple." In the wall-paint section of a large department store one day, two women and a man were examining paint chips. The man with them drummed his fingers restlessly on the counter as the first woman, pairing various color chips with a scrap of carpet material, asked, "Is that ecru?" "No, I'd say it's beige," the second woman offered. The man responded with amusement, "Sure coulda' fooled me. It looks like dirty white," then added with a chuckle, "or tattle-tale gray!"

Men are said to find discussion of color amusing because they consider such matters trivial or irrelevant. They rank color among the minor decisions relegated to women. So words like the following would supposedly be absent from most men's vocabularies: *chartreuse, turquoise, beige, ecru, aquamarine, taupe, mauve.* Unless a man were joking, using sarcasm, imitating a woman, or working as an interior decorator, he might cause raised eyebrows or be viewed with suspicion if he used these fine color distinctions freely in his speech.

There are also work-specific vocabularies for women such as *dart, shirr, kickpleat* (sewing) and *baste, braise* (cooking). Men, of course, have their specialized terms too: *bore, bit, brace* (tools); *points, universal joint* (autos). In addition to a repertoire of words that spring from women's work and interests, women's language is supposedly characterized by the use of certain adjectives and adverbs that connote triviality or unimportance. Examples of such adjectives might include *sweet, dreadful, precious, darling, lovely, adorable, cute, pretty,* or *charming.* Try visualizing the majority of the men you know saying any of the following, and you can see that such language is generally used by women:

What an adorable baby!
That was sweet of you.
That was a lovely dinner.

Women's language supposedly makes more frequent use of intensive adverbs such as *so, terribly, awfully, quite, such,* and *just*.[14] Examples might be: *"so* kind of you," *"terribly* good," *"awfully* nice," *"quite* fascinating," *"such* fun," or *"just* wonderful."

Another supposed feature of women's language is that expletives, exclamations, or expressive words tend to be weaker when spoken by women. Those used by men are often stronger and more forceful.[15] Compare:

Oh dear! My tire's been stolen!
God dammit! My tire's been stolen!

The Cadillac in front, mine? Goodness, no. Wish it were, though.
The Cadillac in front, mine? Hell, no! Wish it were, though.

One difference between using "Oh dear" and "God dammit," or "Goodness, no" and "Hell, no!" is the difference in force and strength of feeling shown. In our culture we're given to understand that women, or "ladies," as we often label them, are not supposed to show temper, but men may express themselves freely. One theory is that because men occupy superior positions of power in our culture, males have a claim on stronger means of expressing feeling. Firestone observes:

As for the double standard about cursing: A man is allowed to blaspheme the world because it belongs to him to damn—but the same curse out of the mouth of a woman or a minor, i.e., an incomplete 'man' to whom the world does not yet belong, is considered presumptuous, and thus an impropriety or worse.[16]

As the swearing in the speech of actress Ali McGraw in the movie *Love Story* pointedly demonstrates, men's language is increasingly being adopted by women. This might be parallel to the greater number of jobs being opened to and filled by women. It is natural that the language style of those with the advantage or the power—men—would be adopted by those in secondary status, and not the other way around. Sentimental audiences would not have smiled so tolerantly had Ryan O'Neal in the movie lamented, "Oh fudge, Jenny."

By being permitted stronger means of expressing themselves, males receive reinforcement of their position of strength. Generally we listen to those who can express themselves most strongly and forcefully. We do not pay nearly as much attention to or take as seriously those who are unable to speak out with strength on matters that concern

For Men   For Women

HELL
DAMMIT
JEEZ

oh dear
(fizz)
darn
oh my

Males are traditionally permitted stronger means of expression.

them. Most women may be unable to speak out. They may be prevented by cultural programming in "correct" or "appropriate" women's speech. The specific features of women's language are neither bad nor good except in relation to certain situations. What is bad is being restricted to these and similar features only, regardless of the situation, merely on the basis of sex.

Some of the claims concerning women's language need to be investigated further. There has not been much concrete research done either to prove or to disprove that women use significantly different adjectives, adverbs, exclamations, or expletives. But the argument that there is a special women's language is compelling. The idea behind it is that some of the features of women's language imply unimportance or triviality and reflect women's weaker position in the power structure.

Exchanges

The preceding discussion dealt primarily with one-way communication. One-way output in the form of descriptions, explanations, directions, or general talk was examined. Now we will turn to two-way communication and talk-exchange situations.

Formal situations

A study was done of free interaction in communication within male-male and female-female dyads.[17] In each pair of conversations, one person was instructed to try to (1) gain the approval or (2) avoid the approval of the other. The talk was recorded. Women used shorter utterances than men, especially when one of the pair was told to avoid the approval of the other. ("You want her to get the idea that you are not interested in becoming her friend.") Also a greater proportion of women's than men's utterances was made up of answers to questions. An interesting incidental finding was that speech disturbances, such as incomplete sentences—for example, "I don't know what—well, anyway I didn't go"—were greater among male than among female subjects.

Female and male communcation behavior was studied in mock-jury deliberations.[18] Jurors listened to a recorded trial, deliberated, and then returned their verdict. Their deliberations were recorded, transcribed, and scored in terms of different behaviors. Four categories are of special interest:

1 Positive reactions: utterances that show solidarity, release of tension, or agreement, such as "That's a good idea."
2 Attempted answers: utterances that give a suggestion, an opinion, or an orientation, such as "Why don't we . . ." or "Well, I think. . . ."
3 Questions: utterances that ask for an opinion or a suggestion, such as "What can we do about. . . ."
4 Negative reactions: utterances that show disagreement, tension, or antagonism, such as "That's a stupid thing to say" or "Are you saying I'm ignorant?"

Females scored significantly higher than males in positive reactions. Males scored higher than females in the more aggressive category of attempted answers. Overall, men originated significantly more speech acts than women. The investigators conclude from this that men "pro-act." They direct "long bursts of acts" aimed at solving the problem. Women "react" to the contributions of others, agreeing, understanding, and supporting. Further, less than one-half as much of the women's talk as the men's showed antagonism or tended to lower another's status. Of the 127 jurors involved, over two-thirds, approximately 67 percent, were men. Yet they contributed practically four-fifths of the talk, considerably more than their share.

Informal situations

Perhaps one of the most provocative studies is one that surveyed the spontaneous talking behavior of a husband and wife in natural settings over a stretch of time.[19] An expense-free vacation at a large midwestern summer resort was offered as an inducement for a couple to volunteer for the experiment. Here samples of their talk were tape-recorded. To pick up the couple's talk, the investigators custom-built a miniature radio transmitter, fitted with a tiny microphone and a foot-long antenna at the upper end and mounted on the shoulder strap of a camera case that contained a power supply. The gear, which was worn by the subjects, weighed only about three pounds and could be slipped on or off with relative ease.

With minor restrictions the couple was free to wander about the community resort. For purposes of transmission, they could not go beyond the high bluff that overlooked the recreational area along the lake. The monitoring station, which stood on the edge of this bluff, had a high-tracking antenna that was able to pick up any point on the grounds and made it possible to tape-record the entire transmitter output. Beyond these limits, however, transmitting was difficult, because of the terrain. Transmitters were worn by subjects 14 to 16 hours a day and on a normal recording day were turned off at midnight. The couple whose talk was analyzed had been married about a year, and both were college educated. Roz, the wife, was twenty, and Jock, the husband, was twenty-five.

The couple's talk was analyzed during a 16-hour day in a number of different ways, including the following four.

1 *Units or episodes.* Talk was broken down according to episodes or behaviors that occurred in a specific place and were devoted to a particular activity. For example, the following were considered to be episodes: breakfast, lunch, packing, craft shop, and rowing.

2 *Amount and length of talk.*

3 *Kinds and uses of talk.* The researchers focused on two main functions of talk, *informational* and *relational. Informational talk* was defined as statements about oneself or one's world. Examples of informational talk taken from Roz and Jock's recordings are:

That is a Modigliani.
His name isn't Karl Schmidt.
It's four miles from here.

Relational talk was defined as talk used by a speaker to manage his or her relations with others. Relational talk reflects the needs of the speaker and may include demands, commands, requests, and so forth. It changes interpersonal relations by getting the listener to take account of and adjust to the state of the speaker. Three main types of relational talk were identified: (a) *directive*, (b) *inductive*, and (c) *quasi-* or partly relational.

a. *Directive* talk controls behavior by demands and prohibitions or promotes action by invitations, suggestions, and permissions. This kind of talk delineates the behavior the speaker wants in order to bring about the desired relation. Examples from Roz and Jock's speech include:

Then get going! [demand]
Why don't you do it right now? [suggestion]
Of course you may. [permission]

Informational Talk
Identifies, classifies, analyzes, organizes, conveys information

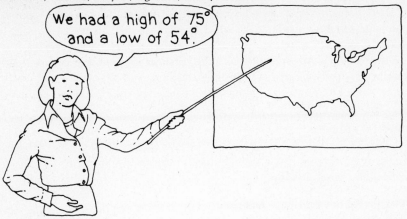

Relational Talk
Directive: controls behavior

Quasi-relational

Inductive: reports speaker's physical or
          psychological state

Two ways to analyze talk.

b. *Inductive* talk does not demand or suggest. Instead it provides information, the knowledge of which may cause the listener to respond with the desired behavior. Inductive messages report the speaker's present physical or psychological state, such as physical sensations, emotions, needs, hopes, wishes, likes, dislikes, and so forth:

I'm cold, tired, hungry.
Now I'm completely confused.
Oh Jock, I like that.

Inductive messages may also include appraisals and statements of obligation like the following:

Yours is the best one here. [appraisal]
What a fool I've been. [appraisal]
You shouldn't do that. [obligation and appraisal]

c. *Quasi-* or partly relational messages are not necessarily spoken to influence the listener. Some are expressive, feeling aloud, and serve immediately to release some feeling, such as, *Ouch! Wow! Darn!*—pure discharge behaviors. Others are best described as thinking aloud, such as:

Hmmm, what have I done wrong here?
I wonder if it would work this way.

The speaker may not aim to communicate with another person, yet these messages tend to have effects on listeners who are within hearing.

4 *Changing intrapersonal and interpersonal relationships as they are influenced by verbal exchanges.* The final type of analysis involved looking at the shifts and variations in their attempts to modify each other's internal and external states. The focus is on the moment-to-moment dynamics of communication behavior as influenced by verbal give and take.

The results of the analysis of Roz and Jock's talk were as follows.

1, 2 *Amount and length of talk in episodes.* Jock's talk consisted of longer units of speech, and he took more than his share of the available talking time. The researchers remarked: "Although his behavior in this respect was quite variable, one tends to remember how easily and how frequently he seized upon available talking time, sometimes quite artlessly assuming the position of the most informed and most interesting member of a social group."[20] Roz was found to be more sensitive to her own impact on the group and to the possible interests and needs of other group members. She frequently acted as a "governor" for Jock, often skillfully, though not always so tactfully, "attenuating his impact on the group." Over a number of different episodes, the share of the talking time Jock took varied from 79 percent in an episode where he was alone with his wife, to 29 percent in a situation in which he was taking golf instruction. Across all the episodes, his total share of talking time claimed was 50.6 percent. This may be the result of the particular selection of episodes examined.

Concerning the average length of different kinds of talk, the longer stretches of talk for both Roz and Jock were, as a rule, information-exchanging messages.

3 *Kinds and uses of talk.* In comparing the kinds of messages Roz and Jock used in different episodes, both used about the same proportion of appraisal relational talk—for example, "Yours is the best one here"; and reports about feeling states—for example, "I'm angry," or "I wish I could go, too." However, Roz produced significantly more expressive or reacting aloud messages—for example, "Ouch!" "Darn!" Jock used more directive statements, "Stop that!" "Won't you join us?" and more informational statements, "It's four miles from here," "That fits over the axle." The wife seemed more explicitly emotive than the husband, whereas he tended to be the more active of the two in structuring and directing interaction between persons. One can only speculate whether these patterns were due to sex differences, age differences, or the particular episodes studied.

4 *Verbal exchanges and changing relationships.* Some interesting patterns emerged. Roz and Jock varied their type of talk from one situation to another. Roz produced a high percentage of emotion-venting messages, "Oh!" "Whoops!", whenever the two were out of the public view. She became noticeably more controlled when others were present. Jock's output of expressive talk was relatively low throughout. Both Roz and Jock tended to produce more directive, controlling talk, "Why don't you get it right now!" only in private or semiprivate exchanges. Roz's output of reports of her physical or psychological states, "I'm tired" or "I like that!" was consistently high in four of five situations analyzed. Jock's talk was more variable, however, and his output of private-state messages was highest in situations where he had placed himself in the role of pupil—for example, with a golf instructor.

In conversation, Roz and Jock differed in the proportion of initiating and responding remarks made. The course of a conversation may be viewed as being directed by initiating or instigative remarks—we shall call them starters—that call forth a series of responses. In samples of the couple's talk each starter was usually followed by a succession of responses from either person, so that the next five or six exchanges were controlled by the initiating remark. For example, "Aren't those cabins nice?" might be a starter remark. A high percentage of starters by one speaker and a high percentage of responses by the second would imply that the first was directing the course of the talk.

Roz and Jock differed significantly in the number of starters and responses they produced. In several of the episodes of speaking, Jock was the more frequent initiator. In a breakfast conversation, for example, seemingly stimulated by the presence of two others, Jock took the lead and controlled the topic of conversation. Yet there was one occasion at lunch, with two others present, when Roz was the more frequent initiator. Fourteen percent of Roz's remarks were initiating at that time, while only 2 percent of Jock's were. This result may have reflected the fact that Jock's conversation followed a single theme, termed ego-elevating experiences by the researchers, for some time. Roz seemed to be trying to shift the conversation to other topics. As the writers remarked, "At times she seemed embarrassed by her husband's tales." The greatest similarity between the husband and wife appeared in social settings, such as lunch or breakfast, which call for a fairly heavy dependence on informational language. The greatest difference between them occurred in situations of greater intimacy where much of their talk consisted of various types of relational language.

Communication strategies

We have referred several times to the view that the asymmetrical power relations between the sexes are reflected in female/male communication differences. Some elements of women's speech that differ from men's speech do not strengthen the position of women in our society. Therefore, it is easy to assume that women's speech is generally bad or inferior and men's good and superior. Techniques of communication that promote individual supremacy, aid in getting the competitive edge, and generate direct action to wrest success or reward from the world appear to be esteemed most highly. These devices embody the predominant value system in our society.

But we must not overlook the fact that a strong alternate value system exists, one which some predict will be the orientation of the future. This has been depicted as the system prescribed for women and lower-ranking members of our society. It stresses the goals and welfare of the group, self-realization, and the importance of who one is rather than what one has accomplished. Techniques of communication most valuable to this system would promote getting along with members in a group and achieving cooperation, interpersonal discovery, and self-expression. These techniques seem to be most frequently used by many women. While they do not represent a center of power, women do have considerable influence in many ways. Their modes of communication should be viewed as positive strategies and explored as useful behaviors, not undesirable opposites of so-called male traits.[21] Of course, the difficulty is that the behaviors and traits of the dominant group in power are the yardstick for measuring what we see as good or bad. So the communication techniques and behaviors of the dominant group are generally sought after and adopted by those in a secondary position. We shall consider several of the alternate communication strategies next.

Tag questions

Lakoff talks at length about the tag question, which she believes women use in more conversational situations than men and which she identifies as a device to avoid making a strong statement.[22] A tag question is its own special animal. It is in-between a statement and a question. A tag question is less assertive than an outright statement such as "Jill wore my clown suit." But it is more confident than a clearcut yes/no question such as "Did Jill wear my clown suit?" A tag question is half and half: "Jill wore my clown suit . . . didn't she?" It is useful for in-between situations where an outright statement is not appropriate and where a yes/no question is not fitting either.

There are situations in which it is legitimate or logical to use a tag question and others in which it is not warranted. Places where tag questions are used and seem to fit include such situations as the following:

1 It is possible to miss seeing and hearing all of a communication and to have only partial information. If the television is turned up loudly, I may not hear clearly when Louise announces to the group she is going to recite Brahman poetry under the stars until midnight. Therefore, I would probably not state with certainty, "Louise is going to recite Brahman poetry under the stars until midnight." Yet I have enough information so that I probably do not have to ask, "Is Louise going to recite Brahman poetry?" I will most likely phrase my utterance in such a way as to get a confirmation of what I suspect to be true, by tacking on a partial question at the end: "Louise is going to recite Brahman poetry . . . isn't she?" This indicates that I think she is, but I am requesting confirmation.

2 On some occasions we feel the necessity to make small talk in order to start conversation or draw someone out. Parties in the conversation know the answer to the question asked already, and it doesn't need confirmation. But it makes up part of the patchwork of small talk that helps us structure much of our daily interaction. I may be put in a social situation with someone I don't know very well. Uneasily trying to fill the awkward silences, I may say "Sure is fun here, isn't it?" or "The walls are unusually perpendicular this evening, aren't they?"

3 Sometimes we use a tag question to request confirmation for something we hope will be accomplished or to try to persuade or wring out a commitment from another. Our daughter may come to us at the table and, leaning forward overcongenially, say overcheerfully, "I can have

Statement

Question

Tag question

Tag questions are part statement and part question.

the car tonight . . . can't I?" Or in measured tones I may address our son, "You are going to clean that disaster area you call a room before supper, aren't you?"

These and similar verbalizations seem to be warranted uses of the tag question. But when a speaker is talking about herself and her feelings or opinions, she has no need to question and get confirmation about them. She, and only she, already knows the correct answer to what her views or feelings are. The following would be ridiculous: "I have a stomach ache, don't I?" or "I hate eggplant, don't I?" The same is true of one's views or judgments about an issue. It would be odd to say "I think Chevy Chase is very profound, don't I?" Only the speaker herself knows if she views something as shallow or profound, or whatever.

Yet compare the following: "Doing syntactic analysis of linguistic transcriptions is fun, isn't it?" Although there are other interpretations, one can take it as an expression of the speaker's own feelings about syntactic analysis, namely, "I feel syntactic analysis of linguistic transcriptions is fun, don't I?" However, only the speaker knows if she enjoys it. Use of the tag in this case implies the person speaking has a definite feeling or opinion in mind but may be hesitant to state it plainly.

The pattern of opinion-giving followed by a tag question is claimed to be more common among women than men. Women's speech is said to be more polite in general than men's.[23] The tag question is a tool of politeness. By phrasing one's opinion indirectly and asking approval or confirmation, the speaker avoids making a strong statement or imposing her views on another. It does not force belief or agreement on the hearer; the tag requests belief or agreement. The decision is left open to the listener. In situations where feelings are strong and persons with opposing views threaten to clash head-on, the use of this device is obvious. It can help avoid conflict and unpleasant confrontation.

But the same device can be a burden as well as a boon to women. It becomes a burden when, because of its obliqueness, the tag question robs communication of force in situations that require vigor and directness. The talker may give the impression that she is not really sure of herself. Overuse of tags puts the speaker in the position of constantly looking to someone else for confirmation or approval of her ideas. She avoids committing herself and never directly reveals or takes a stand on her own views.

One young woman revealed in a discussion:

I often say to my boyfriend, "That's a pretty good album, isn't it?" I suppose I put it that way because I don't want to put my tastes on the line and commit myself like I would if I announced, "That's a good album." Then he could contradict me and say, "No, I don't think the arrangements are good." By tail-ending a question to my statement, I don't come on so strong and I'm putting part of the judgment on his shoulders. Since I don't stick my neck out, I don't lose much. In fact, if he violently dislikes the album I can always say, "Oh, I didn't think so anyway. That's why I asked."

Most of the time we probably use tags without thinking. But we need to be aware that their overuse can make us appear to be wishy-washy, incapable of making decisions, or bland and uninteresting. When our youngest daughter was eleven, she explained why she no longer visited her friend Kathy: "She's really kind of boring. Everything I want to do, she says 'OK' and everything I talk about she agrees with."

There is a paucity of research on the appearance of tag questions in conversation, and there is some difference of opinion concerning their incidence in women's speech. Lakoff's theory that they occur more frequently in women's speech arises out of introspection and her observation of those around her, rather than any quantitative analysis of this phenomenon. In our transcriptions of faculty meetings, there were not sufficient numbers of tag questions occurring in the transcripts to draw any firm conclusions, but there was a tendency for women to use them more. One faculty woman in particular was the source of most of the tags uttered. Most of them involved her opinions or feelings about which only she could provide the correct answer. For example:

That's a great idea, isn't it?
That's disheartening, isn't it?
The way he's getting pushed around isn't right, is it?

A very specialized study of interviews with persons seventy years or older who were born in Maine revealed that the men interviewed used the tag question very little and even then, apparently not in connection with personal feelings or opinion.[24] One of the few tag questions occurred in a discussion about the voting age: "Oh, I think it's eighteen now, isn't it?" Another undoubtedly prompted a smile from the interviewer when the old man, after being stopped during his account several times to explain unfamiliar terms such as *pickpole* or *peavey*, said at one point: "We went across in a canoe. You know what a canoe is, don't you?"

The women interviewed used tag questions more frequently. The researcher felt this feature made their speech seem "hesitant and tentative and polite." Examples of their use of tag questions seemed to cover the range of uses:

Well, most people would say marriage, wouldn't they?
Men had to take it, didn't they?
But she was brave, wasn't she?
Sounds like eighty-six, doesn't it? [her age]

Another study using tape recordings of a small professional meeting varying from 15 to 25 participants, found surprisingly that of the 33 tag questions used, all were spoken by men and none by women. Formal tags, "weren't you?" "does he?" "hasn't it?", and informal tags, "right?" "OK?", were counted in the total. There was approximately the same number of each.[25] However, the researchers did not distinguish between what Lakoff would term "legitimate" tag questions and those that were tied to personal feelings or opinion. It is the latter that Lakoff thinks women use more frequently. Since it is not known whether the males in the study used any personal-feeling tags, we cannot interpret the results as necessarily weakening Lakoff's theory.

There is an additional observation to be made about tag questions. So far the mitigating influence of this device has been stressed. The tag appears to attach a degree of tentativeness and reservation to any statement. But there are a group of tag questions that perform an opposite function. They reinforce and project the strength of the statement, rather than modify and weaken it. For example:

You certainly don't expect me to be happy about this mess, do you!
I've saved and planned for this trip for two years and you aren't thinking of standing in my way, are you!

The emphatic exclamation point used in place of the plaintive question mark indicates the attitude of the speaker in these two situations. Future research of tag questions might categorize the mitigating and assertive types of tag questions in different situations. It is interesting to speculate as to possible trends in the use of these types of questions by females and males.

Qualifiers

Another technique that seems to be employed in women's language more often than in men's is the use of softening, mitigating, or qualifying words and phrases. These are additions to our utterances that can soften or blunt the impact of what we say. They are used to avert or avoid negative or unwanted reactions to our words, and they seem to make our statements less absolute in tone. We use these devices in the beginnings, endings, and sprinkled throughout our utterances: *well, let's see, perhaps, possibly, I suppose, I think, it seems to me, you know,* and so on. Compare the force of the following:

You shouldn't do that.
Perhaps you shouldn't do that.
That's foolish.
It seems to me that's foolish.
You're doing that wrong.
I wonder if you're doing that wrong.
It's time to go.
It's time to go, *I guess.*
No.
Well, no.

Counterbalancing the directness and force of a statement by adding qualifiers makes the speech sound more tentative. Other examples

Mitigating qualifiers may inappropriately weaken utterances, making them tentative and timid (top). Inappropriate use of disclaimers may weaken one's stand (bottom).

include such softeners as *rather, somewhat, sort of, to some extent.* Again, compare:

He's weird.   He's *somewhat* weird.
She's fat.   She's *sort of* fat.

One qualifier that males have been found to use more frequently than females in conversation is *I think.* A study of female-male conversation found that males used *I think* almost twice as often as females. Used more often by the assertive speakers, the device seemed to be employed less as a qualifier than as a way of politely stating one's opinion.[26]

Another device used in smoothing personal interactions is what some term a disclaimer.[27] These mitigators are usually introductory expressions that excuse, explain, or request understanding or forbearance, such as, "I may be wrong but . . ." or "You may not like this, but. . . ." Research has identified different types of disclaimers:

1 "Suspension of judgment," used to ward off emotional judgments: "I don't want you to get mad, but. . . ."
2 "Cognitive disclaimers," used to avoid disbelief or suspicions of poor logic or nonpossession of the facts: "This may sound crazy, but. . . ."
3 "Sin licenses," used to explain or validate supposed misconduct or rule bending: "This may violate the ordinary sense of the law, but not the spirit of these rules. . . ."
4 "Credentialing," used to present special attributes or qualities of the speaker when the reaction is expected to be negative or unfavorable: "Some of my best friends are Indians, but. . . ."
5 "Hedging," used to indicate that the speaker is not adamant about his or her point but is willing to accept other views, or when the speaker does not want to be held accountable for the statement and so hedges to avoid being diminished or damaged in the other's eyes: "I could be mistaken, but . . ." or "I'm not entirely certain, but. . . ."

Disclaimers bear much more looking into, as far as differences in their use by the sexes are concerned. The transcriptions of faculty meetings did not include sufficient numbers of disclaimers to draw firm conclusions, but there was a tendency for women to use more of them than the male faculty members. There were noticeably more disclaimers of the second type, disclaiming poor logic or nonpossession of the facts, and the fifth type, hedging and tentativeness:

I know this sounds silly, but I think. . . . [2]
This may strike you as odd, but we probably should. . . . . [2]
You're going to think this is stupid, but why don't we. . . . [2]
Well, I'm not the expert, but something tells me. . . . [5]
I'm not saying this is a perfect solution, but we could. . . . [5]

All the examples of these two types seem to reflect a presumption that the listener has a basic disregard for or mistrust in the speaker's logic and the soundness of her views. This is not so true of types 1 and 3, which anticipate reactions not so closely related to personal credibility.

We can see the usefulness of disclaimers as verbal strategies to soften negative reactions to what we say or to break some social rules without raising ire. On the other hand, overuse or inappropriate use of disclaimers could weaken one's stand. Why prejudice our case falsely with "I'm not an expert in this, but . . ." or "You may say this is dumb, but . . ." when you feel you stand on a firm base of knowledge and feel confident of your position. We must train ourselves to choose and use disclaimers wisely and sparingly and not to let them tumble from our lips automatically when we are at a loss for words. The Maine study of older women and men mentioned earlier showed that the women's speech was more qualified and the men generally spoke in absolutes.

Lengthening of requests

Another useful verbal strategy that women employ in the mode of politeness is the lengthening of orders and requests through the addition of extra particles. Generally, the shorter a request, the more force or compulsion it conveys. The longer a request, the less it seems to press agreement or compliance on the hearer, to imply threat of consequences for noncompliance, or to suggest a position of superiority or power for the speaker. In the following examples, the more particles that are added, the more the decision is left open to the hearer:

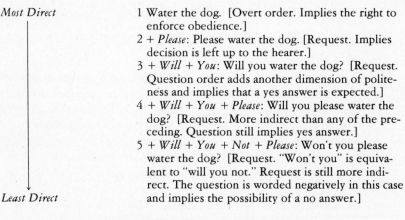

Most Direct

1 Water the dog. [Overt order. Implies the right to enforce obedience.]

2 + *Please*: Please water the dog. [Request. Implies decision is left up to the hearer.]

3 + *Will* + *You*: Will you water the dog? [Request. Question order adds another dimension of politeness and implies that a yes answer is expected.]

4 + *Will* + *You* + *Please*: Will you please water the dog? [Request. More indirect than any of the preceding. Question still implies yes answer.]

5 + *Will* + *You* + *Not* + *Please*: Won't you please water the dog? [Request. "Won't you" is equivalent to "will you not." Request is still more indirect. The question is worded negatively in this case and implies the possibility of a no answer.]

Least Direct

We could carry these examples[28] to an extreme compounding of indirectness as in the superpolite, "It would really help me and I would certainly appreciate it, if you would be able to spare the time to water the dog." These devices are useful in situations where bluntness or direct utterances could trigger hostility, anger, or irrational outbursts from hearers. They are also employed as a way to make one's wishes or needs heard in a situation where others hold the power or authority.

There is no conclusive research on the greater incidence of particles of indirectness and compound requests among women. However, some preliminary observations seem to support the view that women use this style more than men. Previously we mentioned exercises we had done with students instructing group members to draw an arrangement of squares using word cues only. In the cases we observed, there was a decided tendency for most males to be more directive, *telling* the group where to draw the lines, rather than *requesting* that they do so. Note the difference in styles. A male:

. . . . Next! Put your pencil on the bottom left corner of the square. This will be the midpoint of a line you'll drawn. Draw your line at a 45-degree angle to the left side and the bottom side of the square. Now get this! This line is the top side of a second square. Remember! I said the corner intersects the top. Don't get it off center or you'll blow the whole thing.

A female:

. . . . Then I'd like you to construct another box just below the first one, all right? Only this time, try to arrange it so the left point of the first box touches the top of the second box in the middle.

The more direct imperatives of the male, "Put your pencil . . ." "Draw your line . . ." "Remember!" "Don't get it off center or . . . ," contrast with the more polite "I'd like you to . . ." "All right?" and "Only this time, try . . . ," of the female. A student, slightly piqued after the exercise, complained once, "I got tired of his [a male speaker] ordering us around all the time. At some points I felt like throwing my pencil at him!"

The transcriptions of faculty meetings showed most of the participants resorted to indirectness in tactfully phrasing requests or wishes, whatever their sex. More samples of dialogue in meetings need to be analyzed, but the tendency was for men to be more direct. In the case of one woman, the number of politeness particles in her utterances was overdone to the point that she diminished her impact on the group. Several of the more conspicuous examples from her speech were utterances that even asked permission to ask a question:

I'd just like to ask you how many work-study people we have. [Rather than simply, How many work-study people do we have?]
Well, let me just ask this—is there a limit on that item? [Rather than, Is there a limit on that item?]
I was just wondering what it is that we can do to prevent his leaving. [Rather than, How can we prevent his leaving?]

One can argue that the woman was using the introductory phrases as attention-getting prefaces or lead-ins to her question. But the intonation that accompanied her utterances, plus the general roundaboutness of her verbal interaction overall, belied this. Her style suggested an uncertainty of conviction and a readiness to defer to any opposing views or sudden objections. As in the case of the other strategies discussed, unselective or automatic use of polite requests can be detrimental.

Fillers

Fillers used in talk include such verbalizations as *uhm, well, like, you know*. In a study of female-male conversational interaction, females were found to use a much higher proportion of fillers than males.[29] Females used fewest fillers in female-female conversations, although they still surpassed males in the use of this device. This suggests more fluent, less hesitant speech by females talking together and may indicate females are more at ease with a female than with a male.

The investigator suggested that females who talked more may have compensated for their possible "aggressiveness" by "increased indications of hesitancy and increased responsiveness." Women who do take the initiative more in conversations may feel guilty because of their past socialization to docility and their awareness of society's norms of talk for women. Perhaps to offset or play down their taking the initiative, some women try still to give some signs of "proper" nonassertiveness or submissiveness. Use of fillers and hesitations such as *uhm, well,* and so forth may serve as one such sign.

One of the writers had this called to her attention concerning her own style of speech. In making strong or opinionated statements, even within the family, she often makes some false starts; produces a certain number of fillers such as *well, uhm,* and so forth; and then launches into the message, full tilt. During the course of the polemic, listeners are further subjected to intermittent verbal mitigators, qualifiers, and fillers as if to reassure or remind the listener, "Remember, it's just normal, sweet little ole me saying these things."

Suiting style and situation

It is dangerous to conclude that there are rules governing women's style and men's style of speaking. It may even be presumptuous to speak of women's speech and men's speech. But even though we rarely meet a perfect walking-talking version of the female stereotype or of the male stereotype, theory and research point toward some generalizations about the speech of females and males.

1 Women's speech tends to be more person-centered and concerned with interpersonal matters. It is apt to deal with the speaker's own and other's feelings. It is more polite, more indirect, and uses the method of implication. It employs qualifiers and other softening devices to avoid imposing belief, agreement, or obedience on others through overly strong statements, questions, or commands.

2 Men's speech tends to be more centered around external things and is more apt to involve straight factual communication. It is more literal, direct, and to the point. It employs stronger statements and forms that tend to press compliance, agreement, or belief on the listener.[30]

Lakoff has shown that most of the characteristics we list under numbers 1 and 2 can be viewed as two possible conversational styles with various possibilities for shades and mixtures of the two. In this view, most women are seen to use more of style 1, although some occasionally resort to style 2. More men adopt style 2.

The damage comes when women and men cannot readily switch from one style to the other to meet the demands of the situation. To be consistently tied to one style or general mode of talk just because of one's sex limits one as a human being. It predestines the woman or man to a one-sidedness and narrowness in communication. We hope today's children can be encouraged and taught to use both styles early in their communication training.

A consequence of sex differences: frustration and misunderstanding

The second of the two speech styles just outlined has been described as direct, relatively strong in tone, fact-bound, and one which thrives on evidence. This style lends itself well to argument, but it is a mode that does not appear to be comfortable for a number of women. Many females find the argumentative style not only difficult to use, but inhibiting when it is used against them.

Some theory and research on speech patterns suggest that personal opinion, attitudes, and personality are more important for women than fact-bound information. Presumably they prefer talk that is intimate and personal, dealing with how they think and feel. It has been suggested that many women are at a disadvantage in fact-bound talk because they are less likely to have a hard factual background or to be in contact with the world of knowledge.[31]

A study was made of sex differences in intellectual argumentation in the college classroom and the kinds of negative or positive emotive feedback that discussants get.[32] Five types of argumentation contributions were examined: recalling facts, making observations, seeing relationships, hypothesizing, and testing hypotheses. Results showed college males participated more often than females, even though a greater number of females made at least one statement of contribution. Males made significantly more intellectual argumentation statements than females. As for listener responses, males received more positive feedback than females, especially from instructors and female classmates. Both sexes completed a questionnaire and rated the five categories of intellectual argumentation as significantly masculine sex-role standards in society and in the class. So argumentation behaviors were considered primarily male characteristics, rather than standard behavior for both sexes.

Such generalized sex differences may account for the clichés in the way each sex views the other. To some males, women's speech sometimes seems peripheral or off center: "She's totally illogical!" Women's talk may not come sheathed in a protective coating of facts and figures or straight-line reasoning. To men, women's dialogues often seem mindless or superficial, mere recitals of feelings. In reality, the women are sharing a kind of emotional resolution and comfort in their

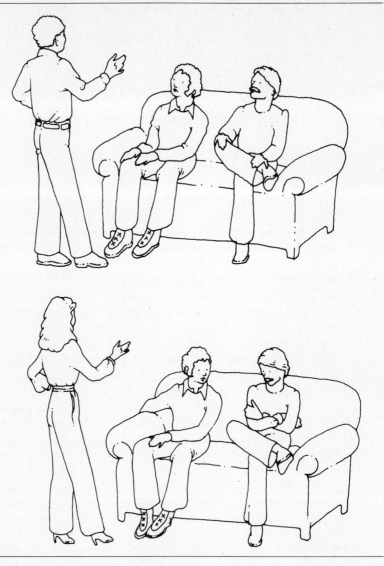

Males usually receive more positive feedback than females for argumentative behavior.

conversation, according to one view.[33] Each woman comments upon the other's feelings by reflecting them in her responses. This occurs in a "very sensitive matching process." Women, on the other hand, may view men's argumentative style as wearing or too competitive: "He takes such obvious pleasure in proving me wrong!" Male dialogue is often weighted by an insistence that statements be based on straight-line reasoning.

One analysis of conversational interaction indicated that, when they talked to each other, the males tended to argue and the females tended to elaborate on each other's utterances. In many cases, males would dispute the other person's utterance or ignore it, while the females would acknowledge it or often build on it.[34]

In verbal conflict situations, women may be at a disadvantage. In some laboratory game experiments, for example, women used accommodative strategies and men used exploitative ones. The women used obliging, favoring, or adjustive tactics, and the men employed more selfish devices calculated for self-advantage or profit. Women strove for a fair outcome, acceptable to all, whereas men were primarily geared toward winning.[35] Research indicates that women seem to shrink from the use of pressure tactics. A study of a philanthropic money-raising activity in a Canadian city found men more amenable to using pressure on prospective contributors, whereas women were hesitant to do so.[36] In competitive and conflict situations, women seem to come out second best by default, by refusing to enter the dialogue arena.

Communication reticence in women apparently cuts across the lines of status and occupation. Even university faculty women may come out second best and fail to speak as frequently or as forcibly as men. Eileen Morley describes some of her own private agonies in communicating:

In a word, I was tongue-tied. Either my mind froze so that I had no thoughts to offer; or if I did have thoughts, I could never find a way into the discussion to make them known. In the latter case I would wait for a speaker to finish talking and open my mouth to respond, but before I had actually produced any sound, someone else would have taken the floor. In the infrequent event that I actually produced words, they did not seem to be experienced as particularly useful by the other people present. I began to feel not so much a silent partner as invisible. And this is particularly tricky in a society which values verbal interchange so highly. To be silent means you might just as well not be there at all. You are a non-person.[37]

Talk is extremely important in our society and has a crucial impact on decision making. A wordless individual, rather than being a silent partner, is in effect invisible. And to be silent is tantamount to being a nonperson in our society. Women's words are not always received the way men's words are. The study comparing male and female argumentation behaviors and listener responses showed a tendency for males to receive more positive feedback and encouraging responses, particularly from instructors and female peers. Subjects considered participation in argumentation to be a masculine rather than feminine activity.[38]

Apparently society rewards males, but not females, for intellectual argument. Perhaps women are even subtly penalized in this regard. Research demonstrated that the same communication coming from males and females got different receptions. In one case, a male lecturer's words were accepted as more authoritative, while identical words from

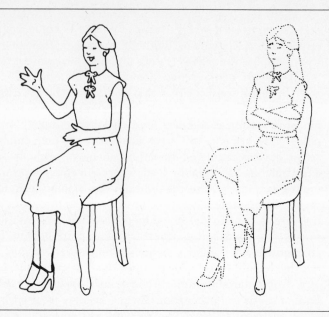

A wordless person is often an invisible person.

a female lecturer were seen as less so. The ideas women advance in a group may be less readily acted upon. Sometimes they are ignored, and the discussion just continues along the same lines as before. Sheila Tobias told of her experience in mixed-sex meetings:

I would go home depressed, thinking about what a communication problem I had. . . . Sometimes I would make a suggestion during the meeting and— nothing! Then later in the course of the meeting I would hear my idea clothed in different words, advanced by a man. And they listened! *Then* it was a good idea.[39]

Even with today's changing attitudes, a woman who displays skill at argument risks losing social acceptance and approval in some situations. Men's self-esteem and acceptability seem to turn on their ideas and actions—what they do. Many women's self-esteem and social acceptability still appear to depend very much on what they *are*—that is, on their personal acceptability in terms of how they look and sound. It has been said that women value the self as a function of reflected appraisals.[40]

Woman's sense of self may be more dependent on the reflection she sees mirrored in others' eyes than a man's is. Her selfhood may be defined more by the approval and acceptance she senses from others. Men may have developed a sense of self-regard that does not depend as much on outside sources.

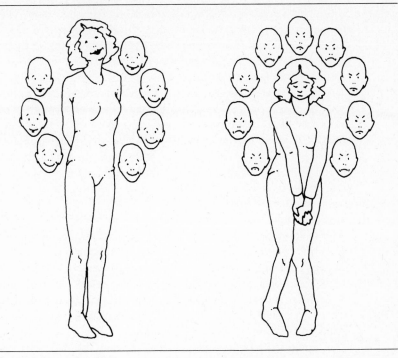

A woman's self-image tends to be based on others' reactions to her.

If so, a woman may take a greater risk in behaving in a way not appropriate to her sex than a man does. If a woman uses an argumentative or unfeminine style, she may risk disapproval, a very real threat to her self-esteem. If certain behaviors make a woman more psychologically vulnerable, one answer may be that she needs to develop inner sources of self-esteem to cushion her against the impact of rejection and criticism.

More training and practice for women in articulating thought processes must be given in the schools. The study on students' argumentation contributions in discussion only underscores what many college instructors have known for some time: women students are often hesitant to put their thinking on the line for consideration. To do so opens oneself to possible criticism of the way one's conclusions were formed.

The person, usually male, with the ready mouth is in one sense at an advantage. He is not so cautious and bound to mental preplanning of every word that his contributions to a group are inhibited. With every contribution—whether it succeeds or fails, is accepted or rejected—he is testing his skill against the whetstone of group process. He is trying out, monitoring, and modifying his explanatory and reasoning powers.

In the very process of talking out his thoughts and verbally walking through his reasoning, he is becoming increasingly aware of his thought processes and train of thinking. The old saw about the woman who blurted out, "How do I know what I think till I see what I say?" may have more truth than fiction in it.

The research cited suggests that women have been victims of years of conditioning. Their speech patterns, their use of tag questions, and their use of qualifiers have relegated them to second-class status insofar as dialogue is concerned. Generalizations about women being more talkative and more rapid speakers have not been supported by research findings. Conditioning and the perpetuation of myths about sex differences have placed barriers to equal communication rights. However, changes are occurring.

Today women are beginning to use male communication techniques. Some are voluntarily putting themselves into intensive training programs to acquire new skills of assertiveness and more open and forceful communication. The best of these programs do more than attempt to resocialize women in the tactics of male communication. They try to strike a healthy balance between extreme aggressiveness and disregard for others, on the one hand, and excessive self-effacement and denial of rights to oneself, on the other.

Some see an imprudent rush to emulate the male by those in the women's movement, with a consequent loss or disregard for the unique and excellent behaviors most often found in women. "Don't throw the baby out with the bath water" is the admonition. One enthusiastic student in a women's communication course summed it up this way: "I think the strategies women have found to use in communication are really neat!"

Suggested activities

1 Listen closely to the verbal interaction of females and males.

    a. Write out verbatim each tag question you hear.

    b. Count the number of tag questions used by each speaker. Does either sex use tags more?

    c. Devise a system of classifying tag questions.

    d. Do you see any difference in the kinds of tags used by females and males?

    e. Monitor your own speech for a day. Do you tend to use many tag questions?

    f. Discuss the significance of your results for women and men communicating.

A suggested format for recording results follows.

Tag Questions Used

Speaker	Age	Female	Male
1	8	"I can go, can't I?"	
2	11		"You can fix it, can't you?"
3	37	"That was messy, wasn't it?"	
4			
5			

2 Listen to some conversations and note all the orders and requests that occur.

  a. Does either sex issue more commands or requests?

  b. Are there differences in the types of requests used by either sex?

  c. What implications do your findings have for female and male communicators?

Suggested format to record results:

Polite: least ——————————————————————————→ most					
Speaker	Sex	Age	Direct	Simple	Compound
1	M	18		+ please	
2	F	45		+ will you	
3	F	9			+ please + will you
4					
5					
6					
7					

3 List all the differences you notice in the way people around you use exclamations or expressions of feeling. Try to include younger children, teenagers, and adults of both sexes in your observations. Some examples are listed:

Woman: Oh dear! You locked the cat in the closet again.
Man: Dammit! You locked the cat in the closet again.
Woman: Oh, no! You've tracked mud in the house again!

Man: Oh, no! My pliers are missing!
Woman: What a charming house you have!
Man: This is a damn fine home.
Woman: This house is great.
Man: Great place you've got here.

Suggested format to record results:

Speakers	Age	Female	Male	Both
1	20–25	Oh dear!	Dammit!	Oh, no!
2	40–50	charming		
3	30–35		damn fine	
4	20–25			great
5				

4 Show several boys and girls of about the same age a magazine picture, photograph, drawing, painting, or sketch and ask each of them to describe it. Take notes and time the descriptions.

a. Who speaks longest and uses most words?

b. Who seems to be more objective, precise, and scientific in the descriptions?

c. Who seems to read meaning into the picture, interpreting or seeing a story or happening in it?

d. Who reads more emotion and feeling into the scene, characters, or setting?

e. Explain what your results tell you about communication and the sex of the speaker.

5 Make a list of words which seem to be taboo for each sex. These would include words not usually spoken by one sex or the other without the possibility of causing prejudice or provoking laughter. Take your list from listening to people around you and from books, magazines, and papers. For example, a student discussion produced these:

Not usually sanctioned for use by females	Not usually sanctioned for use by males
Haul outa' there!	Please move your fanny.
That's one helluva jacket.	What a cute jacket.
C'mon! Step outside a minute.	I'll scratch your eyes out.

3   Why can't a woman be more like a man? communication between the sexes

A concern for the importance of conversation in civilization is not new. Indeed, before 1615, an eager scholar looking in a dictionary for a definition of the word *converse* would have found the following: "To converse: to have sexual intercourse."[1] The sexual act was considered to be the ultimate form of human communication. The fact that such a powerful label as *converse* was used for the terms "talk with," "speak of," and "interchange thoughts and opinions in speech" says something about the importance of conversation.

The importance of talk

Verbal exchange is valued highly in our society. There is some research to support the theory that talk may be as important as sex in marriage.[2] In his novel *The Magic Mountain*, Thomas Mann identifies the essence of talk and stresses the bonding nature of discourse when one of his characters is prompted to say, "Speech is civilization itself. The word, even the most contradictory word, preserves contact— it is silence which isolates."

Conversation is the bonding agent between ourselves and our society. It enables us to reaffirm our own existence. To a great extent our personalities are molded and shaped by our ability to interact verbally with other people. Talk can be used for informing, persuading, entertaining, conveying emotions, and solving problems. It can be ritualistic in what Eric Berne terms "pastimes,"[3] such as greetings or comments on sports, the weather, or politics. In terms of social dialogue, talk is multifunctional.

Yet it is often said that "talk is cheap" and that we live in a "world of words." A common complaint is that we are "drowning in a sea of words." This only underscores the need for us to get inside and inspect this "bubble of Babel." We intend to cast a new light on the very interesting but relatively unexplored phenomenon of talk as it is carried on by women and men.

In this chapter we shall consider the structure of talk and include some provocative models and examples of the social influence of conversation. The first portion lays the background for the studies on female-male communication that are considered later in the chapter. Terms that are important to an analysis of conversation are defined—for example, overlap, interruption, transition cue, turn, and minimal response. In the latter portion of the chapter we shall examine which conversational topics are preferred by each sex and how females and males employ humor. Finally, we shall consider what women and men uniquely contribute to the act of conversation.

The essentials of talk

Observing and recording the talk occurring in task-oriented small groups have served to identify two broad kinds of dialogue—talk that is instrumental and talk that is expressive. Much talk consists of giving information and of soliciting the same—for example, "The person to contact is the acrobatic helicopter flier." "Where is his office?" "Go north to the second street, Upper Stratosphere Drive. It's located in the Skyhigh Center, the big building shaped like an observation tower on the left." This type of conversation is labeled instrumental talk.

Another type of talk functions to help, reward, or raise the status of another, or it may serve to reject, show antagonism, or express negative feelings. This form of dialogue is called expressive talk. Examples of positive expressive dialogue are "You did a fine job!" or "Susan is the world's greatest cook!" Examples of negative expressive talk are: "You look like a million dollars—all green and wrinkled," or "You've got to be the world's worst driver!" Expressive talk covers a wide range of facilitating and debilitating emotional dialogue and includes "purrs and snarls, stroking and striking."[4]

Some writers feel that instrumental talk of the type that prevails in task-oriented groups does not belong under the rubric *conversation*. Sociologist Georg Simmel insists that "as soon as the discussion becomes objective, as soon as it makes the ascertainment of truth its purpose . . . it ceases to be sociable and thus becomes untrue to its own nature."[5] From this perspective, expressive talk is the mainstay and the obligation of conversationalists. Instrumental talk, which stresses the conveying of information, may tend to interfere with the free play of wit and to stifle colorful, creative dialogue development.[6] Conversation becomes "a stroking activity par excellence."[7]

We cannot entirely subscribe to Simmel's view that true conversation is made up only of expressive talk. To do so is to insist that the only factor present in instrumental talk is an intent to convey information. The instrumental assertion can convey a wide range of emotions and feelings via the verbal and nonverbal content. Picture, for example, the gruff foreman of a construction crew admonishing a young, inexperienced workman, "Dammit, George, be careful with that sledge hammer. You're liable to get hurt." To insist that the foreman's warning is strictly information transferal is to ignore the concern that the older man shows for the inexperienced youth. Add to this situation all of the nonverbal elements, and you have a conversational setting involving both instrumental and expressive dialogue.

Structure

Conversation is the transferal of information, attitudes, and emotions from one person to another via oral discourse. It is important to recognize that nonverbal elements supplement, embellish, and even extend the discourse. However, the keystone of conversation is speaking. On closer inspection, we discover that the art of conversation is not monolithic in nature, but instead it consists of elements such as strokes and turns, the mortar that holds the "bricks"—that is, words, together.

Strokes: units of social action "Different strokes for different folks" is a popular shibboleth in society today. Eric Berne has looked at talk from the standpoint of strokes. His insights provide us with the idea that people require differing amounts of strokes, or verbal recognition, in varying situations. A stroke in conversation is what a hug or pat is in physical contact. It is an act of recognition, and Berne calls it a "fundamental unit of social action."[8] An exchange of strokes is a unit of social intercourse or an alternation in turn-taking. In the following example, two women meet in a supermarket:

J: Hello, Rosie. Haven't seen you for awhile.
R: Hi, Jackie! How's everything?
J: Great, great. I'm still in Underwear at Fabulous Fashions. How're you doing?
R: Just fine. I've moved from cheese to vegetables at the supermarket. Well, I have to rush off. Work, work, work, you know.
J: Right! I'll see you around, Rosie.
R: Yeah, 'bye Jackie.

In the second example, additional factors of gratitude and loyalty seem to require more strokes:

J: Hello, Pam. I haven't seen you for awhile.
P: Hi, Jackie! How's everything?
J: Great, great. How're you doing?
P: Just fine. I often think about the good times we had the summer we shared expenses going out to California.
J: Yeah, I really appreciated your taking me along.
P: Oh, I enjoyed it. Besides, you understood car ailments and the signs of motor trouble a lot better than I did.
J: That's what comes of being the only girl in a family with four brothers. And speaking of brothers, I'm on my way to meet Bob now.
P: Well, I'll let you go. Tell Bob I said "hello."
J: I sure will. 'Bye now.
P: G'bye.

The two kinds of relationships in the previous examples call for different amounts of turn-taking. In the first illustration, apparently the two parties mutually felt the situation presented a 6-stroke obligation: recognizing the friend, wishing her well, and then each going on her own way. In the second situation, the recollection of past association and the mutual gratitude for a shared trip called for more, or was worth more, strokes—10 in this case.

Turns: a speech exchange system   Several other researchers have looked at structural aspects of talk. Zimmerman and West[9] see dialogue as a "speech exchange system." It is organized so that (1) one person speaks at a time and (2) change or alternation of talkers occurs. Within this construct, talk can range from the free flow of conversation during a coffee break to the carefully timed exchanges of school debaters or the prearranged formal rituals and ceremonies of the Knights of Columbus or Masonic Order installations. In this instance what distinguishes conversational talk from debate or ceremony is the difference in the distribution of speaking turns, the length of the turns, and the conversational substance of the turns. In debate, the turns occur in a predetermined, fixed order, and the dialogue is conducted in prescribed time modules. In ritual or ceremony, the specific subject matter is also determined in advance.

The dynamics of verbal exchange and turn-taking in any society is useful and fascinating to analyze. For example, a conversational turn involves, not only the time span in which the words are uttered, but also the right and privilege of a particular speaker to talk.[10] Most of the time the turn is prized and actively sought after. For example, at a White House press conference many reporters and news correspondents vie for the opportunity to pose questions, yet status determines who will ask the first question.

Turns seem to be parceled out among speakers in a conversational group. It is interesting to speculate about the tacit rules for determining the length and number of turns each person in a group shall have. Undoubtedly, factors such as status, authority, sex, age, and outside circumstances affect the currency of negotiable turns in any conversational setting. All of us have experienced situations when we were an active, outgoing, possibly dominating participant in discussion; and yet there were other times when we meekly stood on the periphery and timidly offered tidbits of talk while others ruled over the conversational moment.

Some observations can be made about the composition of turns. Ignoring any deep structural analysis, we can think of a conversational turn as consisting of one of several types of units: single words (*yeah*), phrases ("in a minute"), clauses ("if she wants to"), or sentences ("She can borrow the Guy Lombardo album tomorrow"). When each person is given or takes a turn, he or she produces one or more units of dis-

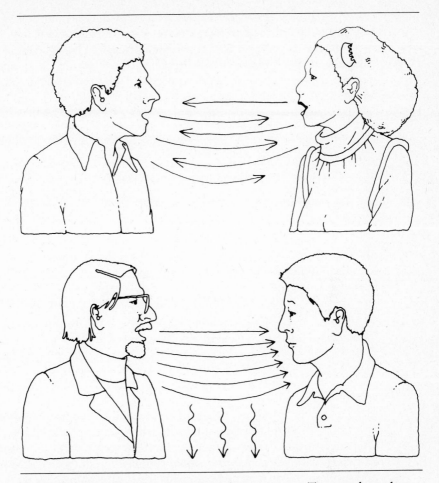

Talk can be thought of as a speech exchange system. *Top:* speakers alternate; *bottom:* one person speaks at a time.

course. As a rule, these spoken units have recognizable boundaries or endings, such as the last word in the phrase or sentence. These boundaries are signals for and places where a turn-transfer to the next speaker can occur.[11]

Listeners can generally sense or anticipate the end of a unit. The beginning of an utterance frequently gives the clue for guessing how and when the turn will end. This clue signals the upcoming opportunity or necessity for a change in speaker. For example,

A: Did you ever see . . . [B anticipates the opportunity or obligation for a new speaker to talk, on the basis of the structural clue which signals that a question is coming.] . . . the Pueblo Grande Ruins in Phoenix?
B: No, what . . . [A, listening, anticipates a further question about the ruins. Structure provides a clue for the next point of speaker change and probable obligation to tell about the ruins.] . . . are they like?

In addition to structural clues for anticipating the end of a unit of talk and the point for a speaker change, vocal intonation can also serve as a signal. A drop in speech melody or a descent in pitch gives a tone of finality and completion to an utterance. Conversely, a rise in pitch can add a tone of request or interrogation to a unit of talk. An example would be

A: I've never 'met Professor Millstone. [Drop in voice is a transition point for the next speaker, who seems to be called upon to identify Professor Millstone through a description or other information.]
B: 'He's the guy with the red 'beard who/always has a 'ten-speed bike propped against his desk. Wears 'shirts with a big 'wheel insignia. [Drop in voice indicates transition point where next speaker is obliged to respond in the affirmative that he/she has seen him or in the negative that he/she has no idea who the man is.]

In the following example, the usual structural clues for a question are absent, but intonation provides the signal:

A: You've met Professor Millstone? [Rise in pitch indicates a question rather than a statement.]
B: Yes, I know him slightly. [Small rise in pitch, leveling off at the end indicates implicit question to the effect of, "Why do you ask?"]

Timing

Even a casual observation of dialogue reveals that change of speakers takes place with split-second timing and with little or no time gap. This exchange suggests a high degree of readiness on the part of the listener. He/she is carefully tuned to possible completion points or places of transition in the dialogue where he/she may, or is obliged to, take a turn; and he/she does so with lightning ease. Such precise timing of speaker exchanges provides interesting insight into what constitutes active listening. It also raises a question of just what happens in interactions when one of the participants later complains, "I couldn't get a word in edgewise," or "I never had a chance to express my views." Is it that the speaker transition cues were not perceived by the listener or listeners? Were the cues of readiness to take a turn consciously or unconsciously ignored by the speaker? Which transition cues were deliberately withheld by the speaker?

Researchers of conversation have come to realize that some responses do not count as fulfilling turns. Brief vocalized sounds such as *mmhm*, *Oh*, or *yeah*, which are emitted by the receiver and interspersed throughout the speaker's talk fall under this category. They are not an alternating turn in the conversation. Rather, these scattered sounds occur at breath pauses, sometimes overlap beginnings or endings of utterances, and sometimes run concurrent with them.

The timing and placement of miniresponse cues indicates attention and encourages the speaker to continue.

A: I met this fascinating woman, see. (Uh huh) And she's been everywhere—Italy, Spain, Greece, Austria, you name it! (Yeah?) I tell you, she is a true international. (Hm!)

Whenever they occur, during a split second of pause or overlapping the utterances of the speaker, these miniresponses neither interrupt the current speaker nor count as turns in their own right. Instead, they are facilitating signs, showing active listening, interest, and understanding. They seem to carry the implicit meaning, "Go on," "I'm listening," or "I'm interested." Their dual function is (1) to indicate listener attention and (2) to give positive reinforcement for the speaker to continue.[12]

Researchers of this phenomenon have noted with interest the verbal dexterity of conversational participants. With nimble ease, listeners insert such supportive signs as *uh huh* or *yeah* between breaths by the speaker, and yet the speaker may never miss a beat in the conversational rhythm. The stream of talk continues without any hesitancy or interruption in flow.

To supply response cues in proper places would seem to require active listening on the part of the respondent. Yet the listener may become adept at almost automatically giving the signs of attention and support, without the existence, in fact, of either involvement or reinforcement. We are all familiar with cartoons in which the husband, struggling to read the paper while his wife speaks at length, still supplies the proper signs of listening on cue. ("Yes, dear, mmhm.

Yes.") Yet he effectively tunes out her message. Occasionally these automatic cues become the butt of humor when they occur at the wrong time. (Wife: "Dear, the children are missing." Husband: "That's good.")

A model for talk

As another consideration of conversation, we shall present a model of talk as a possible framework or perspective in which to view the exchange and interchange of dialogue. This model is based in part on ideas from Zimmerman and West and from Sacks.[13] It focuses on points of possible speaker change. In most casual verbal exchanges, possible points for speaker change are signaled by such cues as reaching the end of a phrase or sentence, using vocal intonation, taking a breath, or pausing or ceasing to speak. Each of these occasions can be viewed as a point for decision making by participants in the conversation, with six alternatives, or courses, to pursue:

1 The current speaker can continue to speak.
2 The current speaker can select the next speaker.
3 The designated speaker can decide to accept the turn.
4 Another speaker can self-select—that is, choose himself or herself and take the initiative without being bidden to do so.
5 The current speaker can decide to terminate the talk and select silence.
6 Another speaker can decide to terminate the talk and select silence.

We will consider each of these alternatives in more detail.

1 Continuation by the current speaker. If other speakers do not respond or take the initiative, the present speaker may continue speaking although he or she is not obliged to.

2 Selection of the next speaker by the current speaker. The present speaker can select the next speaker in ways such as nodding toward, looking at, or fixing eye gaze on that person. He or she can address the person by name or title ("And so that's my opinion, Hilda."), direct a question to the person ("What do you think of that idea?"), or give a command or request ("Tell us your thoughts on the subject.") A combination of the preceding devices are also used.

3 Acceptance of the turn. This is usually an automatic response.

4 Self-selection. Another speaker can self-select and take the initative to speak. Since this course is open to any potential speaker present, it may happen that several listeners will self-select and begin speaking simultaneously. Generally the person who starts first is accorded the turn. But it may also happen that the one who continues talking until the

other, or others, have deferred and become silent will be accorded the turn. In this case, the most persistent talker will prevail.

5 The current speaker can decide to terminate the talk.

6 Another speaker can decide to terminate the talk. Generally terminating a conversation requires tacit agreement from the other member or members of the interaction. Implicitly or explicitly, conversational participants may communicate their wish for the dialogue to terminate. The farewell statement may have been initiated several turns before the actual cessation of talk. The simple ritual of telling another "goodbye" illustrates this well and has been the object of extensive study by some.[14] Through silence, by physically removing oneself from the scene, by looking or turning away, one may end a conversation.

One can see that there are a number of options for the current speaker and the potential speaker. In alternative 1, the current speaker elects to continue, and the process recycles back to the beginning in preparation for the next transition point. In alternative 2, the words of the speaker serve to select the next speaker, in which case, following the transition, the next speaker, at alternative 3, has the right and the obligation to speak.

It may be that the selected speaker does not speak, or that another speaker self-selects before her or him—that is, alternative 4. The cycle then begins again with one of the potential speakers becoming the current speaker. He or she then has one of the conversational alternatives at the next transition point. In addition, alternatives 5 and 6 indicate the option of terminating the talk, which the speakers can exercise by remaining silent or by walking away.

This model represents the regularly occurring features of conversation. Its unique aspect is its focus on the points of possible switch, to another speaker and to the next turn. Such a model can take account of turn size, not only in regard to time span, but also according to the units between possible transition points. These units may link together to form short or long turns. Viewed from this perspective,[15] the conversation process is analyzed according to its internal management. Talk is looked at in terms of the control of turn order and turn size by participants. The complex verbal interaction is influenced by the choices available at each possible change point. It reflects the decisions made by the participants at each of these junctures. This system is subject to the demands of external circumstances. It is influenced by variables such as the number and the status of participants, the time, the setting, the context of the interaction, and the topics of conversation.

The authors believe that the verbal-exchange model suggests exciting new approaches for teaching effective communication. Also, the importance of stroking, turn-taking, and timing have received little attention in speech textbooks. If these communication dynamics could be incorporated into the training of speech students, the very important skills of interpersonal speaking and listening could be vastly expanded and improved for women and for men.

Sex differences in talk

Thus far, our consideration of talk has focused on general characteristics common to the verbal interactions of both women and men. We now turn to the particular social elements of talk that have sexual determinants. We shall examine research studies of women and men speaking. It may be that some time-honored myths about the communication of and between the sexes will be shattered!

Turn-taking

One area in which communication behavior has been found to vary according to sex is turn-taking in conversation. At some point we have all tried to present our ideas in a group and learned that talking does not necessarily mean getting the floor. Many persons of both sexes find interruption during verbal interchange a source of irritation. Apparently, there are some differences between the sexes in this practice.

Not only have men been found to talk much more than women in a mixed group, but they attain their greater talkativeness in part by interrupting women or answering questions that are not addressed to them. Men have been found to interrupt women more often than women interrupt men.[16] Many women have a difficult time getting and keeping attention in a group. Perhaps because their voices are less powerful they have a harder time getting the floor and a harder time keeping it through interruptions. Our informal observation, after teaching communication classes for a number of years, suggests that this is true for many women in college. In discussion groups in college we have often seen women sit wordlessly without participating for long periods of time, unless someone in the group made a special effort to clear conversational space for them.

When speaking in a group, some women feel that men put their listening on a "hold pattern" and do not really hear them. Others complain that when they offer an idea or suggestion, the group takes no notice of it. As one student put it:

It's not so much that the group interrupts you as that they talk *through* you. It's as if your comments really don't penetrate their awareness, and the wheels of group talk just never stop grinding for you even to coast part-way in on your roller skates. They just grind on, over, and around you—and you're left behind with your mouth open, still clutching your skate key.

Listening is a form of stroking behavior, and the stroking role is often perceived as most appropriate for a woman. As an example of this, one study of female/male conversation pinpointed a striking difference between the sexes in the use of *mmhmm*.[17] Females far exceeded males in the use of *mmhmm*, and in fact each individual woman produced more of these words than all the males did put together. As for other affirmative words, such as *right* or *yeah*, both sexes used these about equally. The significant feature of *mmhmm* is that its use in conversation generally implies its user, the listener, is not about to say anything more or initiate a topic. *Right* or *yeah*, on the other hand, is often likely to lead right into an utterance or further talk by its user.

Occasionally, one of the writers will be chided by her family or friends for her running string of *mmhmms*, which punctuate the silence during some one-sided phone conversations: "That must have been an interesting *non*versation," or "That was an interesting view you almost expressed." Some students, mostly females, have monitored their own speech and noted their unthinking overreadiness to agree and support in conversations. They find their reflexive nods of agreement and *mmhmms* are being mechanically acted out at the very moment they catch themselves in disagreement or disbelief. One student said humorously that her head was saying "yes-yes" while her brain suddenly said "no-no": "I want to say, 'Take back that *mmhmm*—I don't agree with my mouth!'" One of the writers found that the best personal counteractive for her own behavior was a good friend and student who on occasion would purposely sprinkle her speech with sudden non sequiturs and say triumphantly in the middle of a nod or *mmhmm* by the writer, "Aha! Caught you, didn't I?"

On the other hand when a woman varies from listening-stroking behavior and becomes more directive, controlling, and goal-oriented in her talk, she may not be taken seriously, and her contribution may be automatically written off as nonessential or easily dispensed with. Rarely, however, do men sit silent while women talk. Chesler points out that when a man is with a group of women, he will speak up and he will question the women, generally from a "superior" position. In many cases, he ultimately controls the conversation.[18]

Perhaps the most interesting study to date on interruptions was done at the University of California, Santa Barbara. The researchers Zimmerman and West took on the staggering task of recording conversations (usually two-party interactions) in coffee shops, drug stores, and other public places in a university community. One or the other of the authors carried a tape recorder. They collected data from male-male, female-female, and female-male conversations. Their analysis of conversation was based on a model of turn-taking that includes a consideration of turn violations. The study centered on the interruption of turns.[19]

Overlaps The investigators thought it important to distinguish between overlaps and interruptions. Overlaps were described as instances of speech during which two persons speak at once. For example, a new speaker may begin to speak at or very close to a possible transition

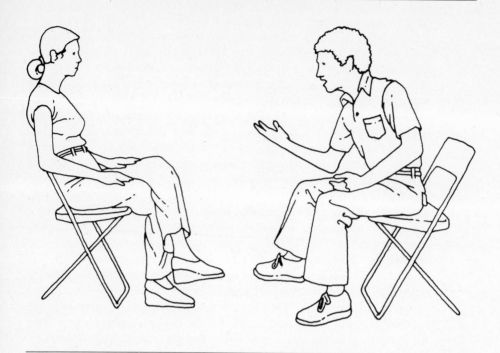

Men tend to talk more and women tend to listen more.

place or ending point in the present speaker's talk. Actors might term it stepping on another's lines. For example,

$$\begin{array}{l} \text{OVERLAP} \\ A\text{: I didn't know you knew } \left(\text{Bob.}\right. \\ B\text{: } \qquad\qquad\qquad\quad \left.\text{Oh yeah, I met him at the Richards'.}\right. \end{array}$$

Here, the next person's response is close to a legitimate, possible point of speaker change ("Bob") in the talk. In this case, it is within the boundary of the last word of the unit. It is this nearness to a legitimate point of change that distinguishes overlap from interruption.

Interruptions An interruption, on the other hand, is a vocalization *before* the last word that could signal a possible end or boundary of a sentence, question, or other unit of talk. For example,

$$\begin{array}{l} \text{INTERRUPTION} \\ A\text{: Today I } \left(\text{met}\right) \quad \text{—(talker may or may not finish his or her sentence)} \\ B\text{: } \qquad\quad \left(\text{Oh,}\right) \text{ I can't talk—Gotta run!} \end{array}$$

Overlaps allow some margin of error in the change between speaker turns. Interruptions, however, can be viewed as violations of the turn-taking system of unwritten rules, which prescribe that the proper place for speaker change is at the end limit of a unit of utterance or possible unit.

The researchers wanted to discover how these overlaps and interruptions were distributed in the speech samples they collected. They found that in same-sex conversations the overlaps and interruptions were distributed fairly evenly among speakers. But in cross-sex (female-male) conversation, the pattern was drastically different. Practically all the interruptions and overlaps were by male speakers, 96 percent and 100 percent, respectively.

They found that 91 percent of the female-male segments showed interruptions. But the few interruptions that occurred in the same-sex conversations were concentrated in only 3 of the 20 segments. So interruptions were clustered in just a few of the conversations for same-sex pairs, but they were evenly scattered across the female-male pairs. Interruption was the rule and not the exception in female-male talk.

The researchers suggest that if interruptions are viewed as violation of a speaker's rights, then continual or frequent interruption can be considered as a disregard for a speaker or for what a speaker has to say. Males may have a different mental set when they converse with females than when they converse with other males. Zimmerman and West comment, "Here, we are dealing with a class of speakers, females, whose rights to speak appear to be casually infringed upon by males."[20] Depending on the interpretation, this can be seen as supporting the contention that sexism occurs even in the common ritual of conversation.

A study done by the authors strongly supported these findings on interruption patterns. In university faculty meetings of the communication department, men averaged a greater number of active interruptions per meeting than did women. One reason for this is that male faculty members took more turns—that is, they verbalized more. However, it was also established that the males' proportion of active interruptions to their total number of turns taken exceeded the females'. It was interesting to note that the one female faculty member who actively interrupted, perpetrated most of her interruptions on other female members. Males were found to be far below females in proportion of their turns being interrupted. The woman with the highest number of interruptions (perpetrated upon her) was the one without a Ph.D. degree. Status, for both females and males, was a significant factor in not being interrupted. For example, the male interrupted least was the departmental chairman.[21]

Silences The occurrence of silence or pauses was investigated by Zimmerman and West. A break in conversational flow is termed a lapse. Some conversations proceed with few lapses, while others may have occasional lengthy gaps between speaker turns. There would seem to be

Silence from females in female-male pairs occurred following three types of situations: delayed listening response (top); overlap (middle); and interruption (bottom).

no reason to expect that one party in a conversation would become silent more than another. Rather, it would appear likely that silences between speaker turns would tend to be evenly distributed.

An examination of patterns of silence revealed that females in female-male segments fell silent most. But for same-sex groups, all females or all males, these lapses of silence were scattered more evenly among all talkers. In accounting for these differences, the authors note first that 62 percent of the females' total silence in female-male conversations followed three types of situations: (1) a delayed minimal response by a male, (2) an overlap by a male, and (3) an interruption by a male.

Some explanation is in order. Minimal responses are those responses which do not count as filling turns, such as "Mmhmm," "Uh huh," "Yeah," or "Oh," but which serve to display continuing interest and co-participation in topic development. In the first case, these responses were given, but their timing was delayed. Normally such verbalizations act as a positive reinforcement for continued talk, but withholding such brief responses as "Yeah" or "Uh huh" until later than their expected utterance could conceivably have an effect the opposite of reinforcement. Most of us have experienced the disappointment of the dampening pause and tardy response:

A: [joyfully] Oh boy! You'll never guess what happened to me today!
B: [long, long pause] . . . What?

The promptly uttered minimal response, with its finely timed placement at various points within the current speaker's talk, is taken as a sign of active attention, encouragement to continue the turn, and support for the speaker's development of a topic. But postponing such responses may signal the listener's disinterest, inattention, or lack of understanding of the current talker. The speaker's silence following the listener's delayed minimal response may reflect the speaker's uncertainty as to her partner's feelings about the current conversation.

A few silences were found to follow delayed minimal responses, overlaps, and interruptions in same-sex conversations. But there were only about one-third as many instances, and the average silence was less than that for females in female-male conversation. In the only two instances in which a female interrupted a male, the interruptions were not followed by silence before the male spoke again.

Conversational control Delayed listening responses, interruptions, and overlaps were used by males and appeared to have a subduing effect on conversational participation of females. Specifically, these three behaviors seem related to the females' noticeable silences right after their occurrence and just before the next speaker's turn. As for turn violations, even after repeated interruptions by males, the transcripts revealed no complaints from the women such as, "You keep interrupting me," or "Let me finish."

Both delayed minimal responses and interruptions may be ways to control conversational topics. For example, if delayed response signals non-support for continuation of a topic, a series of delayed responses should serve to bring the topic to an end. The researchers in fact observed this pattern in some of their transcripts. By the same token, repeated interruption of the partner also tended to be followed by a topic change. These verbal behaviors by males in conversation with females may be an assertion of the right to control the topic of conversation in the same way that adult-child conversations often restrict the child's rights to speak and be listened to. In fact, in comparing some preliminary transcripts of adult-child talk, it has been found that adults interrupt children frequently and that the patterns of these conversations closely resemble those of the female-male patterns.[22]

Males appear to assert strongly the right to control topics, and in so doing they seem to get little or no negative feedback from females. It may be that men, consciously or unconsciously, deny equal status to women as conversational partners in several ways: they may limit women's due in keeping the floor during their turn; and they may withhold verbal-vocal support in women's development of topics.

Zimmerman and West speculate: "Just as male dominance is exhibited through male control of macro-institutions in society it is also exhibited through control of at least a part of one micro-institution."[23] Women seem to be designated the second sex in small things as well as large.

So far, our consideration of sex differences in conversation has concerned itself with verbal devices—that is, overlaps, interruptions, pauses, and control. Now we shall turn to specialization of talk by sex, the topics favored by each sex, and the use of humor by females and males.

The expression of roles

We mentioned earlier that expressive talk functions to raise the status of another, to give help, to provide stroking. Verbal stroking can take the form of asking for opinion, for suggestions, for clarification or of agreeing, reinforcing, and complying. Cultural norms may encourage this verbal behavior in women. For example, in one study of mixed-sex communication pairs, some conversations showed a pattern of females asking questions and males giving answers.[24]

Although researchers use varying labels—expressive, relational, or stroking—this form of talk seems to be used most often by women. A study of mock-jury deliberations revealed that females contributed more positive reactions than males to the discussions. They agreed more; showed more "tension release"—for example, laughing; and manifested more solidarity, as opposed to antagonism. What distinguished the male verbal interaction was the higher number of attempted answers that came from men. They surpassed the women in the opinion-giving and orientation-giving categories of talk. Talk tended to be specialized according to sex, with the preponderance of instrumental, getting-the-job-done speech coming from males and most of the expressive, supportive talk coming from females.[25] The same kind of specialization in talk is also found in studies of husband-wife and husband-wife-child discussions. The instrumental or task role is taken by the husband or father, and the expressive or social-emotional role tends to be taken by the wife or mother.[26]

Specialization of talk by sex may relate to the greater aggressiveness found among males than females,[27] as well as the nurturance that psychologists have found characteristic of many women. In a study that covered 56 societies around the world, women were found to have the expressive role in 46 of them.[28]

A parallel has been drawn between some women's expressive verbal role and the female cichlid's behavior. By showing subservience, the female cichlid performs a stroking function. The human female may transfer this submissiveness to nonsexual relationships such as talking. The findings that women show less antagonism and less willingness to deflate another's status in communication situations may reflect this phenomenon in social interaction, rather than suggest any inherent sex differences. Some studies that compared groups of men and groups of women found more disagreement in the groups of women among themselves. But when the sexes were pitted against each other, women played more cooperatively against men than against women. Men performed in the opposite manner when playing against the opposite sex. They cooperated less when playing against women, as compared with players of their own sex.[29] The introduction of the opposite sex may tone down competitive behavior of women but spark this instinct in men.

The selection of topics

> "The time has come," the Walrus said,
> "To talk of many things. . . ."
> —Lewis Carroll, "Through the Looking Glass"

If, as indicated previously, men speak more and interrupt more, then what at least do they talk about? And do they differ from women? Studies of conversational topics show that sex is high on the list. Baseball, football, and other sports, politics, work, and other men are also discussed. Women, on the other hand, don't appear to discuss sex with each other as much as men do.[30]

Elinor Langer, a customer's service representative for a telephone company, observed the staff in her department for a period of three months. They were primarily women. She concluded that religion and politics were avoided in their conversation. This did not seem to be the case in men's departments of the company, where men had frequent political discussion. Langer suggested that "Women think that such heavy topics are properly in the domain of men." Further, she believed that the women did not wish to let "foolish 'politics' interfere with the commonsense and harmonious adjustments they have made to their working lives."[31]

Some years ago, several studies were conducted by overhearing conversations in various public places. Moore, for example, walked down Broadway in the early evening, listening to conversation fragments.[32] He classified the conversations according to predominant interests of the sexes. In men-men conversations, almost one-half the fragments dealt with money and business; sports or amusement accounted for 14 percent; and other men, 13 percent.

In the case of women talking to women, conversations involved men in 44 percent of the samples, clothing in 23 percent, and other women in 16 percent. In the case of female-male conversations, women talked to men about other men in over 20 percent of the samples and about other women in 13 percent. Men, on the other hand, talked to women about sports or amusements in one-fourth of the samples and about money and business in over one-fifth.

Another study of conversations revealed similar trends, although the investigation was carried on in Ohio. The places frequented were a college campus, department stores, theater lobbies, hotel lobbies, restaurants, barber shops, the streets, and so forth. Conversations, when overheard, were recorded as to topic under discussion, time, place, sex of speakers, and estimated social status. The results were in marked agreement with Moore. Men's most frequent topic was business (one-half the samples); sports and other amusements, 15 percent; and other men, 12 percent. Women's leading topics were men, 22 percent; clothes, 19 percent; and other women, 15 percent.

If the topics "men" and "women" are combined as a single topic, "persons," the frequency was 37 percent in women's conversation, over twice as much as the 16 percent in men's conversation. One might infer from this that women had a greater interest in talking about persons than things.

In a mixed group, men most frequently talked to women of amusements (22 percent) and secondly business and money (19 percent), again comparable to Moore's findings. Men were found to talk to women about themselves 17 percent more than they did when talking to other men. Women spoke with men most often about amusements (23 percent), next about clothing (17 percent), about themselves (15 percent), and about men (14 percent).[33]

So men's greatest conversational interests seemed to be business and money, followed by sports and amusements. Women's leading topics were men and clothes. Persons played a smaller part in men's talk and a larger part in women's. One wonders what results an updated study like this would reveal.

The use of humor

> Oh, when I start to tell a story,
> An amusing anecdote I've read,
> When I start to tell a funny story,
> I get flustered 'cause I know what lies ahead
> (It always happens).
> Just when I start to tell a story,
> It makes no difference where we are.
> When I get where the joke should be,
> You say it just ahead of me.
> I mean to say it drives me mad.
>   —Tom Jones and Harvey Schmidt[34]

Another way in which communication behavior seems to vary by
sex is the use of humor in social situations. It has been said that women
as a rule cannot tell jokes. They kill the punchline or they mix up the
order of the happenings. The telling of jokes and the use of humor
serve as an acceptable outlet for aggression, according to Freud's
theory. If we accept the notion that humor is a form of disguised aggression, then we may theorize that women would use humor less in
female-male interaction, for any show of aggression might be threatening to a male. Says Grotjahn: "The woman has as much natural tendency to enjoy wit as her male counterpart. But if she is clever, she will
not show it."[35] So we would expect that the woman who conforms to
social norms would be "incapable" of telling a joke.

Recently we conducted a workshop on the use of humor in speaking. Eighty percent of the group that enrolled were males. Before the
session, one woman met one of the writers in the hall to tell her she
was dropping out, explaining, "I can't go through with it." The few
women that were in the group appeared uncomfortable. One assignment called for each participant to tell a humorous story or joke for the
group. For one young woman in particular, participation in the session
was obviously an effort. When her turn came, she presented her narrative well until she reached the place of the expected humorous ending.
At that point, she began to speak rapidly and introduce non sequiturs,
laughing nervously through her verbalizing all the while. The group, at
first curious, then puzzled by the narrative, soon become increasingly
amused as her words became more incoherent and her laughter more
convulsive. The situation degenerated, until finally she and the group
dissolved in laughter.

Unfortunately, hers was not enjoyable laughter. It was as if she
were set to get only as far as the closing of her story and then to fall
short of it. She seemed unwilling to place the pointed shaft of humor
herself. Perhaps her verbal fumbling and repetition represented a stall-
ing technique, in anticipation that someone else would intercede and
provide the humorous thrust to conclude her story. Perhaps also she
found some relief in being in on the laughter of the group, even if it
meant laughing at herself. Like her listeners, then, she too could be on

the receiving end, and she could momentarily dissociate herself from the active role of dispensing or imparting humor.

The males in the group seemed to take great relish in recounting their favorite anecdotes. They appeared eager to vie for laughs from the group. Those males who claimed no talent in humor still took obvious pleasure in proving that the opposite was true.

We had an opportunity to observe a comparable situation, but with the proportion of women and men reversed. The class was a communication course in which an overwhelming majority of students were female. The assignment was oral humor, and on the day of the presentations the females, deferring to the few males, sat back and let the men volunteer to speak first. The males performed readily, with perhaps only a little less gusto than the men in the workshop had before. Although a few women still eschewed the role of humorist, the female students this time seemed much freer in their style. Each woman in her turn entered enthusiastically into the storytelling. The verbal and gestural delivery of the women was relatively relaxed and expressive, and some of the constraints in language often noted among females in mixed groups were absent. In this case, with only a few males present, there seemed to be a different status, or power orientation, in the group, and this may have affected the women's perception of their role in the interaction.

Unfortunately, not a great deal has been done in investigating humor and its social functions, and precious little in regard to sex differences. Rose Coser, a sociologist, did a study of laughter among colleagues on the staff of a mental hospital.[36] She recorded conversations containing humor and laughter in staff meetings for three months. The meetings were formally structured and attended by persons of different status: senior staff members, junior staff, and paramedical staff.

She discovered that humor was distributed by status and that there was a tendency for those of lesser authority to make fewer witticisms. Of 90 witticisms made by permanent staff, 53 were made by senior staff, 33 by the junior staff, and 4 by the paramedical staff. There was also a kind of pecking order. A humorist would not direct a witticism at anyone present who was of higher rank, but at someone of equal or lower rank. The junior staff member might direct humor at another junior staff member or a paramedical, but not at senior staff. A senior staff member might aim his wit at another senior staff member, a junior staff member, or a paramedical, and so on. Some surprising sex differences in humor emerged. Men used humor far more often than women. At the meetings, men were responsible for 99 of the total 103 instances of wit! Yet it was observed that the "women often laughed harder."

Coser felt that some of the women staff members had an excellent sense of humor and were capable of making witty remarks or telling jokes effectively. Yet at staff meetings, they scarcely ever used their sense of humor. Rather than reflecting their ability or character, this

Men tend to tell more jokes than women and women tend to laugh more at them.

may indicate that they were yielding to social learning. In this culture women are expected to be passive and receptive, not active and initiating. So a woman who has a good sense of humor is one who laughs ("but not too loudly!") when a man tells a good joke or tosses off a witticism. A man who has a good sense of humor is one who makes witty remarks and tells good jokes.

Coser likened the status of women at the staff meetings to the status of junior staff. Junior staff are expected to learn. Their role is to receive knowledge and acknowledge the intellectual superiority of the senior members. If they use humor too much, this could be interpreted as threatening the teacher-student relationship. Similarly, women are not expected to be witty. Although their humor may be acceptable in some circumstances, it may be disapproved in situations where it could be interpreted as subverting or threatening male authority. In a group meeting, any time that humor is used and the group lapses into laughter, the control is temporarily taken out of the hands of the chairperson or director who is conducting the meeting.

Living with sex differences

Whether in individual in-depth studies or in observation of exchanges in small groups, certain patterns seem to emerge. One basic role separation in communication seems to be that of task-directed versus

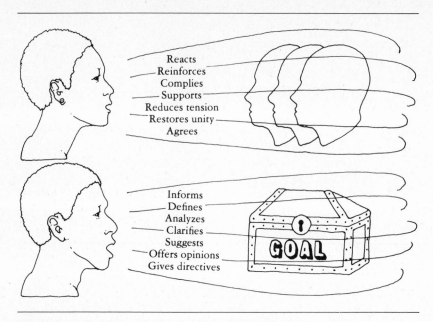

Reacts
Reinforces
Complies
Supports
Reduces tension
Restores unity
Agrees

Informs
Defines
Analyzes
Clarifies
Suggests
Offers opinions
Gives directives

GOAL

Sex roles tend to encourage one-sided verbal behavior patterns.

socio-emotionally directed behavior. Men have tended to perform the task role and women the socio-emotional role. The verbal performance of males is most often a goal-directed, "all-out" effort, characterized by analyzing, clarifying, evaluating, and controlling. Women's communication has involved reacting, positively and negatively, to the general situation and to others, with a tendency to be concerned with the problems of decision making, rather than the decision itself; with reducing tension; and with restoring unity.

Whether the causes are cultural or genetic, sex differences in communication behavior are real. To say that these differences are "just" social or cultural does little good if it is impossible to imagine a society anywhere in which sex differences do not exist. Of what use is it to say that if boys and girls were treated exactly alike, they would be alike, when it has not been possible for a society to do this? Further, one cannot understand communication between the sexes very well if one denies that there are differences between the sexes other than those that can be traced to culture or social structure. It may be that as communicators, females and males are just enough alike to expect more similarities, but they are enough different not to get them. Or, put another way, they are "just similar enough to be intolerant of differences, just different enough to guarantee their presence."[37] Longfellow phrased the eternal and inevitable intertwining of the sexes this way (italics added):

As unto the bow the cord is,
So unto the man is woman,
Though she *bends* him, she *obeys* him,
Though she *draws* him, yet she *follows*,
Useless each without the other![38]

Or, phrased in the time-worn cliché, "You can't live with them, and you can't live without them."

"With them" or "without them," our society's rapid changes, along with the women's movement, are affecting both female and male roles. Both women and men are caught up in a social upheaval they do not fully understand. Much of the force of change is directed against the very things that had previously given people a certain measure of security and identity—their sex roles. Before, when there were problems related to differences between the sexes, one could always shrug them off as inevitable. Today most of us are uncertain ourselves of how many difficulties in our family, social, and work relationships are unalterable and how many we can change.

There seems to be no evidence that either men or women are biologically better suited for either an expressive, stroking role or an instrumental, task-oriented one. Neither role is superior to the other. The instrumental role is important in getting the job done. It requires us to keep things going and prod when necessary. But this type of behavior tends to bring about stress in social groups. Expressive behavior, on the other hand, is supportive and has the effect of lessening stress and anxiety, increasing cohesion, and emphasizing the positive. In the most successful groups, there has to be just the proper balance between the two behaviors—enough push to get the job done and enough support to keep the tension from becoming debilitating.

A healthy acceptance of the value of different roles not tied to sex is beginning to develop. Dr. Patricia Bull, New York consultant to a women's workshop for legislators, lawyers, judges, corrections professionals, and other women in the criminal justice system, commented on sex roles and identity: "I used to ask the men to let me be one of the boys. I no longer do that. I now want to be known as a woman, but still want in on the organization."

Regarding specific traits she said, "Women have special qualities to offer. We may have knocked them in the past, but now we realize they are pretty neat. I mean, the tender things like love, caring and nurturing. Women were confused about that for awhile. They thought maybe they ought to be aggressive instead." Bull does not perceive women and men as fitting just one role or being limited by society's expectations. She advocates a wide range of behaviors for both sexes: "What is best is to be able to choose from the whole spectrum of emotions and attitudes, to be aggressive at times, tender at others. I should be free to be the person I am, not present a half-person because of my womanness."[39]

Suggested activities

1 Observe conversational interaction in a group of three or more persons.

    a. Who takes more turns talking in the group?

    b. Who takes longer turns?

    c. Does number or length of turns have anything to do with sex of the speaker? Explain.

    d. Is age important? Explain.

    e. How does status relate to turn-taking?

    f. Is effectiveness in social situations related to questions a and b in your opinion? Explain.

    g. Describe the personalities of the participants and indicate which person(s) had the most impact on the group. Why?

Suggested format to record results:

Talker	Sex	Age	Status and/or occupation	Number of interruptions made	Number of times interrupted
1					
2					
3					
4					
5					

2 Observe a conversation at length and focus your attention on interruption.

    a. Who interrupts whom?

    b. Who interrupts most?

    c. Who is interrupted most?

    d. How is sex related to interrupting?

    e. Describe any connection you noticed between status or power and interruptions.

    f. What other variables can you suggest to account for differences in interruption?

Suggested format to record results:

Talker	Sex	Age	Status and/or occupation	Number of turns	Average length of turn	Listener reaction
1						
2						
3						
4						
5						

3 Listen to three female and three male comics.

    a. Indicate differences in their styles, topics, and use of humor. Cite samples of their routines to support your contentions.

    b. If you are a female comedian, would you see any restraints in your act, resulting from the fact that you are a woman? What subjects would be taboo?

    c. If you were a male comedian, would you see any restraints in your act, resulting from the fact that you are a man? What taboos?

4 Observe and take notes on conversation at a party or social gathering.

    a. How many males and how many females would you classify as funny or humorous?

    b. Does form or type of humor vary by sex? How?

    c. Does the performance of the funny males and the funny females vary depending on whether they are in small groups or in larger (say over six people) groups? How?

    d. Which persons are at their best in small groups and completely "fade away" in large groups? Which are humorous in big groups but shed their humor in smaller groups? Which do not seem to change?

    e. Is the sex of a person related to use of humor? Use samples and excerpts of the different talkers' humor to support your view.

    f. From your observations, what constitutes a sense of humor in a woman? What constitutes a sense of humor in a man?

5 Listen carefully to some conversations. Try to listen to some same-sex groups (all men or all women) and some mixed groups for comparison.

    a. Keep a running tally of the topics most often discussed. Arrange them by category.

    b. What topics did the all-female or all-male groups discuss?

    c. What topics did the mixed-sex groups discuss?

    d. Who initiated topics? Who changed subjects?

    e. Do the old stereotypes (women discussing mostly recipes, clothing, and gossip and men discussing primarily cars, politics, and sports) hold up?

    f. How did age, occupation, and education influence topic choice?

    g. Interpret your findings concerning women's, men's, and mixed-group conversations, based on your results.

4 Sex patterns in sound

Three things you can be judged by—your voice, your face, and your disposition.
   —Ignas Bernstein

Benjamin Disraeli is credited with having said that there is no index of character so sure as the voice. While some would argue against this generalization, we can be fairly certain of one thing: people tend to make judgments about other people on the basis of voice. Some studies have found high agreement among listeners regarding the personality traits of the speaker. Whether these judgments are right or wrong isn't the important point. The important thing is that our voices help create perceptions of and reactions to us in others. We shall see that there are some interesting sex differences in the reactions voices produce, as well as differences in the vocal apparatus of women and men and the way they use sound.

The impact of voice

It is amazing how much information the voice alone can carry. It has been shown that from vocal cues listeners can fairly accurately distinguish between female and male; persons of high, middle, or low status; short, stocky speakers and lean, slender speakers; big and small speakers; blacks and whites; speakers with a college, high school, and less than a high school education; and speakers of different ages, twenty to thirty, forty to fifty, and sixty to seventy years old.[1]

   The voice also can carry information about the feelings and attitudes of the speaker. Studies have shown that listeners are in considerable agreement both about the type and the strength of feelings portrayed by speakers. In some research electronic filtering is used to obliterate word recognition yet preserve voice cues. The higher frequencies of speech, usually the consonant sounds, are not transmitted, so that the rise and fall and the ebb and flow of the voice is heard but not the actual words spoken. One study that used recordings from the

Army-McCarthy hearings of 1954 showed that listeners tended to be able to distinguish pleasantness and emotion in the word-free speech they heard.[2] In another study, listeners could differentiate between aggressive and submissive speakers.[3]

One of the most complete studies on judgments from voice was done by Addington. Two male and two female speakers simulated 9 characteristics of voice, and listeners rated the personalities of the speakers on 40 personality traits.[4] The speakers varied their voices, simulating breathy, tense, thin, flat, throaty, nasal, and orotund qualities, and changed pitch variety and speaking rate. Particular types of vocal qualities consistently elicited certain common judgments about the speakers. Female and male listeners were similar in the individual judgments they made, but some vocal characteristics were viewed differently when they occurred in male speech than when they occurred in female speech. For example, increased throatiness in male voices caused the speakers to be stereotyped as being older, more realistic, mature, sophisticated, and well adjusted. This quality in females' voices, however, caused them to be perceived as less intelligent, more masculine, lazier, boorish, unemotional, ugly, sickly, and careless.

The elements isolated by factor analysis suggested that the female personality was seen in terms of social faculties and that the male personality was viewed in terms of physical and emotional power. Also in some cases, manipulating vocal qualities in the female voice seemed to change personality perceptions more than similar changes did in the male voice. For example, increased thinness of male voices did not change the listener's image of the speaker, but the same quality in the voices of females created impressions of increased social, physical, emotional, and mental immaturity, as well as increased sense of humor and sensitivity. In some cases, certain vocal characteristics such as breathiness, throatiness, and orotundity caused more negative impressions of females than males. Details of the findings are summarized in Table 4.1.

One conclusion that can be drawn from the research on vocal quality is that women tend to be more specifically judged via voice traits. While some broad, generalized impressions of men are derived—for example, older or younger, more masculine or less masculine—there is little effort to make fine discriminations such as prettier, more petite, mentally immature, high strung, effervescent, naive, humble, neurotic, and so forth. One can then conclude that vocal quality cues are more salient in judging women than in judging men.

Although there is relatively high listener agreement concerning voices and personality traits such as those previously listed, it is generally assumed that these stereotyped judgments are not well grounded. Attempts to match impressions from speakers' voices with results from personality tests have yielded only inconclusive results. The provocative question that remains is: "What, then, are listeners reacting to and making stereotyped judgments about with high agreement?

Table 4.1 Perception of females and males based on vocal characteristics

Vocal characteristics	Female speaker	Male speaker
Breathiness	Seen as being more feminine, prettier, more petite, more effervescent, and more high-strung, while at the same time perceived as being shallower	Seen as being younger and more artistic
Thinness	Perceptions of increased social, physical, emotional, and mental immaturity; increased ratings of sense of humor and sensitivity	Did not seem to alter the listener's image of the speaker; no significant correlations revealed
Flatness	Perceived as being more masculine, more sluggish, colder, and generally more withdrawn	Perceived as being more masculine, more sluggish, colder, and generally more withdrawn; same as for female
Nasality	Wide array of socially undesirable characteristics for both females and males	Wide array of socially undesirable characteristics for both females and males
Tenseness	Seen as being younger, more emotional, feminine, high-strung, and less intelligent	Perceived as being older and more unyielding, cantankerous
Throatiness	Perceived as being less intelligent, more masculine, lazier, more boorish, unemotional, ugly, sickly, careless, inartistic, naive, humble, neurotic, quiet, uninteresting, and apathetic, more cloddish or oafish	Stereotyped as being older, more realistic, mature, sophisticated, and well adjusted
Orotundity	Perceptions of increased liveliness, gregariousness, and aesthetic sensitivity, yet at same time tending to be increasingly proud and humorless	Appeared more energetic, healthy, artistic, sophisticated, proud, interesting, and enthusiastic, more hardy, and aesthetically inclined
Increased rate	Both females and males perceived as more animated and extroverted	Both females and males perceived as more animated and extroverted
Increased pitch variety	Perceived as more dynamic and extroverted	Perceived as more dynamic, feminine, and aesthetically inclined

Source: D. W. Addington, "The Relationship of Selected Vocal Characteristics to Personality Perception," *Speech Monographs* 35 (1968): 492–503.

One writer suggests that the personality or behavioral judgments we make from voice come from common experience and reactions to persons. Perhaps only part of these personality constructs can be defined by tests designed to measure them. Part of the traits may remain unmeasured. It might be that judgments from voice and results of pencil-and-paper scales are both valid measures, but each method may cover a different portion of the total variance of a particular trait or behavioral tendency.[5]

The problem with the Addington study and some others like it is that the voice samples used were monologues. Many of the behavioral traits listeners judge are usually associated with the more animated verbal give and take among persons. The vocal cues of these traits would seem more likely to occur in dialogue than in reading isolated passages, where the vocal animation is often subdued and lacks spontaneity.

Sex and vocal development

Let us now look back to the formation of many of our vocal traits and see what patterns we can determine. Sex differences in the speech of children have often been assumed to reflect sex differences in language development. Some writers are beginning to take a closer look. They speculate that even some of the differences that appear quite early could be due to the different social or verbal climates our culture offers boys and girls.

A sizable body of research shows that girls begin talking at an earlier age than do boys, their speech is more comprehensible at an earlier age, they use short sentences earlier, and they are more fluent than males from 12 months on.[6] The variety of speech sounds used by boys and girls in their first year of life seems to be almost identical, but there is often a difference in control of sounds during the second year in favor of girls.[7] Some studies show girls achieve mature articulation about a half-year earlier than boys.[8] Girls' earlier speech development and greater proficiency in fluency and articulation may be related to the earlier maturation of their speech organs.

There is evidence that although the differences decrease as children grow older, girls generally continue to surpass boys in linguistic skills from elementary school through college. In learning a foreign language and its articulatory coordinations, girls also seem to do better.[9]

There are, however, researchers who do not agree with these conclusions. Some studies do not entirely substantiate the superior skills of girls over boys. Templin found in her language research that while girls tended to receive higher scores than boys, the differences were not consistent and were only occasionally statistically significant.[10] However, her results do support the conclusion that girls achieve articulatory proficiency earlier than boys. She explained that the reduced dif-

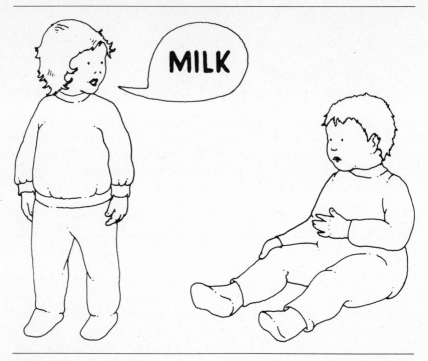

Girls tend to start speaking earlier and progress more rapidly than boys.

ferences she found among the sexes could be accounted for by the shift toward a single standard in child care and training in recent decades.

Other research also minimizes differences. A study of the language of 150 kindergarten children who were matched for chronological age, intelligence, socioeconomic status, and family structure found statistically significant differences in favor of the girls on just two counts: on length of responses, and on one of the fluency measures. The results generally pointed to no difference between the sexes on other fluency measures, vocabulary skills, articulatory skills, structural complexity, and number of different words.[11]

Several recent studies have investigated fluency as measured by length or number of utterances. They reported no sex differences in the amount of speech four-year-olds directed to their child and adult listeners,[12] in the amount of speech by preschool children in conversation pairs,[13] or in nursery school children's amount of talk.[14] In a study of teacher-child interaction, the spontaneous speech of four female preschool teachers and their 38 students was recorded. No differences were found in number of utterances or number of turns in teacher-boy and teacher-girl exchanges. However, girls were more likely than boys to receive verbal feedback or acknowledgment of their answers to teachers' questions.[15]

It seems fair to say that research generally supports the idea that there are sex differences in acquisition of speech sounds, but evidence of structural-grammatical or fluency differences in boys' and girls' speech is indeterminate. Cherry feels that the question of sex differences in children's speech remains open because of shortcomings in the design of early studies and the paucity of research in this area since then. She has taken a second look at some past research in child speech and pinpointed some problems in design which could have biased results of earlier studies:[16]

1 There was no control for observer bias. Generally, no mention was made of number or sex of the experimenters or whether mothers were present or absent during observation. These factors might have some effect on the way the children spoke.

2 The studies did not use audio or video recording in gathering speech samples, and so the accuracy of transcriptions is questionable. Utterances could be missed, shortened, or modified in some ways by the transcriber, with no way to recheck what was heard.

3 No working definitions were given of exactly what constituted an utterance. Transcribers might have been inclined to read significance into speech samples because of their own sex-role expectations, attitudes, or stereotypes. They might have unreliably interpreted some sounds as real speech or heard sound clusters as complete utterances without consistent standards or rules to judge them by.

4 Children's speech was generally not studied in interaction with the speech of others, and the samples were not spontaneous conversation.

5 Results of the research were generally reported as percentages, and no statistical analysis was performed. Therefore, it was unclear which differences were significant.

Some causes of sex differences

It is not certain to what extent some of the sex differences in speech are inherently connected with sex or with differences in the social environments of girls and boys. The research on social and physiological influences presents some interesting material for speculation.

Social causes

Some studies indicate that girls and boys can grow up in seemingly identical surroundings and yet be nurtured in totally different social-emotional climates. In a study of interaction between three-month-old infants and their mothers, more vocal-verbal communication occurred between mothers and daughters than between mothers and sons. Mothers vocalized more to their female infants, and the female infants vocalized more in response to their mothers than the mother–infant son pairs.[17] Research generally indicates that, from the earliest age, mothers look at and talk to their female infants more than they look at and talk to their male infants. One study showed that even in the hospital during the first two days of life mothers looked at, smiled at, and touched their infant daughters more than their infant sons.[18] For the first two years of life, girls are the object of more looking-at and talking-to behaviors.[19]

Observation of spontaneous interaction between mothers and their two-year-old children in a play situation revealed that mother-daughter pairs have a greater tendency to communicate through conversation. Mother-son pairs did not show the same need to maintain conversation and build dialogue.[20] In observations of natural conversations in families with several children, distinctions were found in the way boys and girls from infancy to eight years were addressed. Girls received more gentle verbal treatment, whereas boys received more robust verbal treatment. Fathers, especially, addressed their sons in a boisterous and exuberant style.[21]

Division of play according to sex can provide different verbal environments. Boys may be encouraged to play outside and so are not in as close proximity to the mother. As a result, they may not be exposed to as much adult speech and may get less practice using adult patterns of speech.[22]

The toys girls and boys play with can also create different climates. The play life of girls often includes toys and objects that encourage verbalization rather than action (dolls, tea sets, role-playing clothes to portray mother or nurse, paper dolls, and so forth). Girls' play includes a central dependence on dolls and talk in imitation of mother. In echoing the mother, girls are likely to stimulate more conversation from her and engage in considerable conversational interaction with her.[23]

Boys, despite their inclinations, may see that verbal play is frowned upon for them. It is not "manly" to talk with dolls and use the manner of talk of the mother, who is the adult speech model most frequently at home. Many toys and objects boys use in their play center around action rather than talk: trucks, cars, planes; blocks and building sets; cowboy, Indian, and soldier figures; and so forth. Some toys are associated with mechanical sounds, and boys use these sounds in their play, which is often more violent. Some observation has shown that preschool boys tend to use more sound effects in their speech than do girls.[24]

If we consider comedians and comics who use sound effects in an extension of the play instinct, we can quickly call to mind a number of males: Jonathan Winters, Bill Cosby, Johnny Carson, George Carlin, Jerry Lewis, Avery Schreiber, Charles Callas, Richard Pryor, John Viner, and Rich Little. These men probably first excelled at sound effects when

One study found that preschool boys use more sound effects in their speech than girls.

they were boys playing alone or amusing friends. It is difficult to name female comedians who use mechanical noises or varied sound effects in their routines. When they were little girls they would have been discouraged from using these sounds, which seem to be too rough or tomboyish, and so they now find it inappropriate or uncomfortable to employ sound effects in their routines.

Verbal pursuits of play may be more satisfying in general to girls. Girls can identify more readily with the mother than boys can with the father. The mother is often at home more, and so her talk is heard more than the father's. Girls can come closer to imitating the vocal pitches of the mother than boys can those of the father. Echo verbalization is easier and more satisfying to girls who try to identify with the mother than for boys who try to identify with the father.[25] It could be argued that girls hear the father's voice as much as boys, but girls probably feel less need to imitate and identify with the father. They are already making progress in echoing the mother's speech and are probably getting positive reinforcement and self-satisfaction as they do so.

The fact that the attempts of some boys to identify with their fathers are often confusing, disturbing, and unsuccessful may have some bearing on the finding that boys have more speech problems as they grow older. Also parental attitudes in general are thought to be more favorable toward girls than boys. Disciplinary measures taken with boys are apt to be harsher than those used with girls and to cause more frustration and emotional insecurity for boys.[26]

Physiological causes

> . . . and his big manly voice,
> Turning again toward childish treble pipes
> And whistles in his sound.
> —Shakespeare, *As You Like It* II.vii

> . . . Her voice was ever soft,
> Gentle, and low, an excellent thing in woman.
> —Shakespeare, *King Lear* V.iii

We tend to use different terms when we refer to women's voices and to men's voices. We may speak of a woman's "soft, gentle, and low" voice but refer to a male's "big manly voice." Though we can generally distinguish the voices of male and female speakers of English, it is not clear to what extent the vocal cues we use are dependent on culturally prescribed norms for the sexes rather than on anatomical differences in the speech mechanisms of the sexes.

The larynx, or voice box, of the adult male (its projection at the front of the throat is commonly called the Adam's apple) is generally larger than the female's. Small tough bands of connective tissue in the larynx form the vocal cords. During speech these vibrate when we force breath from our lungs to produce vocal tones for the voiced sounds. Most men have longer and thicker vocal bands than most women. The greater the number of times the vocal cords vibrate, the higher the sound we subjectively hear as pitch. The greater the mass and length of the vocal cords, the less is the frequency of vibration and the lower is our subjective perception of pitch. These small bands of connective tissue range in length from $\frac{1}{2}$ inch to $\frac{7}{8}$ inch in adult females and from $\frac{7}{8}$ inch to $1\frac{1}{4}$ inches in adult males. Since most adult males have longer and thicker vocal cords than the majority of women do, men's voices tend to be lower in pitch. Females usually have higher-pitched voices than males because their vocal bands are shorter and thinner. Their voices are about $\frac{2}{3}$ octave higher than the pitch levels of men's voices.

But pitch, or fundamental frequency, of the vocal cords is probably not the only clue that tells us whether a voice is female or male. Another anatomical factor to be considered is the vocal tract through which the vibrating sound must pass. The vocal tract is an air-filled tube that is divided by the lips, tongue, and soft palate into cavities—the mouth, nose, larynx, and throat cavities. These cavities, or resonators, have certain natural frequencies and respond more readily to sound waves of those frequencies. The cavities act like echo chambers and reinforce or build up the loudness of tones. The resonances, or tones, that are built up or emphasized are termed formants.

Since males and females tend to have different skeletal structures and different-sized vocal tracts, it is likely that different formant-frequency patterns of the resonating cavities would be used as cues in identifying sex. The smaller vocal tract of the average female leads to a pattern of higher formant frequencies than the average male's.

But investigation of acoustic differences in adult female and male speakers has yielded some puzzling results. An analysis of females' and males' vowel formants revealed acoustic differences much sharper than could be accounted for by anatomical sex-differences alone. The researcher concluded that although the formant differences were doubtless related to the size of the average female and male vocal tract, some of the variation must be stylistic and due to linguistic custom, rather than physical make-up. Men and women may modify the sounds they produce to make them conform to male and female archetypes.[27] "In other words, men tend to talk as though they were bigger and women as though they were smaller than they actually may be."[28]

A provocative study dealt with children from ages 4 to 14 years and the identification of their sex on the basis of voice alone. The larynx of preadolescent girls and boys is likely to be the same size if the height and weight of the children are matched, so their fundamental frequencies should probably be similar regardless of sex.[29] Since no difference in jaw length has been found between prepubertal girls and boys,[30] it has seemed logical to assume they would also have the same size vocal tracts. Similar vocal-tract size should mean similar formant frequencies for preadolescent children. One could expect that listeners would not be able to tell the sex of children from their voices before puberty.

The results of the study did not support this expectation. Listeners had little trouble identifying the sex of the children from their voices. Eighty-one percent of their guesses were correct. The investigators speculated about the kinds of cues listeners used in accurately identifying sex. Since the average fundamental frequency was actually a little higher for the boys than for the girls, this was not considered likely to be one of the cues in sex identification. The formant values for the vowels, however, were significantly lower for the boys than for the girls. Since this is the same pattern found in adult speakers, listeners may have used it as an auditory clue.

An interesting finding is that several girls who were most difficult to identify by sex and who were overwhelmingly misjudged to be boys had formant patterns close to the average for boys. In other words, the voices that sounded least girl-like had a pattern of higher fundamentals but lower formants—the same pattern found in the boys' voices.[31] Several possible explanations were offered by the researchers to explain their findings in the study.

First, although recent research argues to the contrary, it is possible preadolescent girls and boys may not have similar skeletal and articulatory structures. Different vocal anatomical structures, even at this age, could lead to different sounds distinguishable by sex. If, however, the average size of boys' and girls' voice mechanisms is equivalent, then the differences found could result from the different ways the children use their vocal apparatus or from hormonal control over certain motor aspects of speech. Or children could be learning cultural patterns that are considered appropriate for each sex. To achieve a certain voice sound, a speaker can vary the size and shape of the vocal resonating cavities by altering tongue position, changing the configuration of the lips, and so forth. For example, rounding the lips will make the vocal tract longer and will lower the formant frequencies. Spreading the lips will shorten the vocal tract and make the formants higher. Some women's characteristic way of talking and smiling at the same time would have the latter effect.[32]

Undoubtedly factors other than formant frequency helped listeners correctly identify the children's voices by sex. Pronunciation, intonation, or vocal quality probably provided clues, also. Several girls with low formants, for example, were not misidentified as boys. But it does seem possible that boys learn to lower their formants in order to sound more masculine and girls to raise theirs in order to sound more feminine.

Children's voices generally undergo changes in pitch and quality between thirteen and sixteen years of age. The changes occur earlier in girls and are less marked than in boys. Girls' vocal cords lengthen and the throat lining becomes thicker and softer. Consequently, female voices often become mellower and richer in quality with the coming of adolescence. They have a longer, slower pubescent period and less laryngeal growth, so they have more time to adjust to vocal changes.

The size and structure of the larynx changes more markedly in boys, so they have to adjust to longer vocal cords and a larger larynx. Their vocal cords lengthen about one centimeter, while the average female's grows only about one-third as much. The angle of the thyroid becomes pronounced in boys, and their vocal cords grow about one-third larger in mass and length, causing their pitch to become lower by about one octave.

With the rapid growth of cartilage and muscle in boys, their vocal mechanism tends to become somewhat unmanageable. Boys' voices may unexpectedly shift from high to low, their vocal quality may change suddenly from hoarse to mellow, and their pitch lapse "into a childish treble as if two sets of vocal folds were vibrating instead of one."[33] The period of adjustment and maturation is estimated to take about 6 months, but it may be prolonged from 18 months to 2 years.

Sex and speech problems

A higher number of males than females are reported to have speech defects in our population. This seems to be true of all age groups and of most types of speech problems, such as stuttering, poor articulation, aphasia, and cleft lip and palate.[34] The differences found in primary grades seem to continue through the college level. A university study found a predominance of male to female speech-defective students ranging from a ratio of 1.6 males to 1 female to as high as 3.4 males to 1 female.[35] The difference in number of females and males with speech defects is probably greatest among stutterers. More males than females stutter, with ratios of from 2 to 10 males for each female reported in the literature. A generally accepted estimate is that male stutterers out-number females by about 4 to 1. Furthermore, stuttering is said to be more severe among boys than among girls and to last longer for boys.[36]

Some explanations have been offered for the difference between the sexes in incidence of speech defects. One explanation is that since girls tend to speak earlier, acquire proficient articulation sooner, and have better language control for their first 10 years of life than do boys, there may be cultural pressure for boys to match girls' performance. Pressure to talk as soon as girls, when they are not ready, may cause some boys to begin to speak defectively. As they grow older, the defects may persist.[37]

Developmental differences may also relate to stuttering problems. If male children develop physically, socially, and linguistically at a slower rate than females, they meet unequal competition that causes frustration in verbal situations. Consequently, they may show more insecurity, hesitancy, and inhibition in their speech.[38] In a male-dominated society, male children are probably under greater duress to achieve. Parents may exert greater pressure to speak well and set higher standards of fluency for boys than for girls and so be quicker to label their sons as stutterers than their daughters.[39]

One investigator tried to find out if stuttering is related to cultural pressure by surveying a society where performance demands on females are increased and those on males are decreased. He believed this type of group exists in the lower socioeconomic strata of our society, so he selected a Southern black population with matriarchal home patterns to survey. He reasoned that if social patterns influence sex differences in stuttering, one might expect a different ratio of female to male stutterers in an environment dominated by a female as compared with one dominanted by a male. A male child imitating the adult male role in the matriarchal home has fewer demands placed on him, while the female child has greater demands placed on her. If unequal environmental pressures are partially responsible for stuttering, greater pressure on females in these homes would be expected to produce a greater proportion of female stutterers.[40]

Results generally supported the hypothesis that the sex differences in stuttering are in some way related to cultural pressure. There were proportionately more female stutterers from matriarchal than patriarchal homes. Conversely, there were more male stutterers from patriarchal than matriarchal homes. Some attribute the higher number of stutterers among males to the general physical liabilities of being male. Maleness has certain biological drawbacks in comparison to females: higher mortality rate at every stage in life; greater incidence of disorders such as chorea, rickets, asthma, tetany, convulsions, and epilepsy; more birth injuries; more structural abnormalities such as cleft palate, at birth. In general, deviations from the norm are more numerous among males.[41]

One theory traces stuttering to delayed myelinization—growth of the white fatty material around certain nerve fibers in the brain that coordinate the muscles used in speech. Research has shown that myelinization in girls is advanced over that of boys in the first years of life, including the critical ages of 2 to 4 years when much stuttering begins.[42]

Sex and speech patterns

We have traditionally categorized speech patterns along geographical lines. Dialects and regional pronunciation patterns have been useful ways of identifying talk. The authors are suggesting a different mode of classifying discourse via sex differences.

Pronunciation

What is in a word—or a word ending, for that matter? Surprisingly, there are some sex differences in the articulation and pronunciation of word endings. These disparities have interesting implications for females and males.

A study of some New England children from 3 to 10 years of age in a semirural town focused on their pronunciation of -*ing* verb endings in interviews. A significantly greater number of girls used -*ing* more frequently; more boys used -*in*. In this community the -*ing* pronunciation seemed to symbolize female speech and the -*in* pronunciation, male speech. Also there was a slight tendency for -*ing* use to be associated with higher socioeconomic status. Personality differences were also associated with the use of the verb endings. For example, a boy regarded by his teacher and others as a "model" boy (successful in school, well liked by peers, thoughtful and considerate) used the -*ing* ending almost exclusively. Whereas a "typical" boy (physically strong, dominating, full of mischief) used the -*in* ending over half the time. Type of setting (formal or informal) also had an effect on speech. In the more formal interviews, the "model" boy, for example, used mostly -*ing* endings, but he dropped the *g* in the informal situation. There was also a tendency for certain formal, reserved, or more sedentary verbs, such as *criticizing, correcting, reading, visiting,* and *interesting,* to have the -*ing* ending. But the more informal verbs associated with physical activity or

Women have been found to use fewer nonstandard or stigmatized forms of speech than men.

movement, such as *punchin, flubbin, swimmin, chewin,* and *hittin,* were given the *-in* ending.[43]

Perhaps without conscious effort speakers both reacted to and produced some vocal cues that signaled social roles and situations; they could sense when a speaker was talking like a female or a male, like a formal person or a relaxed person. Females' pronunciations of the endings tended to be formal and males' pronunciations informal.

Research on adult speech also supports these findings. A study of 700 randomly selected residents in Detroit showed that males tended to use *-in* rather than *-ing* in their speech.[44] In careful speech, women have been found to use fewer nonstandard or stigmatized forms and more of the prestige patterns than men.[45] Another study of an American community showed it was primarily middle-class women who came closest to national speech norms or standards.[46]

Though little research has surveyed black populations, there seem to be similar trends among blacks. One study of black speech in a small Southern community found that the women used fewer nonstandard forms than men and came closer to the prestige patterns.[47] An examination of some of the black population in Detroit revealed that within each social class, black females used speech nearer the standard English norm than males.[48]

Some research suggests that women use more new linguistic forms in their casual speech than men, but they shift their speech to the standard, or so-called correct, forms more sharply in formal settings. This behavior was found to be most extreme in lower-middle-class women.[49] A study showed men had a greater tendency to use nasalized vowels, which were not considered correct.[50]

It is interesting to speculate why women are more likely to use forms that are considered correct, since in some cases the forms used may involve articulatory coordinations that require more effort on their part. Several reasons have been suggested for women's closer adherence to the prestige speech standard:[51]

1 First, women may be more conscious of status and thus more sensitive to the importance of speech in social interaction. Women may feel less secure about their position in society. They are often dependent on males, and their jobs are generally subordinate to, less prestigious, less well paid than those of males. Women may feel the need to secure their position and signal their standing through other ways, speech being one method. This may hold true especially for women who do not work outside the home.

2 Men probably obtain their standing in society more by what they do than by what they are. They are rated by their occupation, their earnings, and in some cases by certain abilities. On the other hand, women traditionally have achieved status by what they are or how they appear—both visually and verbally—they are judged on whether they are attractive, pleasant, cultured, and so on. Since they are not as likely to be rated by their work or occupation, other signals of status such as speech become more important.

3 Another factor may be that use of the so-called rougher language used more by lower economic groups or blue-collar workers may carry positive connotations of masculinity. This language is generally associated with the roughness and toughness that supposedly characterize blue-collar worker life. One researcher, for example, speculated that New York City, although its more formal styles of speech have prestige, "must have an equal and opposing prestige for informal, working-class speech—a covert prestige enforcing this speech pattern." There are, then, hidden values associated with nonstandard speech.[52]

A study of English speakers revealed that more male speakers claimed they used a less prestigious speech than they actually used. Female speakers tended to report they used more prestigious speech than they actually did. The investigator thought this showed that male speakers in his study were subconsciously or privately favorably disposed toward nonstandard working-class speech and women speakers were more favorably disposed toward the prestige, or so-called correct,

Nonstandard speech may carry positive connotations of masculinity for men.

forms. This attitude was never openly expressed, but investigators inferred that a large number of male speakers are more concerned with the hidden prestige of masculinity, which this type of speech supposedly conveys, than with achieving social status.[53]

Apparently men use some substandard speech forms to signal their masculinity and reinforce their group solidarity. In some situations verbally signaling their participation in maleness may be more important to some men than giving the signs of social standing. It would be interesting to monitor the speech of males and females in different settings to see which situations bring out this behavior most markedly and to learn how their pronunciation varies according to the persons with whom they interact.

Pitch

Our pitch and vocal range are not features we can select and change at will as we would our hair style or new clothing. The size, shape, and functioning of our vocal instrument determines our vocal pitch. Cultural pressures, however, can distort some vocal attributes. One such pressure is the premium put on a low-pitched voice in our society. By nature a certain percentage of males are born to have low baritone and bass voices and others to have tenor and high baritone voices. "The result of confusing physical virility with vocal depth is frequently low pitch and poor quality."[54] One needs only to be reminded of the pompous anchor man, Ted Baxter, on the Mary Tyler Moore television program. His concept of "macho," or male virility, is associated with vocal depth. It takes more effort to speak loudly when we are not within our normal pitch range. We can experience fatigue and vocal strain from continued talking below our optimum pitch level.

Cultural pressure for a low-pitched voice can affect women too. By nature a certain percentage of females are born to be altos and others to be sopranos. Our contemporary attitude seems to admire low-pitched women's voices that are slightly breathy in quality. Again, talking below one's normal pitch is vocally inefficient and can take considerably more effort than is necessary at normal pitch.

A high-pitched voice is rarely an asset, for our culture tends to penalize high voices. Especially severe are social penalties for the male with a high-pitched voice. In fact, the old term for an overly high-pitched problem voice was "eunuchoid voice,"[55] a term which stresses the unmasculine connotations of that type of vocal quality. Listeners seem to associate high pitch with undesirable feminine traits. This is exemplified in some of our humor, such as the old joke about the male swimmer being chased by several sharks. "Help! Help! Help!" he shouted in a deep, low-pitched voice. As the sharks streaked by and bit him, he squeaked in a falsetto voice, "Too late! Too late!"

One writer who believes that some television programs for children reinforce sex stereotypes wrote, "Even Sesame Street . . . teaches role rigidity along with the letters of the alphabet. . . . Boy monsters are brave and gruff. Girl monsters are high-pitched and timid."[56] It is not surprising that most of us are likely to submit to, or lean in the direction of, social pressure. We have seen evidence of the social pressure for a so-called masculine voice in our youngest son, who is currently thirteen years old. For the past several years we have heard him singing a full octave below what he should comfortably sing. No amount of remonstrance has been effective in altering his behavior. He seems to feel it is a badge of strength and masculinity to sing in a low voice.

The effect of socialization and the press for low pitch is sometimes evident to us in communication classes. Last semester in several courses, the students studied pitch as one factor in vocal effectiveness. Using a piano, we located the habitual pitch, or level, at which each student normally spoke. Then we determined the optimum or natural pitch for each person. This is the level at which a person can produce vocal tones most efficiently, most comfortably, and with good quality and loudness. We used the general rule of thumb that optimum or

For some people, machismo, or male virility, is associated with vocal depth.

natural pitch is probably one-fourth to one-third above the lowest level of an individual's total pitch range.[57]

Of 34 females and 31 males, we found more speakers of both sexes who tended to vocalize at levels slightly below what we calculated to be their natural level, with 13 females and 12 males demonstrating this tendency. Among those who spoke at levels appreciably higher or lower than what we calculated as their natural pitch, there were twice as many females as males (12 to 6). Seven females were significantly lower and 5 higher than their natural levels. Some of these higher voices sounded like a carry-over from "cute little girl" days. Of the males, 4 were significantly lower and 2 higher than their natural levels.

Intonation

The changes in pitch that occur when we speak are termed intonation. This feature of speech has, we believe, considerable significance for female and male communication in the kinds of messages it conveys.

Intonation is something like a musical melody that is spoken but not sung. When the voice shifts from one definite pitch to another with a break, generally between the syllables of a word or between words, this is termed a *step*:

paper   red paper

Pitch changes that are continuous and occur without breaks in flow are termed *inflections*. These pitch variations may be rapid or slow, rising, falling, or circumflex. Circumflex inflections are combinations of rising-falling, falling-rising patterns:

Oh yeah.   I didn't know.

Studies seem to show that the average pitch level of an individual's voice may be less important to overall effectiveness than variations in pitch. Readers of prose who used a greater range of inflections were selected by listeners as the better speakers. Those rated as poor readers and speakers had narrow inflectional patterns.[58] Among superior female and male speakers, women may have less variable voices than men. For although the women in one study had as great a total pitch range as the men, they did not seem to use their potential to the extent that the men did. The females confined their vocalization more to levels near the bottom of their range. This may be due to a common belief that listeners generally prefer low-pitched female voices.[59]

Variations in pitch patterns are many, and tracking them can be like trying to monitor a kaleidoscope. At the risk of oversimplifying when describing general patterns of pitch, we shall mention some customary patterns of American speech. Phrases or ideas are often introduced with a rising pitch and concluded with a falling contour. Statements of fact and commands or instructions often end on falling pitches, whereas incomplete thoughts and questions are presented with rising intonation.

Just how soon we start to learn these patterns and subtle intonation differences associated with sex is truly surprising. Research suggests that our training is well under way in infancy. Children from three months on have been found to respond positively to friendly tones of voice and negatively to angry tones of voice. In addition, children mimic adult intonation and the average fundamental frequency range. Observations of a ten-month-old boy and a thirteen-month-old girl were reported, in which each child's babbling was recorded in play situations with the father, with the mother, and, in the case of the boy only, alone.[60] Approximately 20 minutes of "conversation" occurred in these settings, and the average fundamental frequencies of the child's voice were measured during babbling and crying.

Results indicated the girl attempted to mimic the fundamental frequencies of her parents. Her fundamental frequency was higher when playing with her mother, 390 cycles per second, and lower when playing with her father, 290 cps. Her babbling was not recorded when she was alone.

The boy showed similar tendencies to mimic intonation signals. The average fundamental frequency of the boy's babbling while he was with his father was 340 cps. The level was 390 cps on the average when he babbled with his mother. He was also recorded when he babbled and cried alone in the crib. The average pitch levels of the solitary vocalizations were higher than when he babbled with both mother and father. The study concluded that the boy lowered his fundamental frequency when he was with either parent but lowered it more when he was with his father.

In our estimation, the way signals of intonation are sent and interpreted is a neglected area of study. These signals can have effects that far transcend the words we send or that contradict or differ greatly from our communication intentions. Intonation can be a signal that identifies one with a certain group—for example, nationality, age, sex, status. One writer, for example, analyzed intuitive impressions of effeminacy in men and gave a behavioral description of the so-called simpering voice: wider pitch-range than normal for men, blending or sliding tonal effects between stressed syllables, more frequent use of circumflex inflections such as rising-falling, falling-rising, and so forth, and switching to an upper or falsetto range from time to time.[61]

Certain intonation characteristics may be identifiable by sex. Women supposedly speak in an overall high pitch, and in many cases women's and children's voices are pitched approximately the same. Also, women are said to use the highest pitch level, the *excited* pitch, more than men and in general to speak with more expressive intonation patterns.[62]

Key relates an experiment conducted by one of her students that involved storytelling by children. Boys and girls in the third, fourth, and fifth grades retold a story. The girls used expressive intonation in their accounts, but the boys were more low-key in their delivery, "playing it cool" even to the point of monotony.[63] Linguists suggest women use patterns of uncertainty and indefiniteness in their speech more often than men. These have been variously characterized as patterns of plight or whining, questioning, helpless patterns. Phoneticians speak of raised, weak syllables as woman's intonation.

One researcher investigated differences in the use of certain intonation patterns by men and women in the midwestern region. She found some definite differences in preferences for and avoidances of some intonation patterns by women and men. Certain patterns of high-low downglides of unexpectedness or surprise were found primarily in women's speech but were generally absent from men's speech. They included patterns such as the following:[64]

1 'Oh 'that's 'awful!

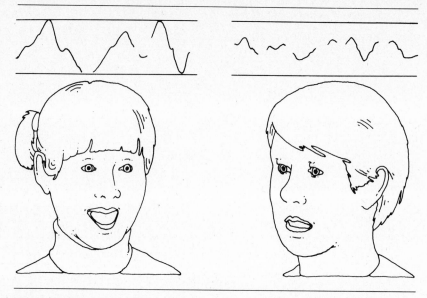

When children were observed telling stories, researchers found that girls used expressive intonation, while boys were low-key in their delivery.

Also used more often by women but lacking in men's speech were request-confirmation patterns like this:

2 You ⌐do!

Other patterns used mostly or solely by women, according to the research include these:

3 The varying-implication nonfinal pattern:

I know he has ⌐gone.

4 The hesitation pattern:

Well, I ⌐studied . . .

5 The polite, cheerful pattern:

Are you coming?

6 Reverse glide, incomplete-deliberation pattern on one syllable (this pattern spread over several words is used by both women and men):

Oh ⌐yes.

7 Polite and cheerful, incomplete-sequence and surprise form:

Won't you come in?
Good ⌐bye

8 Incomplete and unexpected pattern:

What's my ˈnʌame?

Apparently men rarely use the highest level of pitch that women use. Whereas many women use four contrastive levels of intonation, most men probably have only three. Also men seem to avoid final intonation patterns that do not end at the lowest pitch level. If they do use a final raised-pitch step or inflection, it is to signal an incomplete sequence (such as in naming items: "I bought apples, plums . . .") or a question sentence.

Women may use long pitch glides or reverse glides on one syllable, but men usually employ this intonation pattern only when the tone changes are spread out over several words or syllables. Men would not tend to use this variation on one syllable, as in really! But males as well as females would probably use it with several syllables or words, as in I didn't want to go.

An investigator was interested in how female speech might vary with involvement in the women's movement and absence of males. Would these variables affect women's tendency to use the previously mentioned intonation patterns? The expectation was that since the male intonation patterns tend to be associated with authority, women in the feminist setting would use these types of intonation. Instead there were abundant examples of the intonation types just mentioned, which supposedly characterize women's speech: the polite, cheerful pattern; the hesitation pattern; the request-confirmation pattern; and the surprise pattern.[65]

Robin Lakoff discusses a type of uncertainty intonation that she believes is especially restrictive for women. It is used in declarative statements or answers to questions but has the rising intonation of a question. The effect is that of seeking confirmation and at the same time conveying hesitancy.[66] Speaker B uses this pattern in the following two exchanges:

1 A: What time will you be back:
   B: Oh, about four o'clock . . . ?

2 A: What are we having for supper?
   B: Roundsteak . . . ?

At the same time speaker B is supposedly answering a question, her voice (we are assuming the speaker is female) is questioning in its rise in tone. The overall effect, then, is not that of really telling the other that she will be back at four o'clock or that she will have roundsteak for supper. Speaker B is actually asking confirmation or approval, even though she is the one who knows the answer. She is, in effect, saying "Four o'clock . . . if that's OK with you," or "Roundsteak—that is, if you agree."

Lakoff views this pattern of intonation as another manifestation of the politeness that characterizes women's speech. It is a feature whereby the speaker leaves the decision open and does not impose her views or demands on anyone else. There are numerous situations where the polite rise in inflection is useful and desirable. But if this pattern is too widely dispersed throughout one's speech, the overall impression conveyed will be an unwillingness to assert an opinion. It can be difficult to have confidence in a person who communicates a lack of conviction or who seems unsure of herself. Such a person may be seen as incapable of assuming responsibility or as unable to make up her mind or formulate decisions.

Volume

The volume, or loudness, of one's voice is an important factor in communication effectiveness. Obviously, for your message to call forth a response or have an impact upon others, you must first be heard. Though we have gathered no empirical data to support our claim, we have noticed that in our speech classes more females than males need instruction and encouragement to speak more loudly. Both in open class critiquing and individual instructor analysis, more women than men students have to be counseled, "Speak up. Get more force in your speaking."

Our experience is in agreement with the little research that has been done on this subject. In one case a graphic-level recorder was used to record the speaking intensity of females and males who answered five questions: What is your opinion of the zip code? How do you feel about daylight savings time? And so forth. Subjects were at near and far interpersonal distances from the experimenters and spoke with both female and male experimenters. The male speakers in general spoke with greater intensity than the female speakers.[67] When the subjects spoke with someone of the same sex, for example a female to a female, they spoke more softly. When subjects spoke with the opposite sex, a female to a male, or vice versa, they increased their intensity. The researchers interpreted this to mean that subjects probably felt a greater affiliation with an experimenter of the same sex than with one of the opposite sex.

Normally, greater air pressure below the vocal folds is needed to produce louder speech. The will to be heard and proper abdominal breathing supplies sufficient energy to provide this pressure, and the vocal tone produced will be loud enough to be heard easily. It is not surprising to read that some psychiatrists say fearful people often speak in fearful tones or in voices not loud enough to be heard easily.[68] In our culture the voice of authority tends to be a loud voice. If there is no organic defect, it seems probable that a weak voice indicates a timid personality or an extreme reaction to the speaking situation. Many women

Some research has found that males speak with greater intensity, or loudness, than females.

who see themselves in submissive or nonauthoritarian roles seem to reflect their roles in their voices.

One author discusses "the voice as phallus" and suggests that we unconsciously identify the voice as the virile prerogative of the dominant sex. A female can usurp this prerogative when she uses a powerful speaking voice or straightforward speech. She may be viewed by some as repellent in her dominance or by others as attractive. A male may relinquish his assumed prerogative in situations where he is dominated (for example, in the military, on college faculties, in matriarchal homes) and he may develop depressed, hedged, weak styles of speaking, according to the author.[69]

A consequence of sex differences: vocal typecasting

All things considered, the sex communicated by a voice makes a difference in our reactions to what we hear. This was demonstrated to us in a conversation with our oldest son, age 22, concerning a congregational survey on the selection of a new pastor. One of the questionnaire items concerned the respondent's feelings about the selection of a woman as pastor. Our son admitted that he had answered in the negative, commenting, "Personally, a woman's voice wouldn't keep my attention or be as interesting to listen to." In spite of views he had heard expressed at home and his knowledge of professional research, his cultural conditioning and expectations about how a person in the clergy should sound weighed most heavily in his response. Another brother, younger by nine years and reared during a different decade, was more accepting of either sex in the role.

It is interesting to consider how we typecast voices. It is assumed by some that high-pitched voices are not associated with serious topics. A broadcaster gave the following reason why more female news reporters on television are not hired: "As a whole, people don't like to hear women's voices telling them serious things."[70] Perhaps we tend to associate objectivity and accuracy with the deeper male voice and emotionalism with the higher, often more expressive female voice. A writer describes the vocal attributes of the news anchor male: "He sets the tone; with his solemn, low-pitched voice he embodies the wisdom of the world. His commanding presence imposes itself on the material and holds the show together."[71] A former president of NBC News was quoted in *Newsweek* several years ago as saying, "I have the strong feeling that audiences are less prepared to accept news from a woman's voice than a man's."[72] And an announcer's handbook explained that "Women's delivery . . . is lacking in the authority needed for a convincing newscast."[73]

Yet this bias may be more in the minds of the employers than in those of the listener-viewers. A survey on attitudes toward television newswomen taken at the University of Wisconsin does not reflect this view. The sample polled included small-town conservative families. Only about one-fifth of the persons polled said they would be more likely to believe a news report from a man than from a woman. In Europe women do news, and in France their voices are preferred.[74]

Some interesting questions on this general topic merit future research: Do women prefer male voices in the media or elsewhere discussing important issues to the degree that men seem to, and to what extent does this preference exist, if it does exist? At what age does sex preference for voices begin? Do women in broadcasting change their voices during airtime any more than male broadcasters? Do the voices of women in positions of authority show any significant differences from the voices of women in subordinate positions? How do the vocal characteristics of men in these positions compare or contrast with those of women in similar positions?[75]

From our experience teaching communication, we have found that male students tend to come across more forcefully and definitively in their speaking, and many females seem more tentative, less decided, and more open to suggestions and discussion. Both of these modes are extremely useful in communication, but if they are not adapted to the situation and the matter being communicated, they can be not only worthless, but detrimental to either sex.

We once viewed a game show that involved humorous deception in one segment. Some women who, unknown to the game show contestants, were vice presidents of their businesses, were questioned by contestants. Some men who were pretending to be the vice presidents of the businesses were also questioned. The humor in the situation, as far as the audience was concerned, arose from the men's skillful bluffing. Their sometimes illogical and far-fetched statements were delivered in sonorous and decisive tones. Their voices were forceful, with no rising intonation to connote uncertainty. The women, who actually were the authority figures in the businesses and whose answers gave the proper information, did not convey their expertise in their voices, however. They had more questioning patterns in their voices, and except for one, they spoke a little too softly and lacked energy and force. The humorous irony for the audience in this situation was the manner in which the women, the real experts in the subject, came off looking slightly lame and inept in the face of assertive contradictions by male imposters.

A researcher who recorded and analyzed numerous interviews with older women and men in Maine commented on the information the speakers' voices conveyed. She felt that the men she interviewed were sure of themselves and what they had done in life: "Their sureness came across in their intonation patterns. There was an unmistakable firmness to their voices. They held strong opinions." In generalizing about the women, the investigator said: "The women were soft spoken. Everything about the verbal and nonverbal language of most of the women was an acceptance of a second-class status. . . ."[76]

Many women and men need to monitor their voices more carefully to guard against automatic and habitual modes that are at odds with what they are saying and their purpose in saying it. A preponderance of utterances with, say, an upward rising inflection can make a speaker seem wishy-washy or unsure. There is an old pun concerning a theatergoer complaining about an actor who played the part of the king: "He played the king like someone else had just played the ace." Some women need to avoid habitually sounding like the queen limping in after the ace has appeared. Where appropriate, they should affirm their ideas and opinions through confident communication. One way is to avoid patterns or tones that seem to ask for approval, if that is not the intent, and instead use ones that confidently make a statement. Perhaps this is part of what Debbie Reynolds as Molly Brown talk-sings about in *The Unsinkable Molly Brown*: "To show . . . that you know . . . you've got to show you *know* you know!"[77]

If we have a well-grounded opinion, we want it to sound firm and well-grounded, not hesitating and uncertain. After we had worked with a class on voice improvement, one student said at the close of the semester, "I'm beginning to understand about voice. My listeners will never have confidence in me or believe in what I say if I don't sound as if I myself believe in what I'm saying!"

In certain situations males are vocally handicapped. Some men find it difficult to verbally show feelings of tenderness or strong emotions. Many males are not adept at managing their vocal apparatus so that it is responsive to various shades and types of feelings. They may find themselves misunderstood or they may not really communicate

Some men find it difficult to verbalize feelings of tenderness or strong emotion.

what they intend as they growl out endearments, mutter their compliments, or bellow their apologies.

In the final analysis we shall probably feel more comfortable with ourselves and more attuned to others if we can cut through the layer of automatic, unthinking, reflexive vocalic fluff that often obscures, nullifies, or contradicts our words. A vocal mechanism responsive to our feelings and intents should be our goal. This may involve a moment-to-moment awareness such as Carl Sandburg suggests in "Precious Moments":

Speech requires blood and air to make it.
Before the word comes off the end of the tongue,
While the diaphragms of flesh negotiate the word,
In the moment of doom when the word forms,
It is born alive, registering an imprint—
Afterward it is a mummy, a dry fact, done and gone.
The warning holds yet: Speak now or forever hold your peace.[78]

Suggested activities

1 Listen carefully to associates, friends, family members, and children converse.

   a. Keep a record of the degree of precision in speech concerning word endings *-ing* and *-in*. From your observations, do you see any different patterns in precision of speech?

   b. Compare yourself to a person of the opposite sex who is similar in age, status, and educational background. Do you seem to take more or less care in the precision of your speech? Explain why you think this is so.

Suggested format for recording results:

Speaker	Age	Number of times *-in*	Number of times *-ing*
Female 1			
Female 2			
Female 3			
Male 1			
Male 2			
Male 3			

2 Intonation Patterns: Listen to adult female and male conversational speech.

   a. Describe some of the pitch patterns you hear. Draw the patterns if possible.

   b. Which speakers seemed to end their utterances frequently with rising pitch and which with falling pitch? Does this vary by sex? By personality?

   c. Did you hear any of the so-called patterns of plight? In what contexts?

3 Intonation Patterns: Listen to the speech of female and male children of the same age.

   a. What differences do you hear in use of pitch variation?

   b. What do your observations suggest about boys' and girls' use of intonation patterns at this age?

4 Read some sentences to another person, first with your pitch at the end falling and then with the pitch at the end rising. What effect does the rising and falling pitch have on the meaning of what you say for the other person?

5 Many writers contrast the so-called psychological characteristics of females and males. Among the characteristics, "aggressive" is assigned to males and "submissive" is assigned to females.

a. Observe females and males as they speak and interact with one another. What vocal qualities tend to characterize submissive behaviors and which characterize aggressive behaviors? What vocal qualities seem associated with properly assertive behaviors that are neither harmfully aggressive nor self-destructively submissive? Comment on pitch; loudness/softness; speech rate (fast/slow); and quality (harsh, breathy, nasal, and so forth).

b. Compare the speech behaviors of females showing aggressiveness with males showing aggressiveness. What are the similarities? What are the differences?

c. Compare the speech behaviors of females showing submissiveness with males showing submissiveness. What are the similarities? What are the differences?

d. Compare the speech behaviors of females showing assertiveness with males showing assertiveness. What are the similarities? What are the differences?

Suggested format to record results:

Vocal qualities	Behaviors		
	Submissive	Assertive	Aggressive
Speaker 1 Pitch Loudness Quality Rate			
Speaker 2 Pitch Loudness Quality Rate			
Speaker 3 Pitch Loudness Quality Rate			

5 When words speak louder than people: the language of gender

Recently we posed the following riddle to several of our classes: A man and his young son were apprehended in a robbery. The father was shot during the struggle and the son, in handcuffs, was rushed to the police station. As the police pulled the struggling boy into the station, the mayor, who had been called to the scene, looked up and said, "My God, it's my son!" What relation was the mayor to the boy?[1]

Those who had not already heard this riddle or a similar one offered some wild guesses: "He was really the grandfather of the boy but father to the crook who was shot." "He was the twin brother of the man who was killed." "He was no relation, for he was just referring to the arresting officer." "The man had left or divorced his wife who had remarried and this second husband, not the dead man, was the natural father." "He was the reverend who would refer to any of his parishioners as 'my son'." "It's a joke; there is no answer."

The answer is simple and obvious once you develop an unbiased orientation. The mayor was the boy's mother, of course. But why did it not occur to most of the listeners to consider a woman as a possibility? Why did they arbitrarily exclude one-half the range of logical possibilities? "I never thought the mayor was a woman!" some will explain. But the reason is more complicated than a probability ratio of the mayor's sex. It is most likely related to the claim of some scholars that ours is a language dominated by a masculine viewpoint. As early as the 1920's a linguist asserted that English is "the language of a grown-up man, with very little childish or feminine about it."[2]

At most levels of discourse about achievement or activity, women are just not taken into account. If one is wealthy, one is a man of means; if active, a man on the move; if experienced, a man of the world; if average, a man on the street or John Doe; if learned, a man of letters; if socially active, a man about town; if fun-loving, a good-time Charlie; and so on.

The assumption underlying the words we use seems to be that all people are male until proven female. Although there may be women who are doctors, lawyers, mayors, chemists, sculptors, bosses, or dog catchers, somehow they need to be labeled "woman doctor," "female lawyer," or "sculptress," in order for us to picture them in our minds.[3] Of course, there are some words that call up a mental image of a female such as nurse, prostitute, maid, or housekeeper, but they are fewer by far in number.

It is said that language serves as a screen between ourselves and the world. It filters our perceptions of persons and things. Call a woman "a female," "a chick," "a piece," or "a lady." Each term filters our view of the woman differently. But like the two-way window, language also serves as a reflector and reveals the way our culture projects its image upon language.

In this chapter we shall examine the ways language deals with the sexes differently and the way it reflects society's discrepant expectations for them. In looking at both quantitative and qualitative aspects of language, we hope to shed light on some interesting perspectives of our culture.

The numbers game

One telling aspect of the way our language deals with women and men is the number of words allocated for different purposes. The process of constructing the school edition of the *American Heritage Dictionary* occasioned some interesting discoveries by several of the editors.[4] A mind-boggling five million words were computer analyzed in the compilation of the 35,000-entry wordbook. From the computer came 700,000 citation slips, each of which contained a word in three lines of context taken from books and magazines that school children read. In the process came the awesome realization that patterned in the vast numerical array were the outlines of a "culture talking to its children." The pattern that emerged was too striking and the results born of a multitude of words too wide-ranging and too vast in number to be ignored. What was the nature of this monolithic message?

First, it was observed that when the culture talks to its children, it is careful to differentiate them according to sex. In the books and magazines written for children, there were twice as many references to *boy* and *girl* as to the words *child* and *children,* which do not designate sex.

Second, it became obvious that references to girls and women were far fewer than to boys and men. Use of the word *he* was greater in number than *she, him* than *her,* and *his* than *hers* by a ratio of almost 4 to 1. (Even in home economics, *he* appeared twice as often as *she.*) This might not be significant, however, if *he* were used in the generic sense of supposedly referring to all people—for example, in the sentence, "As every person knows, he is in part a product of his own culture." But such was not the case. Alma Graham surveyed an experimental sampling of 100,000 words and found that of 940 citations for *he,* only 32 referred to the generic *he*, as in "someone . . . he." The remaining 908 citations were distributed as follows:

- 744 applied to male human beings
- 128 applied to male animals
- 36 applied to persons such as farmers, sailors, and so forth assumed to be male

A third finding was that, although there are in reality 95 men for every 100 women, in children's books there are seven times as many men as women and twice as many boys as girls. Storybook sons outnumber daughters by over 2 to 1, and all firstborn children are sons. Furthermore, 2 out of 3 mothers in print are mentioned in relation to male children; and 4 out of 5 fathers are fathers of male children. Uncles outnumber aunts by 2 to 1, and four times as many aunts have nephews as have nieces. One can only conclude that in the language of schoolbooks, "whether the subject is reading, mathematics, social studies, art, or science, males command center stage."[5]

There is, however, one area in which females seem to have the dubious distinction of generating a greater number of words and that is the area of sexual terms. Julia Stanley compiled and analyzed a list of 220 sexual terms applied to women.[6] The list is by no means exhaustive, for this semantic set is probably "infinitely expanding." Even though some words may become archaic, new sexual terms for women are constantly being added. The number of these terms plus the impossibility of collecting all of them is a comment on our culture and the screen of language through which it views women, according to Stanley. By contrast, she collected only a small number of terms for males— 22 in all.

Why this proliferation of sexual terms for women? One factor may be our culture's encouragement and pressure on males to live up to, or at least appear to live up to, the masculine morality of machismo, or feminine conquest. Probably many of us use words as a substitute for action or to satisfy what we perceive as a necessity for action. In talking about an action we may obtain the secondhand satisfaction of that action, just as if we had performed it. This may be similar to the vicarious pleasure we get from seeing our TV idol successfully complete an adventure, solve a problem, or triumph in a difficult situation. Feeling the obligation to extend hospitality or special kindness to someone, we may say, "You'll really have to come over some evening for dinner," or "Be sure to give me a call and we'll get together soon, since we haven't talked over old times in ages." Having said these things, we immediately feel better, just as if we have discharged our obligation or lived up to our goals by the very verbalization of these subjects.

The same principle may hold true for males in the verbalization and use of terms that apply to women's sexuality. Observations on the adolescent male's use of words seem to support this. It has been noted that the young male, in the growing awareness of his sexuality, increases his repertoire of words dealing with the sexual aspect of his life, and his vocabulary, particularly of taboo words, is constantly expanding. The abundance of new words and expressions "imparts a feeling, to the youthful males who create and perpetuate them, of ribaldry, vitality, and strength of a masculine character."[7] In short, verbalization of males about sexual matters—the use of obscene terms to describe women as the objects of their sexual pursuit and to boast about their degree of success in sexual encounters with women—serves to establish and maintain their masculine status.

Although the women's movement has influenced attitudes expressed about and by women, there is today probably no female counterpart of the so-called bull session or locker-room rap. Few women boast about their sexual availability, their sexual exploits, or their male lovers. This may be a factor in the small number of sexual terms for males. With new trends in independence and life styles of the sexes, an interesting study would be to monitor the change in number and type of words women use to refer to men.

Word counts and proportions can point up imbalances in spoken or written language about the sexes. But important glimpses of our society can be obtained in other ways. The aspects of language we shall concern ourselves with next involve the use of words to (1) define, delimit, describe, or circumscribe, (2) appraise negatively, positively, or neutrally, and (3) exclude, single out, or include. We shall consider each of these functions separately and in some detail with regard to the sexes.

Definition by gender

Words can be deceiving. Because they define people and things they appear to be objective, and we may overlook the hidden or implied messages they carry. By their very utterance they can suggest meanings to listeners that circumscribe, restrict, eliminate, or enlarge alternatives for persons to whom they refer. It has been said that to name the world is to control the world. That is, through naming we can color or shape persons, things, events, situations to conform to our perceptions or to our liking; we can use language "to push reality into more pleasing shapes."[8]

Labels

The power of naming or labeling has become a significant issue for the sexes. Those with the most power in our society will, consciously or unconsciously, cast their words in the forms most appropriate for them. The language of the favored group is generally accepted and used by those who are less powerful. Through naming, men have defined women's actions, attributes, ideas, and very being in their own male terms. According to Mary Daly, women have had the power of naming taken from them, with no freedom to "name [them]selves, the world, or God."[9] We shall examine naming and labeling relative to the sexes to see how our culture defines them.

Occupational titles, organization and team names Some language analysts indicate that words establish females as secondary and males as primary. First of all, the majority of titles for occupations and professions are male. Historically, males have been active and have been the doers, so these titles carry masculine as an unmarked semantic feature.[10] That is, we do not specify or mark these titles as "male pilot," "man physician," or "male author," for it is generally assumed that males occupy this semantic space. A few titles such as "maid," "nurse," or "prostitute" carry feminine as an unmarked semantic feature, and it is generally assumed that females occupy this semantic space. If either sex moves out of the semantic space reserved for them, they move into negative semantic space—semantic space that is not covered by an appropriate term for the woman or man. For the woman who is a mayor or chemist or the man who is a nurse or housekeeper, the position must generally be marked by a special feminine or masculine marker, which indicates that the person occupying the position is not of the anticipated sex. Thus we designate woman mayor, female physician, or male nurse and male housekeeper.

The point is that aside from the small corner of semantic space that is allocated to women by words that define them—*wife, nurse, mother, prostitute, housekeeper, maid,* and so on—the remainder of the semantic universe belong to males.[11] Beyond her narrow place in semantic space a woman must generally be spoken of or written about using a feminine marker of some kind: *female lawyer, woman pilot.* The addition of a feminine marker, as we shall see later, often casts a term in a more negative form.

Another kind of feminine marker is the addition of suffixes such as *-ess* or *-ette*: *waiter, waitress; poet, poetess; sculptor, sculptress; author, authoress; singer, songstress; drum major, drum majorette;* even (in the *New York Times* in 1969[12]) *jockey, jockette.* Feminizing the titles, occupations, or activities in this manner can have the effect of weakening them, diminishing them, or making them appear trivial. Linguist Alleen Pace Nilsen claims she would prefer to be referred to as a singer rather than songstress, a poet rather than a poetess; an author rather than authoress.[13] For the male terms carry the suggestion of added power or competency. Or, put in another way, *adding* a femine marker ending may *detract* from connotations of potency that such a word normally evokes in people.

Adding appendages to the words reduces women to appendages or extensions of males. It singles out a woman as a special case or exception to the rule, something that does not ordinarily belong. Calling a woman a poetess may not only serve to define her as not belonging to the general order of poets, but may also suggest that her contribution is not equal to a man's—that she is only a pale and lesser imitation. This is also the case with some organizations whose women's divisions have tacked-on extension titles such as "Jaycee-ettes" or "Lionesses." The title has defined the women into lesser status and triviality.

Separate and unequal defining of women is observable in the labeling of competitive sport teams. Male teams have names that suggest force, power, and status: Rams, Colts, Giants, Lions, Tigers, Knights, Pioneers, Raiders. Contrast this with team names for females that seem to trivialize them or imply a tongue-in-cheek attitude toward them: Cindergals, Atomettes, Mercurettes, Michigams, Rockettes.[14]

Terms of address We once encouraged our students to keep a personal record for several days of the various labels and titles by which they were addressed. A fairly consistent pattern emerged: women were generally labeled in more familiar terms than men. First names were used for females more often than for males in similar situations. Social status or professional position was sometimes a determining factor, but more often it was the general status of sex. People may feel free to be more familiar semantically with women. The observations included males and females in parallel positions in real estate agencies, company purchasing departments, public schools, department stores, business offices, eating places. In general, women were addressed in more familiar terms—by first names or nicknames: Rosie, Red, Babe, Honey, Doll, and Joan. Males were generally dealt with more formally by titles or last name: Mr. Kaufman, Supervisor Halders, Eykman, Smitty, Chief, Boss, and Dr. Jones. The asymmetry in address seems to indicate a corresponding difference in status. By the discrepancy in labeling realtors—for example, "Joanie," as opposed to "Mr. McCane"—the two were defined into separate positions. One of the authors recently received university memos from a male colleague penned, "to Barbara" from "JCD." Why not "to BWE" from "JCD"?

Kramer obtained similar results in a study in which university students collected more than 500 phrases or sentences of address from clerks, waiters, or sales people.[15] Female students were addressed by female clerks as "dear," "ma'am," and "miss"; but by male clerks as "lady," "young lady," "kiddo," "ma'am," "senorita," "sweetie," "little lady," "miss," "dear," "lovey," and "baby." Male students were addressed by male clerks as "sir" and by female clerks as "sir" and "dear." Women had a wider range of terms addressed to them and with greater familiarity by males than those terms addressed to males by females.

The owner and the owned: identity by association

Another way in which the sexes are said to be defined differently is that women tend to be given object or possession status in relation to men.

This is supposedly a carryover from the time when females were, in fact, possessions under the power of their fathers and husbands. First, they were someone's daughter and later someone's wife. Yet even to-day, when the legal, economic, and social conditions of women have changed, they are often referred to according to who "owns" them— "John's wife," "Harry's daughter," "Bill's girl"—as if the most significant thing about them is their relationship or possession status in regard to males. In textbooks, although the women may be merely nameless daughters, wives, or mothers, the males with whom they are associated are generally clearly identified by name, occupation, or status: "the mother of Charles Wilson," "Banker Edwards' daughter," "the preacher's wife," "old Doc Smith's wife." The female's identity in each case is dependent upon the identity of the male, with an implication that her identity apart from her relationship to him is relatively un-important.

Robin Lakoff suggests that men are defined in terms of what they do in the world, women in terms of the men with whom they are as-sociated.[16] This identity by association is an albatross that most women carry around their necks for their entire lives. When a woman is mar-ried, the couple is commonly called "man and wife," not "man and woman" or "husband and wife." The position of the man in the world and in relation to other people does not change after marriage. "He was a 'man' before the ceremony, and a 'man' he still is . . . at its conclu-sion." The bride, however, went into the marriage a "woman" and left it a "wife," defined in terms of "the man," her husband. She will probably be referred to much more often as "Eddie's wife" than he will be called "Vera's husband."

A woman who has dissolved her marriage bonds may be referred to as a divorcée, but there is no comparable term for a man to indicate this state. Some may refer to him as a "divorced man," but this seems to be used far less frequently than the "divorcée" label for a woman. Instead, a previously married man is commonly referred to as a "bachelor."

The discrepancy in defining females and males is most marked in the event of a mate's death. A woman whose husband dies is "Ed's widow." But the man whose wife is deceased is not commonly referred to as "Vera's widower." So even after a mate's death, a woman is still defined by her relationship to a man, but the male survivor is not de-fined in terms of his spouse. Linguistically speaking, then, women de-rive their identity from their relationship with men.

In reviewing a computer analysis of words in children's books, at one point the writer lamented, "Where have all the young girls gone?"[17] The computer provided the answer in its tally: even though seven times as many references to men as women appeared, the word *wife* was used three times as often as *husband*, and *mother* appeared more frequently than *father*. The young girls had grown up and been "taken" as wife in marriage by males, who were defined by numerous

Bill Rogers the **lawyer**

Dr. Wong

Bob Polaschak's **daughter**

The Senator's **wife**

Traditionally, males have achieved identity by what they do, females by their relationships with men.

names, occupations, and labels other than *husband* to establish their
identity. The researcher concluded that women are "typecast in the
supporting roles that refer to their relationships to men and children,"
but men can assume any of a number of different roles.

Nilsen relates that, in her perusal of the dictionary, the attitudes
of editors seemed to be that a woman's name should somehow be escorted across a page by a male's name, no matter how famous the
woman in her own right. Thus she found such amusing labeling as:
Amelia Earhart identified as Mrs. George Palmer Putnam; Charlotte
Brontë as Mrs. Arthur B. Nicholls; Jenny Lind as Mme. Otto
Goldschmidt; and Helen Hayes as Mrs. Charles MacArthur. She estimated that more than 50 percent of the women listed in the dictionary
were identified as someone's wife, whereas only one male was identified
as someone's husband. This was Frederic Joliot, who took the last name
of Joliot-Curie. He was identified as "husband of Irene," the daughter of
Pierre and Marie Curie.[18] Accustomed as we are to knowing married
women only by their husbands' names, we sometimes fail to see the
ludicrousness of newspaper accounts that list a charity ball committee
for the Women's League as: Mmes. George Barnet, Rod Harris,
William Davis, and Richard Owen.[19] So strongly are women identified
in terms of the men with whom they are associated that appropriate titles and labels are often omitted. For example, although both authors of
this book hold Ph.D. degrees and are professors in professional and
classroom situations, Gene is referred to as "Professor" or "Dr. Eakins,"
and Barbara is often called "Mrs. Eakins." Our cards, invitations, and
letters are frequently addressed to "Dr. and Mrs. Gene Eakins"—only
occasionally to "Drs. Barbara and Gene Eakins." We know a woman, a
Ph.D., who held a university teaching position for a number of years.
After she married, she continued university teaching, but she had the
return address on her small-note stationery printed, "Dr. and Mrs. . . .

She is/he does

Males tend to be identified or characterized in terms that point up their
occupation, activity, movement, or doing; whereas females are more
often presented in terms of attributes or qualities of being.[20] "He was
the manliest of his sex and she was loveliest of hers," reads a children's
book. Or, "The men are strong, virile, and graceful, and the girls often
beauties." Note that the two descriptions are not really parallel. One
suggests activity and performance, the other appearance. The relegation
of females to an inactive role seems implicit in common utterances,
such as "Ralph is a brilliant young lawyer, and he has a beautiful blonde
wife."[21] Or, "Did you see our new lady manager? What a stacked
broad!"

Perusal of the media can be enlightening, since reflected in the
language one sees a pattern that highlights and values a man for his
mind or activities and a woman for her physical appearance. Men in the

news are generally pictured in a serious, businesslike manner, but women in the news are described in physical terms. If physical attributes have little relevance to the news item, such descriptions can only serve to trivialize, mitigate, and detract from the purpose of the article. A woman running for political office is described as being "a petite grandmother with the figure of a twenty-year-old"; a lawyer being interviewed about her views on the Equal Rights amendment is described as "well put together" and "possessing a feminine demeanor that puts her physically at the opposite end of the continuum from your mannish woman radical"; an artist exhibiting her paintings is portrayed as having a "low husky laugh" and "soft grey eyes"; an athlete is referred to as "a brown-eyed cutie."[22] The women described are not candidates for Miss America or models for whom physical descriptions would be relevant to their jobs. They are women functioning in politics, law, the arts, and athletics. Reports dealing with women in these positions would presumably have little need to include descriptions of their physical or emotional attributes, since the relevant information concerns the women's qualifications and abilities in relation to their roles. Similar descriptions of males in such jobs would be ludicrous. As Hole and Levine quipped several years ago, "When was the last time the *Washington Post* referred to 'the vivacious Robert Finch'?"[23]

In a course, one of the authors spent a class period going through back issues of papers with the students in a headline reversal exercise. We selected headlines or article captions that appeared to focus on irrelevant attributes of people, such as physical or relational features. Almost without exception, the subjects were female. For each such caption or headline, a parallel one was written for a male subject. We came up with pairs similar to the following:[24]

Female	Male
Grandmother Wins Nobel Prize	Grandfather Wins Nobel Prize
Housewife Seeks Council Seat	Unsalaried Husband Seeks Council Seat
Widow Opens Real Estate Office in Phoenix	Widower Opens Real Estate Office in Phoenix
Brunette Holds New City Bridge Title	Bearded Man Holds New City Bridge Title
Blonde Hijacks Airliner	Baldy Hijacks Airliner

If it is unacceptable or ludicrous to have "Baldy Hijacks Airliner" or "Bearded Man Holds New City Bridge Title," why should women be described through external concerns, such as being a housewife, or a blonde, or a widow, or a grandmother?

Active voice/passive voice

Another aspect of defining men as the doers and women as the passive ones who "are" involves the use of sex-marked verb forms. One linguist

examined verb forms in relation to the sexes and found several significant verbal patterns:[25]

1 Women are often referred to in the passive voice, in which they are
recipients of the action. Men are referred to in the active voice, in
which they are the active doers. Compare the following:

Female = Passive
She *was escorted* by him.
She *was picked up* by him in a bar.
She *was romanced* by him.
She *was walked* home by him.
She *was taken* by him to the dance.
She *was taken* [sexually] by him.
She *was given* to him in marriage.

Male = Active
He *escorted* her.
He *picked* her *up* in a bar.
He *romanced* her.
He *walked* her home.
He *took* her to the dance.
He *took* her [sexually].
He *took* her in marriage.

2 Women are often the subjects of intransitive verbs, verbs without direct
objects, which subordinate the action of the female to that of the male.
Men are often the subject of transitive verbs which have women as the
direct objects, a grammatical position which also subordinates the
female. Compare the following:

Female = Intransitive
She *went with him* on a date.
She *walked* home *with him*.

Male = Transitive/direct object
He *took her* out on a date.
He *walked her* home.

The occurrence of these two patterns could indicate a power relation of
men over women, with males the active agents having the power to initiate and females the passive recipients of power asserted by males.
The literal parallel of these active/passive linguistic forms may be the
sex act itself, but this dominant/subordinate relationship apparently carries over into other aspects of life as well.

The female as sex object

Another way in which language is said to deal with the sexes differently
is by assuming that a women's sexuality is the most important thing
about her, whereas men are more often characterized as complete
human beings whose sexuality is only a part of their identity. We often
use language that defines a woman according to the use made of her
sexuality. The act defines the person: as slut, nympho, hooker, trick,
whore, and so on. To define woman as a sex object serves to de-
humanize her by reducing her to her basic sexuality and nothing more.

In what other area of life is there such a variety of terms having
the same meaning? The ingenuity and fertility of imagination employed
in devising sexual words for women appear to be little used in generating similar labels for males. Research on sexual terms for females and
males produced about 10 times as many sexual terms for females as for
males.[26] It is said that rarely is a man defined "so wholly and irrevocably

in a single word" such as "slut." Perhaps the nearest a man comes to this negative reduction is when he offends society and is labeled a "sex fiend."[27] To define, and thereby consign, women primarily to sexual functions through language may discourage them from defining and shaping their own lives. One women's group viewed the problem this way: "We have internalized the male culture's definition of ourselves. That definition views us as relative beings who exist not for ourselves, but for the servicing, maintenance and comfort of men."[28]

Some ironic linguistic situations can occur when words or expressions spoken by or applied to one sex are shifted to the opposite sex, because expressions are frequently interpreted from a sexual perspective when applied to a woman. Compare "You caught me with my pants down."[29] Spoken by a male it is taken metaphorically to indicate embarrassment or being taken unawares. Spoken by a woman, it is interpreted literally and physically and will produce smiles from her hearers, female and male, most of the time.

Label a person a "professional" and, if the individual is a male, the assumption is that he is a lawyer, a doctor, or belongs to one of the other professions. If the person is a female, a reference to her sexuality is immediately assumed. A knowing nod or smile then follows from the conclusion that she is a prostitute, or behaves as if she were. Finally, compare "He's got great legs" with "She's got great legs." In reference to a male, the expression connotes athletic strength and ability, most probably speed in a race. Spoken of a woman, it labels her attractiveness as a sexual object.[30]

Women are also defined sexually in metonymical terms, through reference to specific portions of their bodies or persons: piece, fastfanny, pussy, snatch, lowgap, poxbox, tail, honey pot. There seems to be a scarcity of parallel words in the relatively few sexual terms our culture has for males. Even when a male is termed a "prick," remarks Stanley, it is not a comment on his *sexuality* but rather on his *personality*, akin to such terms as "nurd," "jerk," or "creep."[31]

Sexual metaphors

An examination of the types of metaphors used for females and males reveals ways in which our culture views the relationship of the sexes. The ways in which women and men are compared to different types of things—(1) food, (2) plants, (3) animals, and (4) inanimate objects—identify underlying attitudes about the sexes.[32]

1 Food. Women are often compared to food in a manner that defines them as something to be consumed or enjoyed as good things—"delicious," "a dish," "good enough to eat." They may be fruits or vegetables: "tomato," "peach," "plum," "a peaches-and-cream complexion." Or they may be desserts and sources of sweets: "cookie," "honey," "sweetie-pie," "cheesecake," "cream puff," "cupcake." Males may occa-

sionally be labeled as "big cheese," "meathead," "hunk of meat," "honey," or called a "fruit"; but they are generally not, as Nilsen put it, "laid out on a buffet."

2 Plants. Other metaphoric comparisons used for women, but rarely for males, involve plants: "ramblin' rose," "clinging vine," "wallflower," "shrinking violet." A woman who loses her virginity may be said to be "deflowered." Aside from an occasional allusion to "pansy" (which connotes weakness or unmanliness), males may be seen as too active to be defined in plant-type metaphors.[33]

3 Inanimate objects. In Stanley's categorization of sexual terms for women, she identifies a class of metaphors in which women are compared to inanimate objects. The inanimate objects are subdivided into two classes. The first defines women as passive objects on or through which men take action: "baggage," "mattress," "cotwarmer," "quarter-piece," or "warming pan." The second involves what Stanley views as a basic metaphor that governs women's lives in our "phallocentric culture": "Women have holes; men have external appendages. . . ." In language, she indicates, women exist as "holes for men, as fields to be plowed, as 'pots' full of good things for men." Such metaphors include terms for women like the following: "pipecleaner," "furrowbutt," "honey pot," "bull's eye," "ringer."[34]

4 Animals. The types of animal terms used to define the sexes are significant also. Men are defined by aggressive animal comparisons— "buck," "stud," "wolf," "tomcat" (they go "tomcatting around"); whereas cute, harmless, or pet status is defined for women through such metaphors as "kitten," "bunny," "lamb," "young filly," or "chick," and undesirable standing by "dog," "cow," "sow," or "pig."[35] In her analysis of sexual terms, Stanley found a class of names comparing women to animals, with the underlying concepts of women as something to be hunted ("quail," "canvasback"); to be subordinated and domesticated ("filly," "sow," "dog," "bitch"); to be feared ("bat"); or to be considered vicious ("minx"). Nilsen recounts half humorously how the chicken metaphor tells the whole story of a woman's life: "In her youth she is a *chick*, then she marries and begins feeling *cooped up*, so she goes to *hen* parties where she *cackles* with her friends. Then she has her *brood* and begins to *henpeck* her husband. Finally she turns into an *old biddy*."[36] Perhaps a comparable male metaphor revolves around the deer ("young buck," "stag parties") or stallion ("stud") image.

Letters of recommendation

In subtle ways language can both reflect and perpetuate certain attitudes and affect hiring practices in regard to the sexes. Although in recent years employment opportunities for women have expanded, letters of

recommendation can define a person into or out of consideration for
certain positions in several ways:

Physical and personal descriptions   Description of physical appearance or
personality may appear only incidentally on letters of recommendation
for male job candidates ("dresses well, poised, personable"). Such descriptions are generally only a footnote to the story of the male's
abilities. But a women's commission found that physical descriptions
are given the weight of "a thesis statement" where female candidates
are concerned.[37] Consciously or unconsciously, some letter writers di-
minish the intellectual abilities of a woman by playing up her femininity, her prettiness: "sweet but not saccharine," "shy but very pretty," "a
decoration to the classroom." Social grace is sometimes viewed as a
substitute for intellectual brilliance.

Women candidates apparently have to be both brilliant and chic.
Those who are unattractive or plain do not fare well in recommendations. Often scattered through their dossiers are irrelevant comments such as "____ is a large, broad-boned, somewhat awkward young
woman who . . ."; "her mousiness belies a sharp mind"; "proportioned
like an Olympic swimmer"; "comfortably upholstered" person.

Definitions or descriptions of female and male personality traits
also differ. The following are descriptions quoted from dossiers that we
have attempted to arrange in pairs:[38]

He	**She**
has talent	has warmth, good manners
has drive	is cooperative, sensitive
is at the start of a long career	
will be on the move	
will continue to surpass himself	future career will be a good one
will continue to advance	
a live wire	has humor
dedicated, industrious, dynamic	endowed with lively intellectual curiosity
classroom posture is commanding	particular rapport with students
prose style is energetic, vigorous	writing style is lucid, witty, elegant, graceful, truly readable

Qualities ascribed to a woman candidate can have "a seriously
limiting psychological impact" claims one source, for the stereotyped
language describing the woman candidate has the effect of "damning
her with faint and delicate praise." Men writing recommendations frequently view women as "objects to be regarded, looked at, as mis-
tresses, as wives, as mothers; . . . not as intellectual equal and full
human being."[39] The person writing the recommendation may overlook
the fact that these roles are irrelevant to the role or position for which
the woman is being considered; just as the recommender's own role as
husband, father, or lover is not under consideration in regard to his
professional position or his credibility as a reference.

Indications of marital status Older women entering the job market, in particular, are described or defined in terms of family and marriage. "Let her run her household, not our department"; or "Mrs. _____ has an adolescent son, knows how to treat teen-agers," ran several comments on dossiers. Contrast with this a male of comparable age who, after an army career, was also just embarking on a university career but was described as having "a better preparation for the university than uninterrupted schooling could have been." Another practice is that of praising or describing the candidate's husband, rather than the candidate herself. This, of course, would be ludicrous if done with regard to the male candidate's wife. The spouse of a male candidate is rarely mentioned, but if she is it is as a social adornment.

Letters of recommendation about the married female candidate also frequently compare her with her husband: "Mrs. _____'s husband . . . is an excellent scholar, rather more disciplined and professional in his scholarship. Mrs. _____ complements him with her . . ." Or, "As in the case of her husband, I can recommend. . . ." Or, "_____ and her very able husband." Such letters define the woman as an appendage to her husband, characterize her career second to his, and describe her talents as shining in the light of his.[40]

Indications of political beliefs The third way in which the dossiers defined women was in terms of their participation or nonparticipation in the women's movement: "no fem lib type," "a real gentlewoman," "feminine indeed, but no feminist."

Evaluation by gender

We have pointed out in the previous section that the sexes seem to be defined or labeled in discriminating ways. There are also differences in the way the sexes are evaluated or appraised by language. There tend to be strong, positive connotations associated in language with the concept of masculinity, but negative, weak, or trivial connotations attached to the corresponding feminine concept.

In general, our language terms seem to designate powerful things as masculine but weak, negative things as feminine.[41] All references to God are masculine, and masculine terms are used in prayer books and liturgy: Father, King, Lord, Master. Powerful concepts such as death, hate, and war tend to be referred to as masculine. The sun is often referred to in the masculine, but the moon as feminine. "Old Woman River" does not have the semantic impact of "Old Man River."

Acting or doing tends to be masculine; reacting and passively accepting, feminine.[42] Inanimate objects are frequently feminine, perhaps because they are conceived of as passive things to be owned or managed by men: the engineer's train, the sports enthusiast's sailboat or motorboat, the sailor's ship, the soldier's gun, the driver's car. These are all instruments to be run or "manned" by men. We use expressions such as "fill 'er up" for a car, "rev her up" for an engine.

Things that receive action, are acted upon, or are managed and that are referred to as female include the following: Mother Earth, the land (which is worked, cultivated, or mined), and countries or states (which are ruled or governed). Abstractions, which are supposedly revealed or controlled by men, such as science, liberty, victory, or fortune, are feminine. There is also the suggestion that negative or threatening forces such as hurricanes, tornadoes, or typhoons are given feminine names. Although we may hear someone sing, "Luck be a lady tonight," perhaps just as frequently bad luck or misfortune is credited to the "bitch goddess" success.[43] Larger animals tend to be "he," and smaller ones "she." We commonly characterize dogs as "he" and cats as "she" for reasons attributed to features of the animals' size and temperament.

Nilsen, in skimming through a dictionary, found approximately 500 words that included either a visible feminine marker (*daughter, girl, maid, mistress, queen*, and so forth) or a visible masculine marker (*fellow, son, man, master, king*, and so forth).[44] Masculine terms were clearly in the majority by about a ratio of 3 to 1; 385 masculine terms to 132 feminine ones. In analyzing the terms, one of the features Nilsen considered was prestige, which she defined as designation of either skill or power over others. There were six times as many male prestige words as female prestige words, or double the number of prestige words for males that would have been expected. Most surprising were her results in examining negative connotations. Although there were only one-third as many feminine terms as masculine terms to begin with, the number of negative feminine terms outnumbered the negative masculine terms 25 to 20. That there is some negative connotation attached to the very word *woman* becomes clear when we compare taking defeat "like a man" and taking defeat "like a woman." The former, a positive description, implies strength, fortitude, and endurance; "like a woman" is negative and connotes weakness and whimpering.

Graham makes a powerful point in noting the gulf between the words *boy* and *man*. It is a decided step upward when a boy becomes a man.[45] We talk about things that "separate the men from the boys," experiences that "make a man" out of a boy, and about the pluck that helps one "take it like a man." The giant step upward seems to be absent between *girl* and *woman*. Unlike a boy who greatly enhances his status by achieving manhood, a girl loses status and bargaining power when she loses her youth and becomes a "woman."

The fact that there is little in between is poignantly lamented in the musical *Camelot* as Guinevere sings, "Where Are the Simple Joys of Maidenhood?" Uncertain about her impending marriage to Arthur, she eludes the entire court, which has set out to welcome her, and she hides. "St. Genevieve," she pleads, "where were you when my youth was sold?" Underlining the mood of sadness that accompanies her

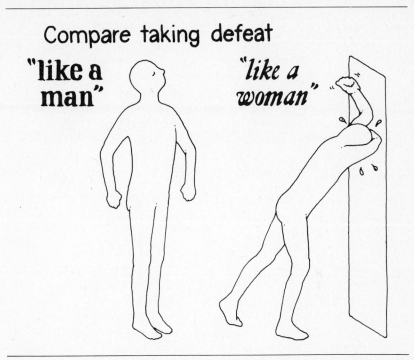

Compare taking defeat "like a man" "like a woman"

The word *woman* carries negative connotations in many situations.

abrupt journey from girlhood to womanhood, she sings plaintively, "Dear Genevieve, sweet Genevieve, shan't I be young before I'm old?"[46] Perhaps Mailer caught the essence of the negative aura that surrounds many feminine terms when he wrote, "Croft's most withering insult is to castigate his subordinates as 'a pack of goddam women.'"[47]

Reverse devaluation

There are several more specific ways of viewing the way language appraises or evaluates the sexes. One is termed my-virtue-is-your-vice.[48] In this frame of reference, the sexes are viewed as polar opposites with mutually exclusive traits. What is considered admirable in one sex is disdained or looked down upon in the other. So a woman who is described in some situations as forceful and verbally standing her ground, features commonly considered male qualities, may be termed "mannish." On the other hand, a man showing tenderness, perhaps shedding tears on some occasion, may be characterized as "womanish" or "effeminate." In both cases the labels carry tones of negative evaluation, because a trait considered typical of one sex has been assumed by the other. But switch the forceful behavior to the male and he will be labeled "masculine," a positive appraisal. Ascribe the tender behavior to the female and she will be termed "womanly" or "feminine."

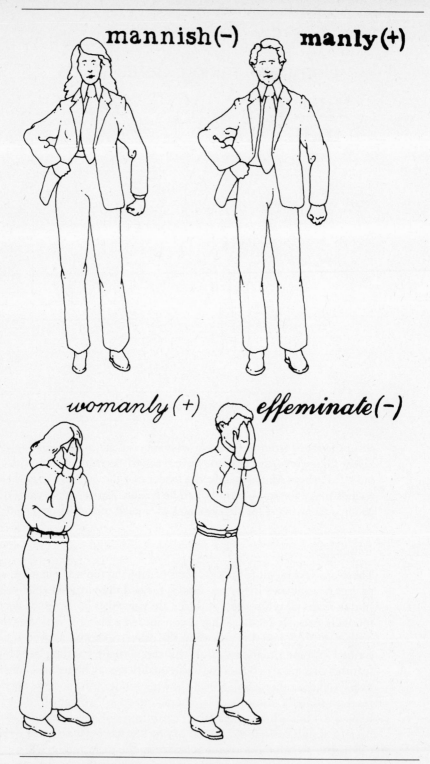

mannish(–)   manly(+)

womanly (+)   effeminate(–)

In the my-virtue-is-your-vice syndrome, what is considered admirable in one sex is looked down on in the other.

Woman's double bind: a no-win situation.

Males may fare the worse in the trade-off of stereotyped traits. Being labeled by terms usually used for the opposite sex is more penalizing for males. Although a female described by so-called male traits may be labeled mannish, unfeminine, or untrue to her sex role, the disdain or negative association is not so great as for a male labeled "womanish." This may be because masculine traits are more valued to begin with and are seen as more positive than feminine traits. Compare "she is a tomboy" with "he is a sissy." It seems to be considered a graver error for males to adopt stereotyped female traits than vice versa. There are probably no equivalent terms for women that have the same negative impact and meaning as "effeminate" or "emasculated" have for men, unless one uses homosexual labels.

Shakespeare put it thus: "A woman impudent and mannish grown/Is not more loathed than an effeminate man." To be told he runs, bats, thinks, or fights "like a girl" or "like a woman" is one of the severest insults for a male. To be termed "womanish," told he acts "like an old woman," or informed he has given "a woman's answer" is likewise insulting. Yet substitute "man" in each of the above phrases and apply them to a woman, and it is much less damning. In fact, there are surely overtones of praise in telling a female she runs, talks, or, most especially, *thinks* "like a man." There is a double bind or dilemma in this, however. At the very moment a woman is being praised for thinking "like a man," the verbal terms also imply condemnation of her for not being fully feminine. And if being fully feminine means thinking "like a woman," a woman is still in trouble because it is commonly held that thinking like a woman is tantamount to being illogical.

There are other ways in which language attests to the illogic of roles permitted to females and males. In our culture males are supposed to be *protective*. To be a "kept" man or one who "hides behind a woman's skirts" is ridiculed. Females in our culture are those who nurture or are *nurturant*. But although the words differ in use, there is an underlying semantic component that is much the same for both: care and concern for another. Declares Key: "It is quite possible that the *desire to take care of* is a human trait which is found in all people at the same time that an opposing trait of *wanting to be taken care of* is also found in all human beings."[49]

Praise him/blame her

Another way in which language deals with the sexes differently in regard to evaluation is summed up neatly as the praise him/blame her phenomenon.[50] This simply means that labels and characterizing terms that are supposedly applied equally in pairs, in similar situations, or with similar concepts to females and males have acquired connotations that are positive for males and negative for females.

Consider, for example: He is a bachelor, but she is an old maid or a spinster. The term *bachelor* may be used as a compliment with positive connotations of romantic desirability, eligibility, and sexual freedom. The parallel term for a woman, *spinster* or *old maid*, implies the opposite: prissiness, fussiness, and undesirability. Modern women have sometimes tried to appropriate the male term and its positive independent feeling by calling themselves "bachelor girls."[51]

Compare the pair *brave* and *squaw*. *Brave* has connotations of youth, courage, and strength. *Squaw* seems to imply the opposite, as the dictionary indicates in its second definition for *squaw*: a term "used humorously or disparagingly."[52] Another set is *wizard* and *witch*. Whereas *wizard* implies wisdom and skill along with magic, *witch* calls up distinctly negative associations of unpleasant appearance and evil purposes along with magic powers. Both *squaw* and *witch* connote old age, which violates the first of the so-called three unpardonable sins of woman: being old, ugly, and aggressive.[53]

There are other examples in which the parallelism in male/female equivalents has broken down, and male terms have retained positive connotations of power, superiority, or prestige, while female terms have acquired pejorative meanings. Compare:

| patron | matron [more apt to refer to woman in charge of a jail or public restroom, a mature married woman, or a socialite] |

landlord	landlady [usually thought of as one who collects the rent and enforces the rules; less dignity than landlord]
king	queen [also used to refer to effeminate homosexual]
sir	madam [has also acquired meaning of brothel manager]
governor	governess [generally thought of as the woman who teaches or trains children, especially in the private home]

There are other pairs, such as *chef/cook*; *tailor/seamstress*; or *poet/poetess*, in which the difference seems to be the lesser degree of expertise or excellence that the female terms suggest.[54]

Witness the divergence through time of the terms *master* and *mistress*.[55] A master was one who had authority or control over others, but more recently refers to one highly skilled in an art or profession. While the dictionary definitions for *mistress* still include "a woman who has mastered a skill," the word is used most commonly to refer to a woman in the narrowest sexual sense: a woman with whom a man cohabits without benefit of marriage. So whereas *master* is a label of approbation and admiration, *mistress* has evolved into one with a stigma. Or, as Robin Lakoff puts it, "It is one thing to be an *old master* like Hans Holbein, and another to be an *old mistress*."

The praise him/blame her tendency can also be seen in our characterization of the same or similar acts by the sexes. A linguistic double standard can produce such varying descriptions as the following: To speak up boldly, one is "aggressive" if female, "courageous" if male. If innovative, one is "pushy" if female, "original" if male. If insistent, one is "hysterical" if female, "persistent" if male. If politically involved, one is "over-emotional" if female, "committed" if male.[56] If amused out loud, one "giggles" or "titters" if female and "laughs" if male. Compare:

She	He
chattered	discussed/talked
nagged	reminded
gossiped	discussed people
bitched	complained/griped
scatterbrained	forgetful
no spring chicken/old biddy/over the hill	mature/distinguished
picky/fussy	careful/fastidious
gabby/talkative	fluent/articulate
has wrinkles	has character lines

Finally, why is it that when recommending a course of action, one who is older is said to "spout old wives' tales" if female and to "give sage, grandfatherly advice" if male?[57]

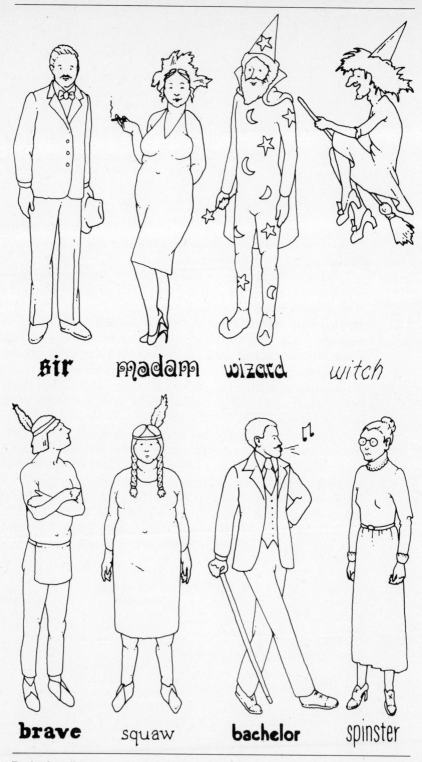

sir **madam** **wizard** *witch*

brave squaw **bachelor** spinster

Praise him/blame her words: why is it that *sir* and *madam* carry very different connotations?

Euphemisms

Along with a discussion of how language is employed evaluatively in relation to the sexes, the term *lady* deserves some mention. *Lady* and *gentleman* make a linguistic pair, as terms associated with persons of refinement, breeding, culture, and high station. But the term *gentleman* is used far less frequently than *lady* today. Lady is actually a euphemism for "woman." A euphemism substitutes for a word that is a source of unpleasantness or embarrassment. It is a mild or softening term used to replace a basic term that seems to be too strong or offensive: "pass on" for *die*, "go to the bathroom" for *defecate*, "expecting" for *pregnant*, "little girls' room" for *toilet*—and "lady" for *woman*. There is little need to substitute *gentleman* for *man* because the word *man* is not a source of strain or negative meaning.[58]

But *woman* has sexual implications that *lady* does not carry. If you think there is no difference between *woman* and *lady* and that they are interchangeable, compare the following sentences:

1 Sally is Mike's woman (lady).
2 She's grown to be a real woman (lady), hasn't she?
3 What Dan needs is a good woman (lady).
4 Act like a woman (lady).

If we substitute the word *lady* in each of the above, we can see that *lady* is a polite term for woman; it tones down the sexual implications by adding a dimension of formality or reserve. For example, in contrast to "a real woman," "a real lady" connotes propriety, politeness, and is not physical in tone. Or in the case of "Act like a woman"/"Act like a lady," there seems to be a contrast between implied sensuality and harmless dignity or fastidiousness.

Some concern has been voiced about the common use of the term *lady* to refer to a woman. Although seeming to confer exalted status on those to whom it refers, *lady* actually has the effect of subtly denigrating those it names. Compare the following:

1 A lady I met is exhibiting her paintings.
2 A woman I met is exhibiting her paintings.
3 A girl I met is exhibiting her paintings.

The use of "lady" in the first example imparts a frivolous, nonserious tone. One might infer the person is merely a dilettante dabbling in painting as a hobby or temporary diversion. Ask a number of persons and you will find that although they defend the exalted status of a "lady," they tend to associate the term with a mental picture of a female in large floppy hat and gloves, perhaps with teacup in hand. They do not picture a woman with sleeves rolled up, bent frowning over an easel, and discussing serious issues. Overlooked in the glow of associating the term *lady* with chivalry is the feeling tone of helplessness, of not being able to do for oneself, which the word carries. So while seeming to be a positive term, *lady* may trivialize the activity—in this case the painting—and faintly ridicule the woman. In the second sentence, "woman" connotes a serious interest in painting. Perhaps it is her vocation. We hear of "one-woman" shows, but never "one-lady" shows.[59]

Another euphemism for *woman* is *girl*. Like *lady*, the label appears complimentary on the surface but has a hidden potential for belittling. For with the word's positive connotation of youth and lightheartedness also come implications of immaturity and irresponsibility. The office worker may be eighteen, thirty-eight, or fifty-eight, but she is always the office "girl." Collectively, she may be addressed in her professional organization as "girls," and though the mother of teenage children she may be variously referred to as "thatta girl," "whatta girl," "girl of my dreams," or "one of the girls we play bridge with." In the third sentence presented previously, the "girl" doing the painting would seem to call forth little confidence in the final product. No matter what the age of the female under discussion, the same mental picture forms of a person who is not to be seriously entrusted with, or expected to make, responsible or serious decisions.

In a class, one of the author's students sampled their family members, friends, and casual acquaintances on two questions about this sentence: "A _____ George knows is coming for lunch. [lady, woman, girl]" The questions:

1 Assuming you are over twenty-one, which of the three people referred to (lady, woman, girl) would you like to be?
2 Which person would you expect to have the most important and useful things to say? Why?

Pooling the responses, we noted some patterns that seemed to support Lakoff's ideas. Whether respondents were children or adults, *woman* was most frequently expected to have "the most important and useful things to say." "Lady" ranked next, and "girl" was far behind the other two. Explanations given were varied and often humorous in implication. The main reasons behind the preference for "woman" seemed to be:

1 Women were more down-to-earth and serious than ladies.
2 Ladies did not have to attend to the basic issues of life as much, for they were occupied with social functions extensively.
3 Ladies had more wealth and thus were more insulated from having to be concerned with important issues of the day.
4 Ladies generally deal with topics such as gardens, charity balls, art collections, and the like.

Results on the other question were more varied. Many older persons, both women and men, but especially those in their late fifties on up, definitely preferred to be the "lady." Reasons included the following:

1 "Lady" is a title or position of more dignity, respect, and refinement than the other two. "Woman" seemed coarser or earthier.
2 Being a lady would ensure better treatment and more privilege.
3 They had been brought up to believe that being a lady was the most desirable thing to be. Any female is a woman by birth. "Lady" is earned through good manners, education, and high moral standards.

Younger females from their teens to their thirties appeared to be influenced by the women's movement and preferred that the term "woman" be applied to them. Some of the reasons were as follows:

1 "Woman" implies little pretense or cultural hypocrisy.
2 "Woman" seems to cut through some of the associations of prudishness or Victorian repression that "lady" suggests.
3 "Lady" sounds stilted.

Young males under thirty also expressed a preference for the term "woman," although not as strong a leaning as their female counterparts. Under-thirty males' reasons for preferring "woman" were similar to the females' and stressed the idea that "woman" implies greater sexual freedom.

Organizational titles

The claim has been made that any organization, activity, or function loses power and meaning when "woman" is added to it.[60] We explored this idea in a pilot study in our classes by presenting lists of hypothetical organization titles with either (1) no gender designation, (2) the term "women" inserted somewhere in the title, (3) the term "ladies" inserted somewhere in the title, or (4) the term "men" inserted somewhere in the title. For example:

• Form 1: Association for American Unity
• Form 2: Association for American Women's Unity
• Form 3: Association for American Ladies' Unity
• Form 4: Association for American Men's Unity

Subjects were to mark their personal evaluation of the significance of each organization on a scale from one to seven.

There was a definite difference in ratings in favor of organizations without gender designations in the titles. Those with "men's" in the titles received slightly higher ratings in general than those with "women's" or "ladies'" in the titles. There was little discernible difference between the ratings when "ladies'" or "women's" was used in the title. Some women, as if to counter the trend in which "woman" as a label devalues, rated the "women's" organizations far above the others.

Female shame/male pride

We referred previously to different ways in which words are used to define or designate the sexuality of women and men. Research supports the notion that most of the terms our culture has available to label women as sexual beings are negative and tend to demean or trivialize them. Note, for example, *hooker, piece, baggage, slut, tramp, whore*. Similar terms for men, which are far fewer in number, have more positive associations in general. Compare: *Casanova, Don Juan, good ole boy, stud, letch, gigolo,* or *Lothario*. Generally the male terms carry positive connotations that seem to reflect the morality of machismo and the prevalence of the double standard. Most terms tend to be used with a "boys-will-be-boys" or "hail-fellow-well-met" feeling and often are employed in good-natured joking.[61]

A common feature of many male words seems to be a reference to male sexuality in terms of degree of success in pursuing women. This pursuit tends to be encouraged in our culture and figures in our assessment of a male's so-called masculinity. Even the term *animal*, though it may be used disparagingly by some women, is connected with our cultural reverence for machismo and is also employed in admiring tones with positive connotation.

Gigolo may have negative connotations when it is used to refer to a man who has flawed the male stereotype of power, strength, and independence and demeaned himself by accepting support or money from a woman. But it can also be used with positive connotations to emphasize the man's masculinity, which is so valued that the roles are switched and it is the female who is paying for his, the male's, favors.[62]

A common feature of female terms seems to be reference to female sexuality in terms of women's accessibility as objects of pursuit and recipients of action. Success in pursuit or encounter has positive connotations for males, but being taken has negative connotations for females. Terms for women who are most available and least costly in money or effort, such as "easy lay," "pick up," "put out," and "two-bit whore," have the most negative connotations.

Almost without exception, sexual terms for women have negative connotations and imply attitudes of ridicule, contempt, and disgust toward female sexuality. As Stanley phrased it, "If a man is a cockhound, one shrugs one's shoulders; if a woman is a slut, the moral fiber of women is in danger."[63]

In accounting for this discrepancy it has been suggested that in our culture a certain amount of shame is associated with sexuality. Women have been socialized to feel embarrassment about their sexuality. In private, men are encouraged to take pride in their masculinity, and this is manifested in talk of physical involvement with women's bodies. An important badge of manhood is a successful sexual encounter. There is really no linguistic counterpart for females of male macho or machismo.

casanova
good ole boy
stud

tramp
slut
whore

Sexual terms are generally positive for men, negative or demeaning for women.

Scholars have noted people's ingenuity and inventiveness in pro-
liferating synonyms for words meaning copulate. Over 1200 English
synonyms have been recorded.[64] This may attest to the "universal fasci-
nation for the creative act." If we look more closely at the contexts in
which we use these terms, we can see that language reflects society's
disapproval of sex, even though it may elevate or idolize the male who
engages in it. Our usage of the various four- and five-letter words for
copulate occurs in contexts with assorted meanings of betray, cheat,
wrong, make a mess of, bungle, take advantage of, deceive, attack, or
destroy. For example, there are various slang usages of *screw*, all of
which are negative: ". . . a *person gets screwed* when he gets the short end
of the stick, when someone betrays him. One says that he worked very
hard when his employer needed him, only to be fired in the slow sea-
son: *his boss screwed him*, or *he got a screwing*."[65] To this we should add
that when intending to curse or denounce another, one may cry out,
"Screw you!"

In language there is evidence of a paradox concerning the sexes'
relation to each other. The linguistic dilemma or double bind that the
sexes face is simply this: "The language is a reflection of a society that
abhors sex while idolizing the male who obtains it and denouncing the
female who offers it."[66]

It has been suggested that the only positive image for women is
asexual—the madonna stereotype. In an analysis of sexual terms for
women, Stanley set up a visual diagram or representation of the
words.[67] To construct the semantic field, she used "length of contact"
(actual contact irrelevant/brief sexual contact/extended contact) as the
horizontal parameter; and cost (free-cheap/cheap/cheap-expensive/
expensive) as the vertical parameter. Following along the diagram from
left to right, one can get a certain perspective of how women are defined and viewed across the spectrum of sexuality.

Beginning with terms that do not require sexual contact for their
use and are in the area free-cheap, we find words that are applied to any
woman: "bitch," "broad," "baggage," "piece," "honey pot." This area
contains a total of 49 terms. Moving into the cheap area and the portion
marked "brief sexual contact," we find the largest number of terms, 151
out of the total 220, exemplified by such words as "hooker," "corner-
girl," "bat," "fastfanny," and so on. Terms in this category refer to the
act of selling oneself cheaply as an object, and the cost may range anywhere from a quarter, as in "two-bit whore," up to $20. In this category
of terms none is positive in connotation, although there is one category
that is neutral, "lady of the night."

In the space defined by extended contact and cheap/expensive and
expensive, there are only fifteen terms. At this end of the spectrum the
terms are less negative in tone: "professional," "prostitute," "Delilah,"
"hetaira," "kept woman." Some are neutral—"entertainer," "con-
cubine," "mistress"—and one, "courtesan," even has positive connotations. These terms, then, are used for women who "place a high price

on themselves in their relationships with men"—"professional," "call girl," "mistress." To Stanley the linguistic message is clear: there is not much respect for the sexuality of women. "But those women who charge the most for their 'services,' whether that charge is direct or indirect, win grudging approval from men."[68]

There is an interesting parallel here with a formula devised by a writer/editor concerning pornography. It involves not the content of the written material but the size, binding, quality of paper and printing, artwork, and most importantly, the cost of the book. Thus, "a book that costs fifteen dollars or more is not pornography but art."[69] Our culture may be more willing to grant its stamp of approval if the price is high enough.

In the diagram, only in the expensive range of the semantic field are "neutral" or "positive" terms found. The categories occupied by "courtesan," "common-law wife," and "wife," in Stanley's view, represent the point at which the state and the church "institutionalize the use of women." Her interpretation of this end of the semantic array is that marriage, signified by the location of the term "wife" on the diagram, is a relationship in which the male "pays and pays, sometimes for life, for his use, and exclusive property rights, of one woman." The movement in the diagram is from general terms which apply to any woman in the world, "broad," "hussy," "floozy," to terms applied to women who relate freely to men sexually, and finally to the specific term "wife." "The more time and money that a man is willing to invest in a woman, the more he legitimizes her existence in our society."[70] Many people find this interpretation jarring and provocative. Obviously a careful investigation and analysis needs to be made of male terms, their use, and parameters. How would the results of such a study relate to or complement the inferences made from this study?

Protests and objections can rarely muzzle speakers in their use of the English language. Words seem to take on their negative or positive coloring through reflecting the views of the most powerful group in society. The question that has been raised is why this inordinate expenditure of time, energy, effort, and versatility in disparaging and diminishing women through language. Perhaps males experience a fear of women and of sexual inadequacy, so they must ridicule and laugh at what they fear.[71]

Exclusion by gender

A third key way in which language deals differently with the sexes involves the potential of language to single out, exclude, or subsume persons or things. In our speech and writing we constantly see, hear, or use generic masculine terms, which are supposed to refer to people in general: "mankind," "the history of man," "the average man," "man-made," "manpower," "a person . . . himself," "each . . . his."

Let us take a look at a day in the life of two people, one a male, Earl, and one a female, Pearl.

Earl

Earl rises in the morning and after dressing puts on his new shoes, removing the tag reading, "80 percent *man*made materials." While eating breakfast, he spreads his bread with margarine "fit for a *king*" and thoughtfully chews the sausages labeled *"man* pleasers" as he reads the newspaper telling about a new archaeological find of a skull and partial skeleton of Neanderthal *man*. (He wonders, Have they ever found any women's skeletons?) Heading out to his car he is intercepted by a pollster who claims to be doing *man*-in-the-street interviews and asks his opinion. After replying briefly, Earl tells the interviewer he must be off, for he is a working*man* and has to get in so many *man*hours per week. Turning on the car radio, he hears a newscast on which a political figure is quoted as favoring a tax bill that will aid the little *man*.

At work, his friend regales him with accounts of the *man*eating sharks he saw on the West coast. At lunch, Earl orders the working*man's* special and tells his friend about his job, which is really a *man*killer. His friend shows little sympathy and urges Earl to "bear up under it like a *man*."

Pearl

Pearl awakens and sets her watch, which is recommended by leading *men* in the field. Unexpectedly, she finds she must use a wrench ("made for handy*men*") to tighten a leaky shower faucet. Perusing the morning paper, she reads that archaeologists have discovered new evidence of *man's* existence three million years ago based on the dating of a woman's skeleton.[72]

After breakfast, she gets in the car and drives past a sign which reads, "Give a kid a job and help mold a *man*."[73] At her law firm she greets Ella, whom her partner calls his "right-hand *man*." Ella tells Pearl she has just been appointed to membership on a five-*man* panel on court reform. Pearl then meets her first client, a woman charged with *man*slaughter in the death of her sister-in-law, who supposedly fell off a ship and drowned when no one yelled *"man* overboard."

Pearl's next appointment is with a woman injured on the job, who is suing for work*men's* compensation. Although, as her partner reminds her, *"man* does not live by bread alone," she decides to leave for lunch anyway. At the restaurant, she orders the business*man's* lunch. On her way out, however, she walks *past* the restroom labeled *"Men"* and enters the door marked *"Women."*

Many ask, "What's all the fuss about *man, he, his,* and *him?"* They insist that these terms refer to *all* human beings, male and female, and that *woman, she,* and *her* are implied in the terms. However, when Graham consulted the computer on this question in regard to children's books, she found only about 3 percent of the citations for *he* referred to subjects who were unspecified as to sex. The rest referred to male human beings, male animals, or persons assumed to be males, such as farmers or sailors.[74] It would be interesting to do a similar investigation on general print material for adults, such as magazines and newspapers.

Linguists have analyzed and categorized the ways in which generic language subsumes and renders woman invisible. These include the following:

1 Usage of the words *man* and *men* to represent human beings or adults in general, as in *"Man's* achievements in the last fifty years are many," or *"Man*made fabrics affect the country's fashion trends."
2 Usage of "a man" or "the man" to represent the average, typical, or hypothetical persons: "If *a man* selects *his* own worktime, under the new flexible work provisions, *he* will tend to be more motivated."
3 Usage of the ending *-man* in occupational or activity terms such as "salesman," "businessman," "statesman," "repairman," "snowman," "hangman," "fireman," "cameraman."
4 Use of *he*, *his*, and *him* with neutral words such as *each* or *everyone*, as in the following: "Each should do the best that *he* . . . ," "Everyone can take *his* . . . ," "A person harms *him*self when. . . ."

What concerns feminists most is the ambiguity that exists in each of the above instances. When someone uses any of these words in a general sense and another interprets the word as specifically masculine, there is a miscommunication and females are unintentionally excluded from the idea or statement. Some consider it a weakness in our language that the pronoun *he* must be used imprecisely to designate both "he" or "she." Those who object to subsuming terms claim that the listener or reader does not form a mental image that includes females upon hearing or reading these terms. When reading about "men of good will," suggests one writer, not many of us are likely to picture "a group of amicable females."[75] So although language experts may declare that generic terms refer to women by implication, the *interpretation* of them may be biased toward the male.

Lakoff feels that emphasis on the problem these terms present for women is misguided.[76] Far more serious in her opinion are the uses of words that define women narrowly in sexual terms or that imply prescribed behavior for women. She feels an attempt to change pronominal usage would be futile. Linguistic imbalances are signals or clues that something is wrong rather than the problem to be solved. Just as a physician will not attack a case of measles by trying to remove the symptoms or to bleach out the red spots, feminists cannot think to remedy social or economic inequities, according to Lakoff, simply by removing the language clues of their existence. She advocates choosing carefully which issues to attack and concentrating efforts where they will be most fruitful. Generic-term issues are "too common and too thoroughly mixed throughout the language."

Nilsen, like Lakoff, is not encouraged by the prospect of changing language, and she predicts that women with this goal face a "very big task." She questions the feasibility of developing a separate language system to accommodate females and implies that even if this were possible, its effect on the actual position of women in society is doubtful. She too feels the women's cause would best be served by concentrating efforts on areas more open to change.[77]

When reading about "men of good will," how many readers will picture a group of amicable females?

Yet language is surely more than a reflection or indicator of the social structure. Speech is a form of action and as such is capable of influencing the thought and actions of its users. "To use *he or she*," remark Thorne and Henley, "rather than *he*, for sex-indefinite antecedents is a *tangible gesture of including*, rather than excluding, women from consciousness."[78] These and other verbal gestures can help transmit, establish, or maintain social structure and also aim thinking and behavior in new directions.

An analogy has been suggested: A physician has the option of prescribing two drugs, Drug A and Drug B, for an illness. Both drugs have the same potential for relieving or curing the illness. But Drug A might cause negative (harmful) side effects, along with its positive results, in some patients. Drug B is capable of bringing about the same positive results but without risk of the negative side effects. Which drug should the physician select?[79] Drug A is suggested as being analogous to traditional language in which all people are male until proven female. It has the potential for negative side effects for certain groups of people that it seems to exclude. Drug B could be compared to improved language usage, which has less potential for harming some groups of people by exclusion.

The possible negative effects of generic terms has been investigated. It seems clear that children, at least, react to language literally. A charming, but very pointed, story is told of a three-year-old child who was unsuccessfully trying to remove a bottle from a cabinet. Because of the size of the cabinet, the bottle had to be tipped sideways to get it out. As the child puzzled over this impasse, her father admonished her, "Use your head!" The child immediately put her head inside the cabinet and pushed at the bottle. She literally did as her father told her.[80]

This kind of literal interpretation of language may lead a child to misinterpret such statements as "Any *man* can succeed in our country," or "Each person should work to *his* full potential." Reference to such occupations or positions as salesman, businessman, chairman, or congressman may cause a child to think that these occupations must be held by males. Traditional language, though we are assured it *intends* to include women, may not be interpreted as inclusive. In fact, it may only reinforce the notion that boys are supposed to choose certain occupations, but girls are not.

Responses of subjects to the term *man* and the masculine pronoun *he* have been investigated, and the results are provocative in their implications. One study used college students as subjects and presented them with a series of statements containing "man" and "he." Rather than responding inclusively by indicating that the terms referred to either or both sexes, subjects tended to designate as male the subject being referred to. Males were selected 407 times and females 53 times. So regardless of whether the words *man* and *he* are intended to be neutral, they apparently are not generally interpreted as neutral by college students. If we infer from this that the intended purpose of these terms is not normally achieved, the question arises, Why continue to use them?[81]

Another provocative study approached the subject from a unique angle. The researchers asked college students to submit magazine and newspaper pictures as illustrations for a projected sociology textbook. Subjects were given two types of topic labels for the illustrations they were to provide: (1) generic labels such as "political man" and "urban man" and (2) sex-inclusive titles such as "political behavior" or "urban life." Of those students who were asked to illustrate "man" titles, 64 percent provided pictures that contained males only. Of the students who were given sex-inclusive titles, only half provided all-male illustrations. As in the first study, a surprisingly large number of respondents do not picture females as well as males when they come across the terms *man* or *he* used in the generic sense.[82]

Probably the most striking indications of the strong effect language has on some people were obtained in a study utilizing job advertisements. High school students were asked to rate 12 job advertisements on an interested/uninterested scale. The language describing several of the occupations was varied so that on one form an inclusive term was used, on a second form a traditional male term such as "frameman" was used, and on a third form a sex-reversed term such as "framewoman" was used. This seemingly simple alteration in language made a significant difference in the interest students expressed in jobs normally considered appropriate for the opposite sex—such as telephone operator, which is generally considered a female job.[83]

When traditional language was used, only 5 percent of the women and 30 percent of the men expressed interest in opposite-sex-typed jobs. But when language that included both sexes was used, 25 percent of the women and 75 percent of the men expressed an interest in opposite-sex-typed jobs. With sex-reversed language, 45 percent of the women and 65 percent of the men showed interest in opposite sex jobs.

More than a joke

Language, as it reveals the position of the sexes and influences their relationships, is a truly fascinating study. The problem of language in relation to the sexes may be, as Paul Gray has suggested, "more than a joke and less than a national crisis."[84]

The thought that individuals with potential interest and/or talent for certain occupations can be encouraged or deterred by a slight alteration in words is indeed sobering. Speculations about the possible impact of our word usage on the precious aspirations, careers, and personal fulfillment of our youth can give us reason to pause. It can cast a chilling pall over humor that points out the awkwardness of speakers addressing the "chairperson, honored guestpersons and personpersons" or of gunpersons who shoot businesspersons in robbery, are apprehended by policepersons, and finally are hanged by hangpersons. Attempts to clarify and free our language from sex bias ought not be the target of idle humor. Certainly any language that insinuates second-class status for roughly one-half the population—the female sex—ought to be changed. We all have the obligation to weigh our words more carefully. There is probably less difference than we would care to imagine between equal and respectful treatment in language and in life!

Suggested activities

1 Keep a one-week record of how you are addressed and what you are called in various situations: being served or working in stores, restaurants, or other commercial establishments; visiting with friends; being spoken to by older persons, by younger persons, by those of the opposite sex, by your superiors, by those over whom you have charge.
   a. Did the titles or terms of address seem to depend on your status? On your sex? In what way? In which situation?
   b. What was a member of the opposite sex called in a similar situation?
   c. What was a person of different status called in a similar situation?

d. What hypotheses have you formulated about women and men and their relative status?
For example:

Record of one day

Position/setting	Male speaker	Approx. age	Female speaker	Approx. age
Grocery checkout clerk			Ma'am	25–30
Department store clerk	Lady	30–40	Honey	40–50
Library assist.			Dr. Eakins	20–25
Phone: student	Mrs. Eakins	19–25	Professor "E"	19
Phone: student	Mrs. "E"	19	Dr. Eakins	20–25
Phone: student	Dr. Eakins	19–25	Dr. Eakins	20
Office sec.			Barbara	25–30
Faculty meeting: associates	Barb	30–35	Barb	30–35
	Barb	45–55	Barbara	30–35
Home: children	Mom	13	Mom	15

2 In descriptions of females in public or professional positions, physical and emotional qualities, rather than qualifications for the job, often receive undue emphasis.

    a. Consult magazines, newspapers, journals, and books to find examples of good and poor descriptions of women. For each item that you clip or record, identify the source from which it came.
Suggested format:

Person	Irrelevant	Relevant	Source
Athlete	brown-eyed cutie	well-coordinated 128-pound runner	

3 It has been suggested that a double standard exists for words referring to the different sexes. Consider the starters below and then add to the list from
    a. your own listening and observation of yourself and others
    b. an informal poll of your friends and family

Concept	He is:	She is:
Bold	Courageous	Aggressive
Assertive	Go-getting	Pushy
Insistent	Persistent	Nagging
Forgetful	Absent-minded	Scatterbrained
Fluent	Verbal	Gabby

6 Silent sounds and secret messages

... People talking without speaking
... People hearing without listening
  —Paul Simon[1]

In addition to the spoken language that we hear daily, a host of silent messages continually occur around us. These messages make up a non-verbal code, which is used and responded to by us all. This language is not formally taught. A substantial portion of the nonverbal communication that takes place is not consciously noted. But it is an extremely important aspect of communication, for we make many important decisions on the basis of nonverbal cues.

Ray Birdwhistell[2] estimates that in most two-person conversations the words communicate only about 35 percent of the social meaning of the situation; the nonverbal elements convey more than 65 percent of the meaning. Another estimate is that the nonverbal message carries 4.3 times the weight of the verbal message.[3] This is not so surprising when we consider the many ways in which we communicate information non-verbally: through eye contact, facial expressions, body posture and body tension, hand gestures and body movements, the way we position ourselves in relation to another person, touch, clothing, cosmetics, and possessions.

Some time ago Freud said, "He that has eyes to see and ears to hear may convince himself that no mortal can keep a secret. If his lips are silent, he chatters with his finger tips; betrayal oozes out of him at every pore."[4] To be more skillful communicators, we need to be aware of nonverbal cues and to use what has been learned to improve communication.

Micro-units of nonverbal communication, such as dropping the eyelids, smiling, pointing, lowering the head slightly, or folding the arms are often considered trivia. But some researchers believe these so-called trivia constitute the very core or essence of our communication interactions. They consider them elements in the "micropolitical structure" that help maintain and support the larger political structure. The larger political structure needs these numerous minutiae of human actions and interactions to sustain and reinforce it. These nonverbal cues fall somewhere on a continuum of social control that ranges from socialization or cultivation of minds, at one extreme, to the use of force or physical violence, at the other.[5] There are some significant sex differences in nonverbal communication patterns and, as we shall see, they have important implications in the lives of women and men.

Sex and nonverbal communication

Zoologists and biologists have begun to see that many animal behaviors, some of which are peculiar to each sex, are not simply mechanical and instinctive responses as previously assumed. Rather the behaviors are shaped and structured by the experiences and environment of the creatures.

Human beings are described as being relatively unimorphic. That is, once we have distinguished the sexes on the basis of their sex organs and the production of ova and spermatozoa, there are not extreme differences between them in secondary sexual characteristics. Although there are differences such as bone structure or distribution of body hair, measurement of these items shows considerable overlap between the sexes. This is in contrast to some species whose physical differences are so extreme that only experts can tell that the male and female belong to the same species.

In addition to primary and secondary sexual characteristics, there are tertiary sexual characteristics, the learned, situationally produced characteristics. They are cultural or human-invented traits. Birdwhistell postulates that humans, and other species weakly differentiated by sex, evolve or develop certain tertiary nonverbal characteristics such as position, movement, or expression that display or point up gender. He worked with persons from seven societies and found that women and men distinguished typically female communication behavior from typically male communication behavior, as well as distinguishing feminine males and masculine females. Each culture's stereotypes could be acted out or roughly described. These positions, movements, and expressions are apparently culturally coded. What is viewed as feminine behavior in one culture may be different from what is considered feminine in another or may be seen as masculine behavior in yet another.[6]

The important point for our discussion is that tertiary sexual behavior is learned, socially patterned communication behavior that apparently functions to identify both the gender of a person and the social expectancies linked with that gender. Rather than being natural, or a logical consequence of biology, some of our nonverbal behavior has probably been shaped and patterned to exhibit and point up sex differences. The asymmetric model described in Chapter 2 underscores the part power plays in female and male communication. But perhaps we have gone to cultural extremes: ". . . The either-or type of sexual behavior demanded of men and women by the mores of Western culture under threat of severe penalty is not in line with the trend of sexual adjustment as it has developed throughout biological evolution."[7] Perhaps in so sharply delineating behavior appropriate for each sex, we have, as a result, too narrowly channeled our sexuality. We shall now turn our attention to learned, situationally produced tertiary characteristics.

Sex differences in nonverbal communication

Women seem to be more sensitive than men to social cues. Research has shown that female subjects are more responsive to nonverbal cues, compared with verbal ones, than males.[8] Not only have women been found to be more responsive to nonverbal stimuli, but they apparently read it with greater accuracy than males. One study used the Profile of Nonverbal Sensitivity, a test that utilizes film clips of a series of scenes involving people using body movement and facial expression and showing face, torso, both, or neither. Subjects heard scrambled voice, content-filtered speech with intonation features preserved, or no sound. They were to select the best of the written interpretations of the nonverbal cues after each scene. Females from fifth grade to adulthood obtained better scores than males, with the exception of men who held jobs involving "nurturant, artistic, or expressive" work. When body cues were included, women did better than men. Sensitivity to nonverbal cues appeared to be independent of general intelligence or test-taking skills.[9]

One could hypothesize that nonverbal awareness is an inborn trait and that females are more sensitive and responsive to nonverbal cues from birth. However, it seems more likely that females learn to become nonverbally sensitive at an early age because of their socialization. Their greater receptivity to nonverbal cues from others may be related to their lower status in society and the necessity of this skill to their survival. Blacks, for example, have been shown to be better than whites at interpreting nonverbal signals.[10]

When a group of teachers took the Profile of Nonverbal Sensitivity, those more sensitive to nonverbal communication scored as less authoritarian and more democratic in teaching orientation. Females were relatively better than males at interpreting negative attitudes.[11] Since females may be placed in subordinate positions or be dependent on others in social situations more often, they may be forced to become adept at reading signs of approbation or displeasure from those on whom they depend. Perhaps more than men, they need to know what expectations for them are. Developing the ability to pick up small nonverbal cues in others quickly may be a defense mechanism or survival technique women unconsciously use. It is much more important to someone in a subordinate position to know the mood, the feelings, or intentions of the dominant one than vice versa. The office worker will immediately note and relay to other office subordinates the information that "the boss is in one of his moods again." Just a look, the manner of walk, or the carriage of the arms and shoulders may provide the clue for that anxious observer. Rare, however, is the authority figure who notices employees' moods or is even aware that they have them.

We are not taught nonverbal communication in school. Our schools emphasize verbal communication. Because we seldom examine how we send and interpret nonverbal messages, the nonverbal channel is a very useful avenue for subtly manipulating people. The manipulation does not have to be consciously perceived.

We are prevented from getting knowledge or understanding of nonverbal communication because a delineation of looks, gait, posture, or facial expression is not legitimate in describing interaction. Such items are surely not accepted as valid data in an argument. ("What do you mean, I look as if I don't approve? I said 'all right,' didn't I?") And yet nonverbal cues have more than four times the impact of verbal messages. Not only are women more sensitive to such cues, but their position in society and their socialization to greater docility and compliance may predispose them to be more vulnerable to manipulation and thus make them ideal targets for this subtle form of social control. It behooves both women and men to learn as much as possible about how nonverbal cues can affect people and can serve to perpetuate status and power relationships in society.[12] With this concern in mind, let us examine the categories of nonverbal behavior.

Eye contact

Research in the use of eye contact has shown sharp differences according to sex. In studies involving female and male subjects, women have been found to look more at the other person than men do. In addition, women look at one another more and hold eye contact longer with each other than men do with other men. Women look at one another more while they are speaking, while they are being spoken to, and while they are exchanging simultaneous glances. Whatever the sex of the other, women have been shown to spend more time looking at their partner than men do.[13] What might account for this asymmetry, or difference, in looking behavior of the sexes? The usual explanation given is that women are more willing to establish and maintain eye contact because they are more inclined toward social and interpersonal relations. The gaze may be an avenue of emotional expression for women.[14]

Another reason has been suggested for sex differences in eye behavior. Some experiments have found that in orienting their bodies in space women are more affected than men by visual cues. In other words, in tests where subjects must make judgments about horizontal and vertical position, women tend to use reference points in the environment rather than internal body cues.[15] This physical characteristic could be generalized to social situations.

Women look more at the other person than men do.

Let us consider the paradigm of asymmetrical behavior as an indicator of status. Among unequals the subordinate is the one most likely to want social approval, and it has been shown that people have more eye contact with those from whom they want approval.[16] The kinds of clues or information women may get by observing a male's reactions or behavior are important in helping them gauge the appropriateness of their own behavior. Women may value nonverbal information from males more than males value nonverbal information from females.[17] Furthermore, it has been found that in conversation, the listener tends to look more at the speaker, whereas the speaker often looks away while talking. Since some studies show that men tend to talk more in female-male pairs, women would spend more time listening and, therefore, probably more time looking at the other.

Also it has been shown that the more positive an attitude toward the person being addressed, the more eye contact there is. Increased eye contact with the person being addressed also occurs if that person is of higher status.[18] In some cases males use more positive head nods, but females use more eye contact, when they are seeking approval.[19] In an investigation involving mixed-sex pairs, when women were told their partner's eye contact exceeded normal levels, they had a more favorable evaluation of him. But when men were told their partner looked more than usual, they had a less favorable evaluation of her.[20] These studies suggest that women may be using eye contact to seek approval and that perhaps both women and men perceive women to have less status than men. Perhaps, as one student commented, "They almost *ask* for the subordinate position by their very behavior."

In our personal experience, we became acquainted with a graduate student and the woman he had just married. There was a discrepancy in educational background between the man, who was just beginning work on his Ph.D., and the woman, who had a high school education. Not only her uneasiness but her heavy reliance on nonverbal cues to her husband's reactions were evident at social gatherings. During conversation, her eyes would continually stray to his face. When speaking with her, it was difficult to establish eye contact, for during her comments or her answers to questions, her eyes would dart to her husband's face, as if to measure the appropriateness of her remark by his approbation or lack of it.

Some writers have observed that women tend to avert their gaze, especially when stared at by men.[21] Although mutual eye contact between persons can indicate affiliation or liking, prolonged eye contact or staring can signify something quite different. Back in our youth, we sometimes engaged in "double whammy," a game in which we tried to outstare our partner. The first one to break the eyelock by looking away, dropping the eyes, or closing the eyes was the loser. It has been suggested that this kind of competitiveness is involved when two persons' gazes meet, such that "a wordless struggle ensues, until one or the other succeeds in establishing dominance."[22] Dominance is acquiesced to and submissiveness signaled by the person who finally looks away or down. We might ask ourselves, in our last encounter with the boss, someone in very high authority, or a person whom we felt greatly "outclassed" us in position or wealth, who was the first to break the mutual gaze and glance away? Indeed, this is a "'game' . . . enacted at [subtle] levels thousands of times daily."[23]

Jane van Lawick-Goodall has observed behavior of chimpanzees for a number of years and has noted striking similarities in the behavior of chimpanzees and people, particularly in nonverbal communication patterns.[24] She points out how a greeting between two chimpanzees generally re-establishes the dominance status of the one relative to the other. She describes how one female chimp, "nervous Olly," greets another chimp, "Mike," to whom she may bow to the ground and crouch submissively with downbent head. "She is, in effect, acknowledging Mike's superior rank," says Goodall. This would seem to be the extreme of avoiding eye gaze with one of superior rank. Goodall also indicates that an angry chimpanzee may fixedly stare at an opponent.

Some years ago, when our oldest daughter was quite young, she asked us earnestly, "Why is it baboons don't like you to stare at them?" The family was amused at this, and it became a standing joke at our home for years. But we had been to the zoo and, young as she was, our daughter had apparently noticed that the baboons she saw reacted in a disturbed manner to staring.

Research with humans has shown that staring calls forth the same kinds of responses found in primates and that it serves as threat display.[25] Observations of averted eye behavior in autistic children suggest that the averted glance or downcast eyes may be a gesture of submissiveness in humans. Researchers noted to their surprise that autistic children were rarely attacked by the other children, although they seemed to be "easy targets." They concluded that the autistic child's avoidance of eye contact served as a signal much like the appeasement postures used by certain gulls, for example. That is to say, turning away the gaze and avoiding eye contact seemed to restrain or check aggressive behavior or threat display.[26]

The power of the direct stare and the strength of the message it conveys, as well as the acquiescence that turning the eyes away can signify, was illustrated to us by a humorous incident at a cocktail hour for new faculty. One young couple was eager to please and be accepted because it was the husband's first position after finishing graduate school. The wife was a hearty, direct young woman who had been reared in Iowa. She had a bluff, good-natured sense of humor and an amusing way with idioms that refused to stay tucked under the sedateness she tried in vain to assume for this "important" occasion. She was in a tight little circle with some of the tenured and dignified "old guard," when one of them commented upon the great pleasure of discovering that his young colleague had such a lovely wife. The young woman was pleased and began animatedly telling her elderly admirer she felt "as grateful as the cow who remarked to the farmer, 'Thank you for a warm hand on a cold morning.'" As she spoke, her husband fixed upon her a direct and piercing stare. The young woman then stopped her talk and turned her head slightly as she lowered her eyes and became very intent upon sipping her punch.

There may seem to be a contradiction in reporting that women tend to look at others more than men do and yet claim that they generally follow a pattern of submission in one-sided behavior interactions. But several explanations may be offered.[27] First, more of women's looking consists of mutual eye contact. It is possible that during mutual eye contact women are the first to turn the eyes away, the signal of submission. For example, one observation in which a male stared at 60 females and males showed that females averted their gaze more often. About 40 percent of the females would return the stare, then immediately break eye contact, and then reestablish it—as many as four times in an encounter. Only one male of the group made repetitive eye contact in this way.

Second, it may be useful to identify the nature of the gaze and distinguish between subordinate attentiveness and dominant staring. Women may do more looking or scanning of the other person's face for expressive cues when the other person's gaze is directed elsewhere, just as subordinates in the animal world must stay alert to cues from the powerful. But when that person returns the gaze, a woman may drop hers. Intermittent and repetitive eye contact may be the female's response to two conflicting tendencies: the inclination to avert the eyes in submission and the need to watch for visual cues from the powerful.

Third, people tend to do more looking while they are listening to another speak than when they themselves are speaking; and we have learned that women are listeners more often than talkers. So women may be doing more of their looking while listening (in the submissive role) to the other person talk.

Fourth, looking that is done by subjects in experimental lab situations may function differently from looking that occurs in more natural settings. Some informal studies of eye contact by persons passing one another in public showed that 71 percent of the males established eye contact with a female but only 43 percent of the females established eye contact with a male. Other observations have shown a pattern of females averting the eyes from both female and male starers. In contrast, males generally stared back at female starers, although they avoided eye contact with other males.

Apparently two types of eye behavior characterize both dominance and submissiveness, but in different ways.

1 Dominant staring and looking away. Staring can be used by a superior in some situations to communicate power and assert dominance. But in other instances staring may not be needed. With subordinates, one can feel comfortable and secure in one's power. A superior need not anxiously scan the inferior's face for approval or feedback, but can instead look away or gaze into space as if the underling were not there.

2 Submissive watching and averting of the gaze. Careful watching by an underling can be used to communicate submission and dutiful attentiveness, as well as to gather feedback or attitude cues from the dominant. But in some cases looking is not useful or appropriate. When receiving the fixed stare of a powerful other, for example, a subordinate may signal submission by averting the eyes.

Finally, it is said that while looking directly at a man, a woman will often have her head slightly tilted. This may imply the beginning of a "presenting" gesture, or enough submission to render the stare ambivalent if not actually submissive.[28]

It is interesting to note that in a "Dear Abby" survey on what women notice first about men and what men notice first about women, the eyes rank third for both sexes. Comments included such sentiments from women as, "The eyes tell everything," or "You can tell more about a man's character from his eyes than from anything else. His mouth can lie, but his eyes can't." Males' comments included explanations such as, "It tells me whether or not she's interested in me," or "The eyes show kindness, cruelty, warmth, trust, friendliness and compassion—or a lack of it."[29]

Facial expression

Women have been found to be more prone to reveal their emotions in facial expressions than men. A psychologist who conducted an experiment on this subject found that men tended to keep their emotions "all bottled up." Subjects in the experiment (students) were shown slides calculated to arouse strong feelings or emotions. The pictures included scenes that were unpleasant, such as a victim with severe burns; pleasant, such as happy children; unusual, a double-exposed photograph; scenic; or sexual. While the subjects were viewing the slides, their own facial expressions were being picked up over closed-circuit television. The researchers found that it was easier to tell what kind of picture was being shown from viewing the women's facial expressions than from viewing the men's expressions. They concluded that men are "internalizers." Some of the evidence suggesting that men keep their emotions inside were the faster heart beat and greater activity of the sweat glands of males during the experiment.[30]

It is significant to note that while preschool children were found to react differently to pictures, this difference did not seem to occur according to sex but on the basis of individual personality differences. The implication is that while they are growing up males are conditioned by society not to show or express their feelings and females are conditioned to reveal theirs more freely. While perhaps less advantageous in terms of power, it would seem to be healthier to express one's emotions.

Women have been found to be better able to remember names and faces, at least those of high school classmates.[31] A study tested subjects from ages 17 to 47, with men and women put into nine categories, depending on the number of years since they had graduated from high school. In all categories the women's memories were superior to men's in matching names and faces. One would conclude that women are conditioned to associate names with physical characteristics more so than men.

From her study of chimpanzees, Goodall has observed that many of the submissive and aggressive gestures of the chimpanzee closely resemble our own. The chimpanzees have some facial expressions for situations that seem to provide insight when considering the human social environment.[32] One facial expression is the "compressed-lips face" shown by aggressive chimpanzees during a charging display or when attacking others.

Another expression is the "play face" shown during periods of frolicking. The front upper teeth are exposed, and the upper lip is drawn back and up. A "full open grin," with upper and lower front

During a slide show, females revealed their emotions through facial expression more than males did.

teeth showing and jaws open, is displayed when a chimpanzee is frightened or excited, such as during attack or when a high-ranking male "displays" close to a subordinate. A "low open grin," with the upper lip slightly relaxed to cover the upper front teeth, is shown when the chimpanzee is less frightened or excited.

When the chimpanzee is less frightened or less excited than in the previous situations, "a full closed grin," with upper and lower teeth showing but with jaws closed, may be shown. It is also displayed by a low-ranking chimpanzee, when approaching a superior in silence. Goodall remarked, "If the human nervous or social smile has its equivalent expression in the chimpanzee it is, without doubt, the closed grin." Elsewhere it has been observed that apes use a "rudimentary smile" as an appeasement gesture or to indicate submission.[33] It apparently signals to an aggressor that the subordinate creature intends no harm.

Some writers have pointed out that women smile more than men do, whether or not they are really happy or amused. The smile may be a concomitant of the social status of women and be used as a gesture of submission as a part of their culturally prescribed role. Supposedly the smile is an indicator of submission, particularly from women to men. Silveira indicates two instances in which women are more likely to smile: when a woman and a man greet one another, and when the two are conversing and are only moderately well acquainted.[34] In these situations, rather than indicating friendliness or pleasure, the smile supposedly shows that no aggression or harm is intended. One study found that women tended to smile and laugh more than men during labora-

Women smile more than men do, whether or not they are happy or amused.

tory conversations. Women may have smiled more to cover up uneasiness or nervousness or to meet social expectations. The men who smiled generally did so only after they felt comfortable and to express solidarity or union.[35]

In an investigation of approval seeking, one member in each pair of communicators was instructed to try to either gain or avoid the approval of the other. Those who tried to gain approval used significantly more nonverbal acts, including smiles. There was no difference between the sexes in use of smiles in approval seeking. However, when subjects were instructed to behave so as to avoid the approval of the other, the women avoiding approval tended to smile more often than the men avoiding approval. Perhaps the women were unwilling to withhold this gesture because they believe smiling is expected of them socially, whatever the situation. Or it may be that the forced or ready smile was so much a part of the female subjects' socialization that they used it unconsciously, even when inappropriate for their purposes.[36]

Research has shown that children tend to respond differently to female and male smiles. Children five to eight years old responded to women's smiles, as compared to men's smiles, in a neutral manner.[37] Furthermore, children five to twelve years old tended to react to "kidding" messages, which included a negative statement spoken with a smile, as negative; and the negative interpretation was stronger when the speaker was a woman.[38] Young children's different responses to the smiles of women and men in these studies probably reflect sex differences in the smiling communication patterns of adults.

In another experiment videotapes were made of parents with their children. Half the families in the sample had disturbed children and half had normal children. Ratings were made of the parents' words and smiling during interaction with their children. Results showed that fathers made more positive statements when they smiled than when they did not smile. But mothers' statements were not more positive when they were smiling than when they were not smiling, and sometimes in fact were even slightly more negative when smiling. The pattern was not related to child disturbance.

Mothers in lower-class families smiled considerably less than their middle-class counterparts. Whereas 75 percent of the middle-class mothers smiled more than once, only 13 percent of the lower-class mothers smiled more than once. There was no significant difference between lower- and middle-class fathers in amount of smiling.[39] From the results of this study, it appears that fathers are more sincere when they smile, and they are more likely to be saying something relatively friendlier or more approving when smiling than when they are not smiling. When mothers smile at their children, they may be saying something no more evaluatively positive than when they are not smiling. One may conclude that children are probably "reading" adults accurately when they interpret more friendliness in a male's smile than in a female's smile.

What does the middle-class mother's public smile mean? The researchers suggest that the mother is trying to meet middle-class expectations for a "good" mother, which discourage open expression of negative feelings. Her culturally prescribed role calls for "warm, compliant behavior in public situations." The smile may be used as a kind of softener, or mitigator, of critical statements. Another explanation is that the woman may use a smile as "socially ingratiating behavior," rather than as an indicator of friendliness or approval. One writer suggests that both women and men are "deeply threatened" by a female who does not smile often enough and who is apparently not unhappy.[40]

A class project by Henley featured a field study in which students smiled at about three hundred persons (half females, half males) in public and recorded whether each individual smiled back or not. Seventy-six percent of the time people returned smiles. But different patterns of smiling could be identified for each sex. Women returned smiles more often, about 89 percent of the time; and they returned smiles more frequently to males (93 percent of the time) than to other females (86 percent). Males returned smiles only 67 percent of the time to females and were even more inhibited in smiling back at other males, which they did only 58 percent of the time. Henley concluded that some short-changing occurs in the tradeoff of smiles between the sexes: "Women are exploited by men—they give 93 percent but receive in return only 67 percent."[41]

Shulamith Firestone represents an extreme but thought-provoking view concerning the smile as a "badge of appeasement." She terms the smile "the child/woman equivalent of the shuffle," since it indicates the acquiescence to power, and she describes her youthful efforts to re-socialize herself. "In my own case, I had to train myself out of that phony smile, which is like a nervous tic on every teenage girl. And this meant that I smiled rarely, for in truth, when it came down to real smiling, I had less to smile about." Firestone describes her "'dream' action": "... *a smile boycott*, at which declaration all women would instantly abandon their 'pleasing' smiles, henceforth smiling only when something pleased them."[42]

Posture and bearing

It has been observed that among nonequals in status, superordinates can indulge in a casualness and relative unconcern with body comportment that subordinates are not permitted. For example, one researcher observed that doctors in the hospital had the privilege of sitting in undignified positions at staff meetings and could saunter into the nurses' station and lounge on the station's dispensing counter. Other personnel such as attendants and nurses had to be more circumspect in their bearing.[43] We need no handbook to tell us that in most interactions the person whom we observe sprawling out, leaning back, or propping feet up while the other maintains more "proper" bearing probably has the authority or power role.

A number of nonverbal sex differences in bearing and posture seem to parallel this asymmetry between nonequals. Birdwhistell describes some posture differences between the sexes involving leg, arm, and pelvis positioning. He believes these are among the most easily recognizable American gender identification signals. In fact, he indicates that leg angle and arm-body angle can be measured exactly. Women giving off gender signals are said to bring their legs together, sometimes even to the extent that their upper legs cross or they stand knee over knee. The American male, however, tends to keep legs apart by a 10- to 15-degree angle.[44] Anyone who has ever participated in physical fitness exercises and assumed "attention" and "at ease" stances knows that the male stance is a more relaxed one.

As for arm-body carriage, females are said to keep their upper arms close to the trunk, while the male moves the arms 5 to 10 degrees away from the body in giving gender cues. Males may carry the pelvis rolled slightly back and females slightly forward. In movement, females supposedly present the entire body from neck to ankles as a moving whole. Males, in contrast, move the arms independently from the trunk and may subtly wag the hips with a slight right and left movement involving a twist at the rib cage. The male bearing seems the more relaxed of the two. Johnny Carson once said of Dr. Joyce Brothers, "She sits as if her knees were welded together."

That these are socialized positions may be inferred from the fact that often as women and men grow older or become ill, their gender

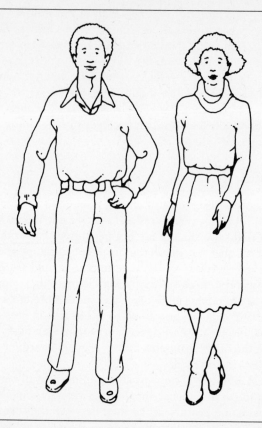

American males walk with their legs apart by a 10- to 15-degree angle, their arms 5 to 10 degrees away from the trunk. American females walk with legs together, their upper arms close to the trunk.

positions may become underemphasized or indistinguishable. An elderly woman may, for example, sit relaxed with her legs apart. Because this is an inappropriate gender signal, such an action often appears bizarre or may be the object of humor. Carol Burnett, portraying an old woman in one of her comedy routines, sometimes uses this position to get laughs.

Research indicates that in social situations, men assume a more relaxed posture than women, no matter what the sex of the other partner is.[45] Males have been found to assume more asymmetric leg positions and more reclining postures than females.[46] Generally females tend to position their bodies more directly facing the person with whom they are communicating than male communicators do.

In one study males and females were asked to imagine themselves communicating with different persons and to sit the way they would if addressing those persons. Torso lean proved to be a distinguishing difference in some cases. There is less sideways lean in communications with high-status persons. Torso lean was more relaxed, more backward,

Males tend to assume relaxed postures and expand into available space. Females tend to assume tense, condensed postures, taking up as little space as possible.

when communicators addressed persons they disliked. Torso lean of the males was farther back than that of the females. Women used less arm openness with high-status persons than with low-status persons. Males showed no difference. Leg openness of female communicators was less than that of male communicators.[47]

It appears from these and a number of related studies that males are generally more relaxed than females, just as higher-status persons are more relaxed than those in subordinate roles. Research also shows that communicators in general are more relaxed with females than with males. They show less body tension, more relaxed posture, and more backward lean. By their somewhat tenser postures, women are said to convey submissive attitudes. Their general bodily demeanor and bearing is more restrained and restricted than men's. But society seems to expect this. Greater circumspection in body movement appears to be required of women, even in all-female groups.

It is considered unfeminine or unladylike for a woman to "use her body too forcefully, to sprawl, to stand with her legs widely spread, to sit with her feet up, . . . to cross the ankle of one leg over the knee of the other." And depending on the type of clothing she wears, "she may be expected to sit with her knees together, not to sit cross-legged, or not even to bend over."[48] Although restrictions on women have relaxed recently, these prescriptions of propriety still seem to be in force. Women who break them are not fully accepted.

The public posture, stance, and gait prescribed for and expected of women can be extremely awkward. In an effort to demonstrate to our classes how inconvenient some of the expected behaviors for women are, the authors have borrowed a six-item list of exercises for men for our male students to perform in class. While the result has often led to merriment over the inability of some males to deftly and convincingly perform these actions, the exercises have served to make both the women and the men aware of the extent to which many of our learned behaviors are unexamined.

The following six sets of directions illustrate the inconvenience of the public postures permitted to women:

1 Sit down in a straight chair. Cross your legs at the ankles and keep your knees pressed together.
2 Bend down to pick up an object from the floor. Each time you bend, remember to bend your knees so that your rear end doesn't stick up, and place one hand on your shirt-front to hold it to your chest.
3 Run a short distance, keeping your knees together. You will find you have to take short, high steps.
4 Sit comfortably on the floor. . . . Arrange your legs to that no one can see [your underwear]. Sit like this for a long time without changing position.
5 Walk down a city street . . . . Look straight ahead. Every time a man walks past you, avert your eyes and make your face expressionless.
6 Walk around with your stomach pulled in tight, your shoulders thrown back, and your chest out. . . . Try to speak loudly and aggressively in this posture.[49]

Gesture

"Every little gesture has a meaning all its own." So go the lyrics of an old song. And though students of kinesics, like Birdwhistell, hasten to warn us that no position, expression, or movement ever carries meaning in and of itself, research in nonverbal communication seems to indicate that patterns of gesture can tell us a good deal about ourselves and others. An important consideration is this: "The more men and women interact in the way they have been trained to from birth without considering the meaning of what they do, the more they become dulled to the significance of their actions."[50] Outsiders who observe a culture different from their own can sometimes spot behavioral differences, and the significance of these differences, which those engaged in the behaviors are not conscious of. Some observational studies help us get outside ourselves and draw our attention to details we might otherwise not notice.

In viewing nonverbal gestures of preschool children, one investigator discovered that girls exhibited more pronounced bodily behavior when they were with other girls than when they were with boys. When they were paired with boys, they tended to be quieter. She concluded that society's expectations of sex differences in social behavior are evident even in the very young child and that different behavior is expected from boys than from girls.[51]

Hand gestures are generally considered to function as illustrators, and they also serve to reveal our emotional states, intentionally or unintentionally. Hand and foot movements can sometimes signal messages at variance with our words. There seems to be some indication that in approval-seeking situations, women use more gesticulations than do males.[52] Since some studies have shown males talk more, interrupt more, and in general dominate conversations more than females, perhaps women resort to nonverbal expression more frequently. Some have concluded that women are molded into more patterns of behavior than are men, for there are more implicit and explicit rules as to how females should act and behave. Although initiative, innovation, boldness, and action are encouraged in males, such qualities are discouraged in women. "Forced to submerge their individual impulses and energies, women tend to express themselves more subtly and covertly."[53] The nonverbal channel may be an outlet for women's covert and more subtle expression.

Peterson did a videotaped study of nonverbal communication that occurred during verbal communication between male-male, female-female, and female-male pairs. Subject pairs were university students, and each pair held a two-minute conversation on the topic of their choice. She studied number of gestures, kinds of gestures, gestures used primarily by females, and gestures used primarily by males. She focused on hand, leg, and foot movements.[54]

She found that overall, the number of gestures displayed by males exceeded the number exhibited by females, regardless of the sex of the conversation partner. Males displayed about the same number of gestures when conversing with either sex. However, females displayed significantly more gestures with males than with other females.

As for differences between the sexes in the kinds of gestures used, she observed the following:

Females
• tend to leave both hands down on chair arms more than males do
• arrange or play with their hair or ornamentation more

Males
• use sweeping gestures more than females
• use arms to lift or move the body position more
• use closed fist more
• stroke chin more
• sit with ankle of one leg crossing the knee of the other more

- tend to exhibit greater amount of leg and foot movement
- tap their feet more

In addition, certain gestures seemed to be performed exclusively by females and others by males in this study. An asterisk indicates a more frequently performed gesture.

Female
- hand or hands in lap
- tapping hands
- legs crossed at knees*
- ankles crossed, knees slightly apart

Male
- stretching hands and cracking knuckles
- pointing*
- both feet on floor with legs apart
- legs stretched out, ankles crossed
- knees spread apart when sitting*

General observations that Peterson made in regard to nonverbal gestures and the sexes include the following:

1 Both males and females seemed to be more relaxed with the same sex than with the opposite sex, except in two cases where subjects knew each other previously. Subjects exhibited more nervous gestures with the opposite sex.

2 Exclusively male and exclusively female gestures seemed to be reserved for conversations with the same-sex partner. Pointing generally occurred only between males, and hands in the lap between females.

3 Some traits appeared related to gender display. Females handled their hair and clothing ornamentation a great deal more in front of men than women. Men were significantly more open with their leg position and kept their feet on the floor with legs apart when conversing with other males. With females, however, the men nearly always crossed one ankle over the other knee.

4 Both males and females tended to display a greater number and greater diversity of gestures with the opposite sex. There seemed to be more foot movement with the same sex.

Peterson believed her study indicated that nonverbal communication fills a dual role in conversation for the sexes. Gesture serves as an illustrator and supplement to the verbal channel, and it acts as a means of gender display. Since certain movements occurred exclusively in same-sex pairs, it is possible that separate nonverbal languages are occurring. There seemed to be a greater display of dominant gestures by males—closed fist, pointing, sweeping gestures. Open and dominant gestures may be signals of power and status.

Clothing, grooming, and physical appearance

Physical attractiveness and the artifacts that contribute to appearance affect communication and communication responses. One study explored the use of physical attractiveness by females as a means of obtaining higher grades from male college professors. The researcher found no differences in the scores of females and males on a Machiavellian scale, which attempts to get at traits associated with those who use any means (cunning, duplicity, or whatever) to achieve a goal. He hypothesized that cultural and social norms may prevent females from using obvious exploitative or deceptive tactics, so they utilize more socially acceptable, but more covert, means and take advantage of their physical attractiveness.[55]

After comparing faculty ratings of women's pictures with their grade-point averages and position in the family, he found a correlation between physical attractiveness, grade point average, and being firstborn and female. Women who used more exhibiting behavior were probably more memorable to professors and thus fared better on grades. They tended to sit in the front of the room more often or come to see the professor after class or during the instructor's office hours more frequently. Using a series of questions about body measurements, the researcher determined that, as he had hypothesized, the firstborn females did indeed seem more aware of and socially concerned about their looks.

In some respects, claimed the researcher, he found the results "not at all surprising," for "the suggestion that *men* live by their *brains* and *women* by their *bodies* was made as far back as Genesis." He found the implications of these results "rather frightening" since the results suggest that the male college professor is a "rather put-upon creature, *hoodwinked* by the *male* students (later born) and *enticed* by the *female* students (first born)." (Italics added.) Whether the reverse is true for female college professors ought to be a subject for future research. As consolation, however, the writer noted that when a sample of 22 faculty members was given the Machiavellian scale, their average scores, compared with the scores of students in the study, showed them to be significantly more manipulative.

In another experiment, a girl was made up to look unattractive in one setting and attractive in another. The girl read aloud and explained some questions to listeners. Results showed the attitudes of the male students were modified more by the girl in the attractive condition than in the unattractive condition. However, this result was true for a male audience only.[56]

Several years ago, the authors videotaped two women and two men speakers giving persuasive pro and con speeches about the merits of debate. Each gave his or her speech twice: once when made up to look unattractive with nose putty; subtle, unflattering make-up touches; and poorly styled hair and again when made up to look attractive. Clothing was kept constant. The speeches were such that, in the first set, the pro speech was constructed as a cogent and well-reasoned talk and the con speech as poorly reasoned and dogmatic. In the second set, the pro speech was poorly reasoned and dogmatic, and the con speech was cogent and well-reasoned. Listeners, who were college students, took a pretest concerning their attitudes on the subject and then took a post-test following the talks.

Results showed that physical attractiveness did have a persuasive effect on both sexes in their acceptance of the views of the speakers. Both speakers of the well-reasoned talks had a greater persuasive effect when made up in their attractive state, as was anticipated. An interesting result was a difference in persuasiveness that occurred between the females and males in their unattractive states, whether they gave the poorly reasoned or well-reasoned talk. The males made up unattractively were only slightly less effective than in their attractive state. However, there was considerable difference in the influence of the females, depending on physical state. Unattractiveness in the female caused a decidedly more negative reception of her views. In fact, in one of the videotaped versions the unattractiveness of the female who delivered the cogent pro talk weighed so heavily that the attractive female who answered with the poorly reasoned and ill-constructed con speech had the greater impact on listeners. Both females and males seemed more accepting of arguments or views from an unattractive male than from an unattractive female. Males were most negative toward the unattractive female's stand. Another study showed that regardless of sex, attractive people are rated high on character in credibility scales.[57]

In a "Dear Abby" reader survey mentioned earlier, readers were asked to indicate what they noticed first about the opposite sex. Results indicated that women noticed physique first. Added the columnist: "But nearly every female who wrote that it is the first thing she *notices* about a man also wrote that it was certainly not the most *important*." A close second was grooming, including attire. Most women who wrote that they noticed a man's physical attributes first emphasized that it is "what's on the inside" that counts. Women placed much more importance on behavior than the men did in their survey. Responses from men indicated that men noticed bosoms first. After bosoms, a woman's figure, or whole torso, ranked next in importance, with some male respondents terming themselves "leg men" or "fanny fanciers."[58]

These studies, as well as the casual responses to the "Dear Abby" column, seem to reflect our cultural emphasis on a man's activity—what he does—and on a woman's being—how she appears. This was graphically illustrated last year at Arizona State University, where one of the

In one experiment, the views of unattractively made-up males were accepted more readily than those of unattractively made-up females.

authors teaches. Several men stationed themselves in front of the student union with signs numbered from 4 to 9. They proceeded to rate women on campus by holding numbered signs over the women's heads as they passed. After the university police were summoned to investigate complaints, one of the self-appointed raters explained lamely, "It seemed to me that everyone in the area enjoyed what we did, except for one woman who asked for a sign so she could rate one of us. Of course I refused."[59]

Perhaps women in our society are expected to be more visible and to reveal more of their bodies than men are. Men are sometimes described as more modest than women. This, at least, was the view of Hollywood dress designer Edith Head during an interview. Head has dressed stars from Cary Grant to Robert Redford, and Carole Lombard to Elizabeth Taylor. "Men for the most part are annoyingly modest in the fitting room if a woman is present," she says. "Women, however, will peel off to their panties and bras with male fitters present without batting an eye." She cited Clark Gable as one who was extremely modest. He could bare his chest, but if he had to unzip his trousers and expose his shorts, "he would bluster and blush and make amusing remarks about what he had to go through for his art." Head mentioned a friend who was the head nurse in a urology clinic. "She faces up to male modesty all day long and it's a bore. Women, for the most part, do not have false modesty about their bodies." The references to modesty in all instances refer to mixed company.[60]

The significance of clothing should be noted in passing. Different clothing types for the sexes is believed by some to have important social ramifications. Of course, pants suits for women have been and are worn extensively today, along with skirts, yet pants remain the symbol of the male and skirts the symbol of the female. Some writers question the notion that skirts should be worn by females. The roles of both sexes are changing. Women are moving out of old patterns, acquiring more education, exercising control of their childbearing, and getting political power. Yet, say some, they are still dressed in an archaic manner, with hips, thighs, and stomach skirted protectively or defensively hidden. Specialists in the history of dress indicate that the differentiation of pants and skirts goes back many years.[61] Skirts may have been important once to protect the one who bore children because in early ages humans were more at the mercy of the elements, dangerous animals, human enemies, and high infant mortality. Presumably then, men were in awe of women's life-giving power and felt it necessary to "protect women's gateway to birth with skirts."

The division of pants from skirts may have been made originally because men needed freedom of leg movement when hunting and working the soil. Women needed skirts to hide their children under if danger threatened, to protect their own bodies, and to form convenient carrying places to convey children or food. Moira Johnston, a clothing historian, believes that skirts later became a male constriction for females because men feared the power a woman's childbearing ability gave her. So they consigned her sexuality to hiding. Later on the skirt became a form of modesty and an attempt to conceal seductive areas.

According to Johnston, the silhouette loosens when morals are lowered, as for example in the Roaring Twenties with the loose flapper dress. After the Second World War, when women went back to the home and to childbearing, fashions became more constrictive and restrictive. Women wore clothing cinched at the waist, with long, full skirts and high-heeled shoes. In looking at the history of feminism, one writer notes the significance of clothing.[62] Before the 1920's women's clothing was confining and cumbersome. Casting aside the old corsets and long skirts may have had more significance for women's emancipation than women's suffrage had.

Henley notes that women's clothing today is fashioned to be revealing, but it still restricts women's body movement. Women are not supposed to reveal too much, and this requires guarded movement in many cases. Another concomitant of clothing designed to reveal physical features is that, unlike more loose-fitting men's clothing, there are not convenient pockets in which to carry belongings—hence women's awkward purses. Some men's clothing styles today are styled for closer fit, and this may account for the carrying bags and purselike cases made and sold for males in some places. A clothing historian hypothesized that women have not freed themselves more from skirts and other restrictive women's clothing styles because they fear "terror of disorientation, and dissolution of identity."[63]

In reflecting upon contemporary feminine clothing styles, the authors of this book would add this thought: The popular pants suit has had a liberating effect upon females. No longer must knees be tightly drawn together when sitting. Pants allow much more freedom of movement when walking, sitting on the floor, or lounging on the arm of a chair. The traditional need to cover and protect the female genital area by posture and apparel has been reduced considerably.

The so-called unisex look in clothing has freed women's bosoms from the protective slouch and the provocative thrust. It would be interesting to do research on how attitudes of the wearer are changed when clothing habits are modified. Perhaps it is true that we are what we wear!

Use of space

The way we use space can convey nonverbal messages. It has been observed that dominant animals and dominant human beings keep a larger buffer zone of personal space surrounding them that discourages violation than do subordinate animals and humans.[64] Dominant persons are not approached as closely as persons of lesser status. But research has shown that women are approached by both sexes more closely than men.

In one study, university students carried tape measures with them and when approached by anyone who began a conversation, each student measured the distance nose-to-nose between themselves and each speaker.[65] Distances between pairs varied according to sex, age, and race. It was found that generally women were approached more closely than men by both women and men. Perhaps the envelope of inviolable space surrounding women is generally less than men's, and women are perceived as less dominant. Further, compared with men, women stand more closely to good friends but farther away from those they describe just as friends. It has been suggested that perhaps women are more cautious until they have established close relationships. In addition, it has been found that less distance is maintained between women and members of both sexes when they are sitting.[66] There are indications that compared with men, women perceive their own territory as being smaller and as being more open to influence by others.[67] Both sexes have been found more wary of the approach of males than of females.[68]

Studies on crowding offer some insight on differences in personal space between the sexes. One researcher observed groups of people in crowded and uncrowded rooms during one-hour periods of time. Re-

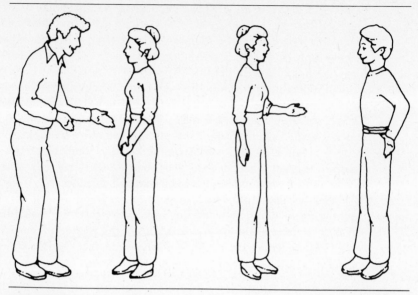

Research shows that women are approached more closely than men by both sexes.

sults showed that generally men had more negative reactions to crowding. They liked others less and considered them less friendly. In general, they found the situation more unpleasant, and they became more contentious and distrustful. In contrast, women found the experience pleasanter, liked others more, and considered them friendlier than men did.[69]

It appears that women's territory is perceived as smaller by both males and females. Women may be more tolerant of, or accustomed to, having their personal space breeched by others. This may also be an indication that they are considered to be of lower status by those with whom they interact.

Certainly control of greater territory and space is a characteristic we associate with dominance and status. Superiors have the prerogative of taking more space. They have larger houses, estates, cars, offices, and desks, as well as more personal space in body spread. Inferiors own less space and take up less space personally with their bodies. Females generally command less space. For example, a study showed that women are less likely to have a special and unviolated room in the home.[70] The male may have his den where "nothing is to be touched." Some will counter that the woman has her territory—her kitchen or sewing room. But this space is often as infinitely invadable for the woman working in it as her time while she is doing so. We are all familiar with Archie Bunker's special chair. While men may have their own chair in a house, women rarely do.

Seating arrangement is another space variable. Research shows that female/male status is evident in the way people seat themselves.[71] At rectangular tables, generally the "head" position (the seat at either end of the table) is associated with higher status. Subjects in a study were shown paper-and-pencil diagrams of rectangular tables and asked how they would locate themselves with regard to a person of higher, lower, or equal status and of either sex. When subjects were asked to choose the seat they would take upon arriving first and then to name the seat the other would then take, approximately twice as many females as males would sit side by side, and this was more frequent in relation to a low-status than a high-status person. When asked to choose which seat the other would take upon arriving first, respondents tended to put others at an "end" chair. This tendency was greater for a high-status male authority figure. Subjects were also told to imagine that either Professor Henry Smith or Professor Susan Smith were there. Twice as many subjects would choose the head chair for themselves when the female professor was there as when the male professor was there.

Students in one of our classes did some observational studies of female and male students walking across the Arizona State University campus during peak class-change times in the heavily trafficked mall areas. They found people of both sexes tend to cut across females' paths more frequently.

When female-male pairs approach each other on the street, apparently women are expected to walk around men, according to the results of one study.[72] Nineteen woman-man pairs were observed, and in 12 out of the 19, the woman moved out of the man's way. In only 3 cases did the man move, and in the remaining 4 instances both moved. When women approached women or men approached men, however, about half of the time both moved out of each other's way. The rest of the time only one person moved.

Also in regard to space, it has been observed that women's general body comportment is restrained. Often their femininity is judged according to how little space they take up. Women condense or compress; men expand. Whereas males use space expansively, women, by the way they cross their legs, keep their elbows to their sides, and maintain a more erect posture, seem to be trying to take up as little space as possible. Novelist Marge Piercy, describing a character teaching movement to a theater group, put it well:

Men expanded into available space. They sprawled, or they sat with spread legs. They put their arms on the arms of chairs. They crossed their legs by putting a foot on the other knee. They dominated space expansively. Women condensed. Women crossed their legs by putting one leg over the other and alongside. Women kept their elbows to their sides, taking up as little space as possible. They behaved as if it were their duty not to rub against, not to touch, not to bump a man. If contact occurred, the woman shrank back. If a woman bumped a man, he might choose to interpret it as a come-on. Women sat protectively using elbows not to dominate space, not to mark territory, but to protect their soft tissues.[73]

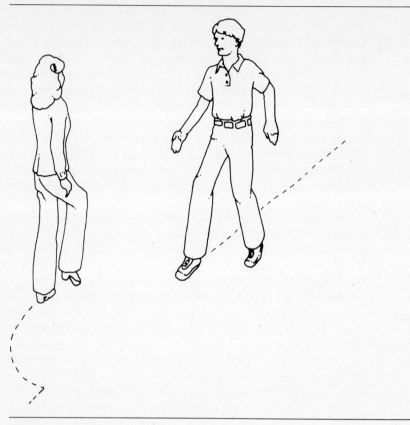

Females tend to move out of a male's way.

Touch

Touch has been the object of some investigation. Most research seems to show that females are touched by others more than males are. Mothers have been found to touch their female children more than their male children from the age of six months on.[74] In one study of touch, the researcher gave a questionnaire to students concerning which parts of the body are touched most often and by whom. He found that females are considerably more accessible to touch by all persons than males are. Friends of the opposite sex and mothers did the most touching.[75]

Further investigation showed that mothers touched their sons more than fathers did, and fathers touched their daughters more than their sons. Daughters touched their fathers more than sons did, and sons touched their mothers more than they touched their fathers. In other words, fathers and sons tended to refrain from touching each other, but other touching interaction in the family was about equal. As for body regions, mothers touched daughters in more places than they did sons. Fathers touched daughters in more places than they did sons. Fathers also were touched by their daughters in more places than they were by their sons. Males touched their opposite-sex best friends in more regions than females reported touching their opposite-sex friends. So in three of the four comparisons, touch by fathers, touch by mothers, and touch by opposite-sex friends, females were touched more. The mean total being-touched score for women was higher than for men. Also, whereas women's opposite-sex friends touched them the most, men's opposite-sex friends touched them the least.[76]

The pattern of greater touching by males has been interpreted by some as a reflection of sexual interest and greater sexual motivation of men. Henley does not accept this, since she finds research does not support greater sexuality in males than females. Rather, she regards touching as a sign of status or power. Touching is an invasion of one's personal space and involves the deference or lack of deference accorded to the space surrounding the body. Touching between intimates can symbolize friendship and affection. But when the pattern of touching is not reciprocal, and both parties do not take equal touch privileges, it can indicate power and status.[77] An observer of the touch system in a hospital noted that although the doctors might touch other ranks to convey support or comfort, other ranks tended to feel it would be presumptuous to return a doctor's touch, and particularly to initiate it.[78]

One investigation of touching involved some 60 hours of observing incidents of touching in public. Intentional touch with the hand was recorded, as well as whether the touch was returned. Sex, age, and approximate socioeconomic status of the persons observed was also noted. Results showed that higher-status persons touched lower-status ones significantly more frequently. Comparing touching between the sexes, men touched women at a greater rate, when all else (age and apparent socioeconomic status) was equal. When other things were unequal, for example if women had a socioeconomic status advantage, the woman would be the more likely one to initiate touch.[79]

The pattern of sexual status showed up primarily in outdoor settings (shopping plaza, beach, college campus, and so forth) rather than in indoor interaction (bank, store, restaurant, doctor's office, and so on). It was suggested that because outdoor interaction is more public, it may necessitate stricter attention to signals of power. Indoor interaction is more informal and encourages more relaxed power relationships. When people are indoors, power can probably be more easily communicated by other cues than touching. Subtle cues, such as eye movements, gestures, and voice shifts, can convey reminders of status easily. But outdoors gross, larger physical acts, such as touching, seem to be required.

Goodall describes one use of touch among chimpanzees.[80] A chimpanzee, after being threatened or attacked by a superior, may follow the aggressor around, screaming and crouching to the ground or

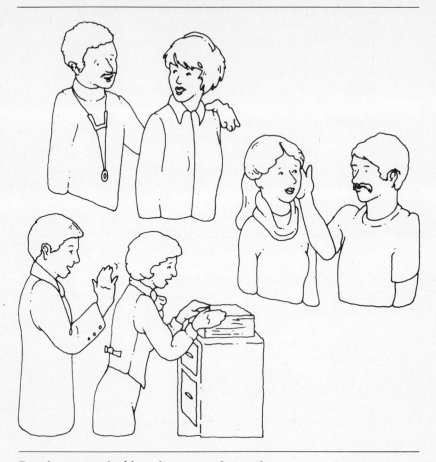

Females are touched by others more than males are.

holding out his or her hand. The chimpanzee is begging a reassuring touch from the superior. Sometimes the subordinate chimpanzee will not relax until he or she has been touched or patted and embraced. Greetings also reestablish the dominance status of one chimpanzee in relation to the other. For example, Olly would greet Mike by holding out her hand toward him. By this gesture she was acknowledging his superior rank. Mike would touch, pat, or hold her hand or touch her head in response to her submission. These gestures of dominance and submission observed in primates seem to occur among humans as well. As with apes, the gestures are probably used by humans to maintain and reinforce the social hierarchy by reminding lower-status persons of their position in the order and by reassuring higher-status people that those of lesser rank accept their place in the pecking order.

An informal test of the significance of touch that is not reciprocated and the authority it symbolizes would be to ask ourselves which person in each of the following pairs would be more likely to touch the other—to lay a hand on the back, put an arm around the shoulder, tap the chest, or grasp the wrist: master and servant; teacher and student; pastor and parishioner; doctor and patient; foreman and worker; executive and secretary; police and accused; lawyer and client.[81] If status can explain touch differences in other groups, it seems reasonable to accept this as a factor in female/male touch differences as well.

A considerable amount of touching of women is so much a part of our culture that it goes virtually unnoticed. It occurs when men guide women through the door, down the stairs, into the car, across the street; when they playfully lift women; when they pat them on the head, or playfully spank them; and in many other instances. Males seem to have greater freedom to touch others. When used with objects, touching seems to connote possession. This may apply to attitudes about women as well. As Henley and Thorne express it: ". . . the wholesale touching of women carries the message that women are community property. They are tactually accessible just as they are visually and informationally accessible."[82]

It is interesting to consider the difference in interpretation of touch by the sexes. This difference seems to support the idea that touch is used as a sign of status or power among the sexes. The difference in female/male perspective can be shown by an illustration which Henley relates.[83] A woman was at a party one evening and saw a male friend of both her and her husband. At various times in the evening he would come up and sit with his arm around her. This she interpreted as a friendly gesture, and she reciprocated the action with friendly intent. However, later the man approached her in private and made sexual advances. When the woman expressed surprise at his suggestions, he replied, "Wasn't that what you were trying to tell me all evening?" The point is that women do not interpret a man's touch as necessarily a sexual invitation, but men often interpret a woman's touch in that way. Touch, of course, can be either. It can be a gesture of power or of intimacy. But touch as a gesture of power will appear to be inappropriate if it is used by one not having power.

Since women are often subordinate, touching by women will be perceived as a gesture of intimacy or sexual invitation rather than power. One would not anticipate that they would be exercising power. In addition, viewing a woman's gesture as a sexual invitation is not only complimentary to the man, but it can put the woman at a disadvantage. By putting a narrower sexual interpretation on what she does and placing her in the position of a sex object, she is effectively placed outside the arena of primary social interaction.

Status and nonverbal communication

We have looked at a number of nonverbal behavior differences exhibited by females and males. One theoretical thread running through

Table 6.1 Asymmetrical Nonverbal Cues

Cues	Superior [male]	Subordinate [female]
Eyes	Look or stare aggressively Look elsewhere while speaking	Lower eyes, avert eyes, look away, blink Watch speaker while listening
Face	No smile or frown Impassive, not showing emotions	Smile Expressive facial gestures, showing emotions
Posture Bearing	Relaxed, more body lean Loose legs, freed arms, non-circumspect positions	Tense, more erect Tight, legs together, arms close to body
Gestures	Larger, more sweeping, forceful, such as pointing	Smaller, more inhibited
Touch	Touches other	Does not touch other or recip- rocate touch, cuddles, or yields to the touch
Use of space	Expands, uses more space	Condenses, contracts, takes as little space as possible
Distance	Maintains larger envelope of space Closer Approaches closer, crowds Cuts across other's path Walks into other's path	Maintains smaller envelope of space More distant Approaches more distant, re- treats, yields Gives way Moves out of the way
Clothing	Loose, comfortable	Constraining, formfitting

Source: Some of the material in this table was suggested by Nancy Henley, "Examples of Some Nonverbal Behaviors with Usage Differing for Status Equals and Nonequals, and for Women and Men," *Siscom '75: Women's (and Men's) Communication,* ed. Barbara Eakins, Gene Eakins, and Barbara Lieb-Brilhart (Falls Church, Va.: Speech Communication Association, 1976), Table 1, p. 39; and Henley, "Gestures of Power and Privilege. Examples of Some Nonverbal Behaviors with Usage Differing for Status Equals and Nonequals, and For Women and Men," *Body Politics: Power, Sex, and Nonverbal Communication* (Englewood Cliffs, N.J.: Prentice-Hall, 1977), Table 5, p. 181.

much of the discussion is the concept of asymmetry, or nonreciprocality of behavior, that exists between nonequals in status. Female/male differences have been seen to roughly parallel those between superiors and subordinates in status, suggesting a status and power differential behind the socialization of the sexes. Table 6.1, which is based on theory and some research cited previously, categorizes behavior cues used by females and males.

To a certain extent we may say that behavior is cued. Perhaps women give gestures of submission because they have been shown gestures of dominance. In some situations some people may use gestures of dominance because they have been shown gestures of acquiescence or ingratiation by the others with whom they interact. One writer had some sobering pronouncements to make concerning many of the so-called womanly gestures.[84] She indicated that submission in women is conveyed by such behaviors as smiling, averting the eyes, or lowering or turning the head. Self-improvement specialists would grow pale on hearing her definition of charm: "Charm is nothing more than a series of gestures (including vocalizations) indicating submission!" Staunch feminists would probably add a hearty "amen."

Changing or manipulating the signals and indicators of power or subordination may not go very far toward transforming the inequities of society. But perhaps by becoming aware of what we are signifying or are responding to nonverbally, we can better gain control over our lives and more readily ensure that our actions and responses are more conscious, more voluntary or, at least, less automatic. We may surprise ourselves by the extent to which we can affect the patterns and relationships in our lives.

Suggested activities

1 Observe smiling and frowning facial expressions of persons interacting with each other in various settings: a classroom, the checkout line at a grocery store, a restaurant, a bank, a gas station, a coffee break, a meeting of an organization.
   a. Who smiles most frequently? Least frequently?
   b. What purposes do smiles and frowns seem to serve?
   c. What relation do sex, status, and personality bear to smiling and nonsmiling behavior, in your opinion?
Suggested format for recording results:

Persons interacting	Sex	Approx. age	Estimated socioeconomic position	Smiling when	Unsmiling or frowning when
1					
2					
3					
4					
5					

2 Observe hand gestures of persons during conversational interaction.
   a. What differences do you see in hand movements of females and males in conventional gestures (commonly understood through

custom and convention), such as pointing, fist-clenching, palm open, palm downward, warning gesture, and so forth?

    b. What differences do you see in descriptive gestures (so big, this high, shaped like this, moving thus)?

    c. What differences do you see in the number of gestures used?

    d. What differences do you see in the size of gestures— large or small, sweeping or restrained?

3 Compare female and male children in use of gesture. How do they differ in use of gesture
    a. in same-sex groups?
    b. in opposite-sex groups?

4 Observe pedestrian traffic on the street, in grocery or department stores, in shopping malls, in corridors and halls of buildings—wherever people are forced to encounter one another on the move.

    a. Which persons tend to give way or walk around the other?

    b. Which tend to persist or continue on their course, claiming the right of way?

    c. Formulate some hypotheses on the basis of your observations. Suggested format to record results:

Walkers	Sex	Approx. age	Estimated socioeconomic status	Claimed right of way	Gave way
1					
2					
3					
4					
5					

5 Heighten your awareness of touch in relation to those around you.

    a. Keep a careful record for a period of several days of the following facts:

        (1) Who touches you? Do you reciprocate?

        (2) Whom do you touch? Does the person reciprocate?

    b. What significance does sex of the person seem to have in your results?

    c. How does status figure in your findings?

    d. Does setting appear to influence your results in any way?

    e. What insights have you developed about touch and its use in our culture?

Suggested format for recording results:

	Sex	Age	Socioeconomic status	Returned	Setting
Toucher Person touched					
Toucher Person touched					
Toucher Person touched					

7 Speaking up: communicating with confidence

In this concluding chapter, the temptation is almost irresistible to impose upon the reader's consciousness layer after layer of communication prescriptions. Certainly, the investigation of the subject of women's and men's communication has left both authors with a set of conclusions, some shared and some held individually, about how to improve discourse between the sexes. As a result of our research, one assumption that we initially held as a tentative and tenuous hypothesis has crystallized into a clear belief—that arbitrary role assignments in a sexist society are barriers to communication between all people; women, men, and children. So-called sex-role socialization has created and has perpetuated attitudes and behaviors that are injurious to all.

We recognize that many women and men are content with the old order and have no wish to alter or to radicalize their modes of communication. It would be simplistic and naive to state that they should feel perfectly free to continue in these accustomed ways. The point is that communication involves everyone in society. Generally, we are not free to pick and choose those with whom we communicate. To the degree that one person communicates in a style that demeans and subordinates another; to that degree is human dignity eroded. Since we cannot choose to live and communicate in a vacuum, we must recognize that we all share the burden of freeing our discourse from sex-role power wielding.

In attempting to collect and organize our suggestions for improving female-male communication, we must confess to experiencing a certain degree of frustration and apprehension. So much consideration needs to be given to a variety of issues. To this end, we offer the following suggestions distilled from our research and conclusions. To arrange these suggestions into some meaningful form for consideration by the reader, we have divided the material into verbal and nonverbal categories.

Verbal behavior

It seems obvious that the improvement of communication between the sexes requires attitudinal and behavioral changes. Certainly attitude and behavior are interdependent, and any alteration of one will mean consequential change for the other. Just where to interrupt the existing chain from thought to deed is debatable. It seems to us that the most positive change ought to begin with altering attitudes. In recent times we have seen much lip service paid to the concept of equal rights in the form of token behavioral modification, but little real progress toward human equality has been effected. The consistent theme running through this book is that an asymmetric relationship exists between women and men in society. The research in all areas of human communication consistently underscores the dominant power status of males and the dominated, subordinated status of females. One of the most compelling appeals for human equality in communicating is made by J. B. Priestley:

I am convinced that good talk cannot flourish where there is a wide gulf between the sexes, where the men are altogether too masculine, too hearty and bluff and booming, where the women are too feminine, at once both too arch and too anxious. Where men are leavened by a feminine element, where women are not without some tempering by the masculine spirit, there is a chance of good talk.[1]

One of the ways to alter the asymmetric power relationship is to expose myths and stereotypes about female-male communication. The common belief that women talk more than men is not supported by research. If this very obvious stereotype is false, then how many other popular notions about female-male communication can stand the test of powerful inquiry? We need a massive program of on-going empirical study about our traditional beliefs concerning talk between and within the sexes.

In business the attitudes of women and men about women need to change. Right now the business organization fits the male experience. Nancy Conklin, talking about discourse in the organizational setting, notes the difference between women's and men's talk. Women's talk is often characterized as gossiping, an activity of low value. If they try to elevate themselves above gossiping—that is, to be like men—women are said to be carrying on conversation, which is still regarded as a form of entertainment. Men, in contrast, are said to have discussions in conferences and meetings, and they talk "straight from the shoulder" in "a businesslike way." Conklin urges women to develop strategies for dealing with the new interactional situations presented by board-room and locker-room talk. Women should either acquire the style of speaking accepted for these occasions or establish their credentials as group members with their own forms of communication. Women must "recognize, legitimize, and creatively develop their own speech genres. Clearly the back-slapping joke will never be a female vehicle."[2]

The point has been made that technology is having a homogenizing effect on women and men. The mystique of the great fighting male and the earth-mother female is one of the casualties of modern change.

This iconoclasm ought to be accelerated and encouraged. Especially in the world of work a spirit of androgeny should be encouraged. Women and men ought to be encouraged to accept whatever business position or to enter any profession they prefer without any social stigma attached to their selection of these roles.

In small-group communication men are expected to "pro-act." They analyze, clarify, evaluate, and control the flow of conversation. Women are expected to react. They stroke, positively reinforce, listen, reduce tension, and restore unity. There is no evidence that men or women are more biologically suited to pro-act or react. Nor is either role superior to the other. Courses in effective group communication should stress listening as a passive skill for men to acquire and using humor as an active skill for more women to acquire.

Also, women need to take another look at their existing communication skills. Instead of deprecating them and wishing to be more like their male counterparts, they need to expand these skills, as well as to acquire so-called male techniques.

Conklin argues that women have "acute sociolinguistic sensitivity," whereby they become attuned to the behavior of others, relying on external norms. As a result, women may allow themselves to be defined by standards that are not necessarily their own. They may become estranged from their own culture and from other women. But women's sensitivity to the behavior of others can be turned into a powerful advantage for them. There are strengths in their skills in manipulating language, in their repertoire of stylistic devices, in their attentiveness to others' communication. "Both in dealing with the power structure, and in dealing with other women, an awareness of the ebb and flow below the surface of the interaction is a useful tool and also a valuable weapon."[3]

It is easier to identify biases in language than to remedy or eliminate them. To change male-oriented language, some writers suggest replacing the traditional generic *man*, *he*, or *himself* with inclusionary language or sex-blind substitutes. The following are possibilities:[4]

1 Words such as *people, human beings, humanity, the human race, citizens,* or *inhabitants* can substitute for *man* or *mankind*.
2 Occupational, activity, or other kinds of terms ending in *-man* can be replaced by words that can include persons of either or both sexes. For example, "insurance man" can be replaced by "insurance agent," "cameraman" by "camera operator," "mailman" by "mail carrier," "foreman" by "supervisor," "workman" by "worker," "cleaning woman" by "office cleaner," and so on.
3 Terms such as *one, you,* "she and he," or "he and she" can be substituted for the masculine pronoun *he*. For example, "As for the new employee, *she or he* can . . . ," or "*one* can . . . ," or "*you* can. . . ."
4 The sentence can be recast in the plural. Use "Students can program

7.1 Inclusive pronouns

	Miller and Swift	Densmore
Nominative replacement for "she or he"	*Tey* "Each should do as *tey* pleases."	*She* (which includes in one word "she and he") "Each should do as *she* pleases."
Objective replacement for "her and him"	*Tem* "Each will get what is coming to *tem*."	*Herm* (includes *her* and *him*) "Each will get what is coming to *herm*."
Possessive replacement for "his and her"	*Ter(s)* "One should make *ter* own way." "One should normally claim only what is rightfully *ters*."	*Heris* (includes *her* and *his*) "One should make *heris* own way." "One should normally claim only what is rightfully *heris*."

their studies themselves," rather than "Each student can program his study himself."

Some writers favor creating new forms. They find "he or she" or "he/she" awkward, the use of "they" or plural construction ungrammatical or inconvenient at times, and exclusionary tactics absurd in some instances. Several have suggested some new generic personal pronouns. Miller and Swift and Densmore, for example, have suggested sets of personal pronouns to replace the old male-oriented ones.[5] They are shown in Table 7.1.

Other authorities, however, hold the opinion that it is unrealistic to expect to get rid of generic masculine terms and that it makes more sense to adjust to them. While suggesting that we try to avoid misleading use of the word *man*, Nilsen advocates concentrating efforts on educating people to the way language is.[6] She feels that special efforts should be directed toward using illustrations that include both females and males whenever a generic masculine term such as *man* or *he* is used, to emphasize its use as an all-inclusive term.

Of course, new word usage seems awkward at first. But as Paul Gray commented in *Time*, the words that survive over time are generally those that are useful, "and the useful ones sound better as the years go by."[7] Certainly we are all aware of the vigorous campaigns waged over the past few years to eliminate sexist terms from our speaking. We recall the awkward early attempts to use the term *chairperson* in place of the familiar *chairman*, and we note that the word falls rather easily from the tongue and on the ear today. It is probably not too difficult to adjust to new, nonsexist words.

One of the authors willingly admits that the experience of writing this book has made him extremely conscious of the inequities imposed upon women by our language. There is a tendency to dismiss the importance of eliminating sexist references from our communication primarily because the overall massive effect of biased language usage is missed when one considers only one or two specific examples of linguistic prejudice. To insist on eliminating the generic *man* from *chairman* appears to be nitpicking until one realizes the impact on behaviors and attitudes of thousands of such references in our language.

We have seen at least some of the ways that language is used in relation to the sexes. Although language is regarded as a monolith that is not readily shifted or remolded, some suggestions have been offered for chipping away the rough spots in regard to some of the presumed inequities in naming and describing women and men:

1 More gender balance should be obtained in language usage. More examples featuring females could be added in our discourse and some of the active, courageous, assertive, and confident traits traditionally reserved for males could be attributed to females as well. Conversely, some of the sensitive, caring, amenable traits generally ascribed to females could be portrayed in males.

Graham writes of a "new archetypal woman" that took form when she was involved in composing a wordbook for children.[8] This new woman appeared in many of the examples used to clarify word definitions. The new type of woman had brains and courage. From the *A* page, where for the word *abridge* she quoted the Nineteenth Amendment, to the *Z* page where "she zipped down the hill on her sled," she exhibited active and participative characteristics in addition to being gentle, kind, and understanding: "When she 'plunged into her work, her mind began to percolate' (not her coffee). . . . 'She prided herself on her eloquence' (not on the sheen of her freshly waxed floors)."

Along with the "new liberated woman" to be depicted in our communication, writers have suggested a new liberated man. Such a man could be described with more than the one-sided tradition-bound male characteristics of being active, courageous, and ready to compete. Like his female counterpart, he too could be vulnerable. Like the examples contained in the wordbook for children, he could be portrayed variously with human traits: "striving to attain mastery over his emotions"; "his resolve began to waver"; or "tears welled up in his eyes." His career options can be expanded, as in "He studies typing at night," or "He teaches kindergarten."

2 Another suggestion is to guard against language that treats either sex as objects or things in a dehumanizing manner. Women should be described in terms other than their physical or sexual attributes, especially in contexts where men are described by their skills, professional positions, or mental attributes.

3 Language that treats women as possessions or extensions of men or solely in terms of their relationship to men should be avoided.

4 Some publishers' guidelines have been formulated to help writers to utilize language that provides fair and balanced treatment for the sexes and to avoid language that can reinforce sexist attitudes and assumptions. These guidelines, of course, are helpful in oral communication as well. The adoption of many of the feminists' suggestions in leading publishers' guidelines has lent support to the feminist position on language. We have summarized one such set of guidelines, which seems to be quite broad in scope, issued by McGraw-Hill. See "Nonsexist Treatment of Women and Men," pages 186–187.

An ideal system of human communication ought to stress the following values:

1 cooperation
2 interpersonal discovery
3 self-realization
4 self-expression

However, until such a utopia emerges, women need to recognize the predominant male value system that governs communication. This system includes

1 promoting individual supremacy
2 getting the competitive edge
3 generating and directing personal action to wrest success and reward from the world

Such a value acquisition will require a special, ultrasophisticated form of assertiveness training for females who wish to acquire the concomitant communication skills. Many behavioral forms will need to be changed.

Stylistically, women will be perceived as more authoritative and sure of themselves as they learn to use fewer tag questions. These expressions give the impression that a woman is not sure of herself or hesitates to express an opinion. Though their use may indicate politeness, it can be a sign and a statement of weakness. The same holds true for qualifiers and disclaimers. They indicate a willingness to be disputed and also convey the speaker's wish not to be held accountable for the statement and willingness to accept other views.

With regard to their speaking voices, women need to recognize that male intonation patterns are currently associated with authority. Many women will need to develop authoritative vocal patterns. Especially they should strive to avoid using the intonation of a question when making a declarative statement, since this connotes uncertainty.

Nonsexist treatment of women and men

1 Avoid typecasting in careers and activities.

    a. Avoid typecasting women in traditional roles.

    b. Avoid showing men as subject to the "masculine mystique" in interests, attitudes, and careers.

    c. Attempt to break job stereotypes for women and men.

    d. Show married women who work outside the home and emphasize the point that women have choices about their marital status.

    e. Address course materials to students of both sexes.

    f. Portray women and girls as active participants the same as men and boys, and not only in connection with cooking, sewing, shopping.

2 Represent members of both sexes as whole human beings.

    a. Represent women and men with human (not just feminine or masculine) strengths and weaknesses. Characteristics praised in males should also be praised in females.

    b. As in portraying men and boys, show women and girls also as active, logical, accomplishing.

    c. Sometimes show men as quiet and passive, fearful and indecisive, just as women are sometimes portrayed.

3 Accord women and men the same respect and avoid either trivializing women or describing them by physical attributes when men are described by mental attributes.

    a. Avoid: (1) girl-watching tone and sexual innuendoes; (2) focusing on physical appearance; (3) using female-gender word forms, such as "poetess"; (4) treating women as sex objects or as weak and helpless; (5) making women figures of fun or scorn (not "the weaker sex" but "women"; not "libber" but "feminist").

    b. Avoid references to general ineptness of males in the home or dependence on women for meals.

    c. Treat women as part of the rule, not the exception (not "woman doctor," but "doctor"). Avoid gee-whiz attitude toward women who perform competently.

    d. Represent women as participants in the action, not as possessions of men. (Not, "Pioneers moved West, taking their wives and children," but "Pioneer women and men moved West, taking their children.")

    e. Avoid portraying women as needing male permission to act.

4 Recognize women for their own achievements.

5 In references to humanity at large, use inclusive language.

    a. Avoid the generic word *man,* since it is often not interpreted broadly. (Not "mankind" but "humanity"; not "manmade" but "artificial"; not "primitive man" but "primitive peoples."

b. Avoid the generic pronouns *he, him, his* in reference to a hypothetical person or humanity in general.

> (1) Reword sentence. (Not "The average American drinks his coffee black," but "The average American drinks black coffee.")
>
> (2) Recast into plural. ("Most Americans drink their coffee black.")
>
> (3) Replace the pronoun with "one," "you," "he or she," and so forth.
>
> (4) Alternate male and female expressions and examples: "I've often heard supervisors say, 'She's not the right person for the job,' or 'He lacks the qualifications.'"
>
> (5) If the generic *he* is used, explain in the preface and in the text that the reference is to both females and males.

c. Replace occupational terms ending in *-man* by inclusive terms. (Not "businessman," but "business manager"; not "fireman," but "fire fighter.")

d. Avoid language that assumes all readers are male. (Not "you and your wife," but "you and your spouse.")

6 Use language that designates and describes the sexes equally.

a. Use parallel language for women and men. (Not "man and wife," but "husband and wife" or "man and woman." Not "Billie Jean and Riggs," but "King and Riggs" or "Billie Jean and Bobby.")

b. Identify women by their own names, not in terms of their roles as wife, mother, and so forth. (Not "Nehru's daughter," but "Indira Gandhi.") Avoid unnecessary reference to marital status.

c. Use terms that include both sexes; avoid unnecessary references to gender.

d. Use nonsexist job titles. (Not "maid" and "house boy" but "house-" or "office cleaner.")

e. Avoid linking certain pronouns with certain work or occupations. Pluralize or else use "he or she" or "she and he". (Not "the shopper . . . she," but "shoppers . . . they"; not "the breadwinner . . . his earnings," but "the breadwinner . . . her or his earnings.")

f. Do not always mention males first. Alternate the order: "women and men," "gentlemen and ladies," "she or he."

Women need to talk up more in business and social settings.

In terms of language, women need to expand their semantic space. Any labels that mark women as secondary beings should be vigorously expunged. Such innocuous-sounding words as "poetess," "songstress," and "authoress" denote the feminine referent and connote a reduction of potency. They innocently and insidiously mark the special female example, which does not belong to the general masculine order and is, consequently, inferior by implication.

Women are recognizing that too often their identity depends on a male. She is "John's wife" or "Mrs. James Smith" or "Harry's widow." Even the contemporary practice by feminists of hyphenating their maiden name with their husband's name seems less than satisfactory to some. They are just adding another male-derived name—that is, their father's surname—to their husband's name.

The Buckley law has guaranteed everyone freedom of access to personal letters of recommendation and dossiers. One can anticipate that letters describing men only in terms of their work capabilities and women in terms of their social graces will be discarded in favor of descriptions that stress performance capabilities equally.

These are some of the techniques of verbal behavior that women need to acquire. Now let us turn to a consideration of nonverbal behavior.

Nonverbal behavior

What kinds of correctives can we apply to our nonverbal behaviors? It has been suggested that it is easier to change nonverbal interaction patterns than it is to alter speech patterns. Some possible suggestions for women include the following:

1 Examine your own style of nonverbal behavior for sex-stereotyped patterns and particularly for self-defeating and destructive patterns. Try to recognize when you are intimidated. If you do respond with submissive behaviors, perhaps then it will be because you have made the conscious decision that this is appropriate behavior, and it will not be an automatic or reflexive response on your part.

2 Monitor yourself for the ever-present nervous grinning and uneasy smiling that is often cued by dominance behavior from another. Smile when you are happy, when you feel good. Phony smiling may weaken your position because your smile will be relatively meaningless.

3 When someone looks at you, don't drop your eyes. Look back. Stare someone in the eye, if appropriate.

4 Touch others when you feel it is appropriate and be aware of who is touching you. Refuse to accept tactual assertion of authority. Do not submit to another's will because of the subtle implication of that person's touch. Remove your hands from the grasp of persons who hold them too long and remove another's hands from your person when such a touch or grasp is unsolicited and unwanted.

5 Be more relaxed in demeanor and assume an open posture. Do not be afraid to claim moving-around space for yourself.

6 Do not be too quick to make way for the other person as you approach one another. Expect some "give" from the other as well. Establishing eye contact or looking at the other, rather than averting the eyes, is useful in such a situation.

7 Free your gestures to express your feelings. Avoid histrionics but do not hesitate to point, clench your fist, or use other forceful gestures if they convey your ideas well.

8 Be aware of small gestures, such as the head tilt, that can do you a disservice when you are looking directly at another. Tilting your head can mitigate the directness of your gaze by giving it an air of submissiveness.

9 Remember you have some responsibility for socializing the next generation. Be aware of what you are nonverbally teaching children, in terms

Women should refuse to accept subtle tactual assertion of authority.

of submissiveness and acquiescence to power and privilege, through nonverbal communication.[9]

Possible suggestions for males include the following:

1 Begin to develop an awareness of what you are signaling and signifying nonverbally.
2 Restrain your invasions of others' personal space if it is not by mutual consent.
3 Avoid touch when it may be unsolicited, is not likely to be reciprocated, and seems to be used as an assertion of status or authority.
4 Keep in mind you may sometimes benefit by "losing your cool" and feeling free to express your emotions.
5 Monitor your reactions to being touched by women.
6 Remember you have some responsibility for socializing the next generation. Be aware of what you are nonverbally teaching children in terms of dominance, power, and privilege through nonverbal communication.

Because of women's apparent disadvantageous position in society, many writers feel women should develop supportive gestures with other women. Positive ways for women, and people in general, to give attention and support nonverbally to other women during communication interaction include the following:

1 Look at women when they speak.
2 Respond and react.
3 Do not interrupt.
4 Do not distract with noises or gestures while they are talking.
5 Develop gestures of mutual support, such as these behaviors: eye contact, leaning forward, nodding (where appropriate and genuine), and smiling (where appropriate and genuine), open posture.[10]

One of the authors, who had the opportunity to interview Nancy Henley on an educational television program about women and communication, put a question to her concerning some practical nonverbal communication behaviors. Her answer was particularly cogent and so we present part of the transcribed dialogue here, with the interesting detail she gave:

Eakins: I'd like some practical advice. It fascinates me that you type nonverbal cues either as a sign of power or as ways to manipulate. Take me. Let's say I'm a teacher and I'm going to a faculty meeting. I have an idea that I particularly want to communicate to that superior. Now starting me at the doorway, how do you suggest that I use nonverbal communication for myself in a way that is useful in this group?
Henley: Now this is certainly good practical application. When you walk in the door, it would be best not to be encumbered with a lot of things that you would drop or would be falling off of you in various ways. You may turn things around and give an appearance of ineptness and awkwardness that sometimes hampers you. I think men have evolved ways of carrying or moving more efficiently with things they have to carry. Of course, we know ways of striding through the door, standing up straight, with a kind of military bearing. You don't want to look like you're sneaking in, slumped over. . . .
    It depends on whether it's a room with fixed chairs. . . . If it's a conference room of some sort, this is an environment that can be modified. I mean things can be changed. . . . [Because] if there's a way you can change something, it gives you more control. [You have] a feeling of power in your environment, if you have created it in some way yourself: if you want chairs closer together or farther apart, if you want to sit at a particular end of the table. Look where people are sitting. If you feel there are two sides, . . . look at how the other side is sitting. . . . Will it be to your advantage to have your side infiltrate, in order to keep them from talking to each other? Or does your side need more organization so that you should sit together for solidarity? When in the meeting, try to move and jiggle as little as possible. The demeanor of the professional is this unmoving, unruffled kind of air. . . . The person . . . does not [confuse] things by . . . random movement, putting things [in] and taking things out and moving things around. Sitting quietly [he] is still . . . himself and shows some power. When people are talking, discussing things, making points, certainly it's good to be attentive at all times. If you have to let your attention stray

Women should not hesitate to use forceful gestures that convey their ideas well.

at times, it's better to let your attention stray when the opposition is speaking. (General laughter)

Show support for people on your side, of your position. Or if you are the one who is putting the position forward, see that people who are supporting you show attentiveness. Attentiveness is shown by leaning forward, by looking at the speaker, by not making noises. I have been at a meeting, a board meeting, when in fact women were on one side and the board of directors . . . were on the other. And there was one, an executive officer I think, who had a pipe. And he used it, whether he knew it or not, in very cynical ways. There are so many things you can do with a pipe, if you're a man, [that] affect the situation. He had them all down pat. That's where I realized that manipulating the amount of gestures and the noise you make affects the interaction of the situation. He would bang his pipe; he would fool around with it . . . when we were talking. He would get up and go to the water cooler . . . when we were speaking. . . .

And then I realized that [it is] important [that] none of us do that to each other; that we show respect and stay in our seats. And if we have to get up and go get something, wait until someone else, someone on the other side, [has the floor]. It's a matter of both showing solidarity and believing [in] yourself putting forth the point. When you get up to speak . . . don't hesitate. Speak straight out. The question of interrupting may come up. If someone starts to interrupt, women are very likely to give in. Recent research [done] in public places, where two people are speaking together, showed that 96 percent of the interruptions are done by males. It was just fantastic. Women almost never interrupted, and with very little overlap of speech, even in women. When someone else starts talking, they stop. Now if you're speaking and someone starts talking when you have the floor, . . . just train yourself not to shut up. It's new; it's going to be a difficult feeling; you just have to not give in. Keep talking. What happens with some men, or other people who interrupt, [is that] you may go on talking together for a long time. And it may be embarrassing. But you have at least illustrated or demonstrated to them that you are talking, you have the floor, and they have interrupted.

. . . If you notice powerful people or men who have a lot of confidence, you find they do not smile often when they're making their case. I don't say that people shouldn't smile. What advice I do give to women is to smile when they're happy and feel like smiling. And do not smile if they're not happy, because this is when a lot of smiling is done. That does weaken your position.[11]

Conclusion

Our intention in writing this book has been to assemble a body of meaningful research on women's and men's communication, to suggest the implications of this research, and to draw some specific conclusions from this research. Certainly much more study needs to be done to clarify how and why sex roles are power related and how these roles affect human communication and, indeed, our personal happiness.

All the communication variables that were examined—voice, language, nonverbal behavior, verbal strategies, and so forth—are interrelated. We intuitively feel that, if at various points along this interlinking chain, some positive alterations are made, the whole communication network will be changed for the better. The alterations will be difficult and they will be painful. However, it has been said that no personal growth occurs without pain, and lack of personal growth is even more painful.[12]

Suggested activity

Decide for yourself. You have been looking at and cataloguing many differences in communication behavior.

a. Describe the communication behaviors that are characteristic of you now.

b. Indicate what new verbal and nonverbal elements you plan to incorporate into your communication behavior in the future.

c. Draw up the complete communication profile that you believe is best suited to you.

Notes

1 The sexes: discriminations without differences and differences that discriminate

1 "You Are Woman, I Am Man," *Funny Girl* (New York: Columbia Records), side 2. Copyright © 1963 and 1964 by Bob Merrill and Jule Styne. Chappell-Styne, Inc. and Wonderful Music Corp., owners of publication and Allied rights throughout the world. Chappell & Co., Inc., sole and exclusive agent. International Copyright Secured. *All rights reserved.* Used by permission.

2 Susan Fogg, "The Ups and Downs of Human Behavior Cycles," *Chicago Daily News*, 20 April 1973, p. 23, reporting on research by Michael Wallerstein, Jr., and Nancy Lee Roberts; Estelle Ramey, "Men's Cycles," *Ms.*, Spring 1972, pp. 8–15.

3 Some of the preceding material was suggested in a discussion by Letha Scanzoni and Nancy Hardesty, *All We're Meant to Be: A Biblical Approach to Women's Liberation* (Waco, Tex.: Word Books, 1974), pp. 74–75.

4 Ray Birdwhistell, "Masculinity and Femininity as Display," *Kinesics and Context* (Philadelpha: University of Pennsylvania Press, 1970), pp. 39–46.

5 Ann Oakley, *Sex, Gender and Society* (New York: Harper & Row, Publishers, 1972), pp. 16–17.

6 Sheila Tobias, "Educating Women for Leadership" (KNOW, Inc., P.O. Box 86031, Pittsburgh, Pa. 15221).

7 Inge K. Broverman, Donald M. Broverman, Frank E. Clarkson, Paul S. Rosen-krantz, and Susan R. Vogel, "Sex-Role Stereotypes and Clinical Judgments of Mental Health," *Journal of Consulting and Clinical Psychology* 34 (1970): 1–7.

8 Estelle Ramey (Address before the National Association for Women Deans, Administrators and Counselors, Spring 1973). Reprinted by permission of the National Association for Women Deans, Administrators, and Counselors and the author.

9 Cheris Kramer, "Female and Male Perception of Female and Male Speech" (Paper delivered at the Annual Meeting of the American Sociological Association, San Francisco, August 1975).

10 Alex C. Sherriffs and John P. McKee, "Qualitative Aspects of Beliefs about Men and Women, *Journal of Personality* 25 (1957): 451–464. Copyright 1957 by Duke University Press.

11 Paul S. Rosenkrantz, Helen Bee, Susan R. Vogel, Inge Broverman, and Donald M. Broverman, "Sex-Role Stereotypes and Self-Concepts in College Students," *Journal of Consulting and Clinical Psychology* 32 (1968): 287–295.

12 H. J. Ehrlich, *The Social Psychology of Prejudice* (New York: John Wiley & Sons, 1973); Inge Broverman, Susan R. Vogel, Donald M. Broverman, Frank E.

Clarkson, and Paul S. Rosenkrantz, "Sex-Role Stereotypes: A Current Appraisal," *Journal of Social Issues* 28 (1972): 59–78.

13 Sheila Tobias, "Educating Women for Leadership" (n.p.).

14 Michael M. Reece, "Masculinity and Femininity: A Factor Analytic Study," *Psychological Reports* 14 (1964): 123–139; Helen Franzwa, "Woman's Place in Semantic Space" (Address to the Speech Communication Association Convention, Chicago, 1974).

15 Helen Franzwa, "Woman's Place in Semantic Space"; Kay Deaux, *The Behavior of Men and Women* (Belmont, Cal.: Brooks/Cole Publishing Co., 1976), p. 37.

16 "Up the Ladder, Finally," *Business Week*, 24 November 1975, pp. 58–68.

17 Jessie Bernard, *Academic Women* (University Park: Pennsylvania State University Press, 1964), pp. 255–257.

18 Phillip Goldberg, "Are Women Prejudiced against Women?" in *Toward a Sociology of Women*, ed. Constantina Safilios-Rothschild (Lexington, Mass.: Xerox College Publishing, 1972), pp. 10–13.

19 Joan M. Gaulard, "*Mary Hartman, Mary Hartman*: An Analysis of Satire in the Violation of Soap Opera Stereotypes" (Address to the Speech Communication Association Convention, San Francisco, December 1976). Stephanie Harrington, "Mary Hartman: The Unedited, All-American Unconscious," *Ms.,* May 1976, pp. 55, 98. © Ms. Magazine Corp., 1976. Reprinted with permission.

20 Stephanie Harrington, "Mary Hartman: The Unedited, All-American Unconscious," pp. 55, 98; Joan M. Gaulard, "*Mary Hartman, Mary Hartman*: An Analysis of Satire in the Violation of Soap Opera Stereotypes."

21 Jessie Bernard, *The Sex Game* (New York: Atheneum, 1973), pp. 328–329.

22 Georgie Anne Geyer, "New Female Value System Throws the Men," *Los Angeles Times*, 11 February 1976, p. 7, reporting Matina Horner's research. Copyright © 1976, Los Angeles Times. Reprinted with permission.

23 Ibid., p. 7.

24 William Labov, *Language in the Inner City: Studies in the Black English Vernacular* (Philadelphia: University of Pennsylvania Press, 1972).

25 Sheila Tobias (Address to a Workshop for Faculty Women, Arizona State University, April 1975).

26 The idea for this illustration came from Nancy Henley, "Nonverbal Interaction and Personal Growth," *Siscom '75: Women's (and Men's) Communication*, ed. Barbara Eakins, Gene Eakins, and Barbara Lieb-Brilhart (Falls Church, Va.: Speech Communication Association, 1976), p. 144; see also Nancy Henley, *Body Politics: Power, Sex, and Nonverbal Communication* (Englewood Cliffs, N.J.: Prentice-Hall, 1977), pp. 92–93.

27 Ramey (Address before the National Association for Women Deans, Administrators and Counselors, Spring 1973).

28 Nancy Henley mentions this among other possible factors in "Power, Sex, and Nonverbal Communication," *Siscom '75: Women's (and Men's) Communication*, pp. 36–38.

29 Birdwhistell, "Masculinity and Femininity as Display," pp. 39–46.

30 Henley, "Power, Sex, and Nonverbal Communication," *Siscom '75: Women's (and Men's) Communication*, p. 37.

31 Birdwhistell, "Masculinity and Femininity as Display"; Nancy Henley, "Power, Sex, and Nonverbal Communication," *Berkeley Journal of Sociology* 18 (1973–74): 2–3.

32 Henley, "Power, Sex, and Nonverbal Communication," *Siscom '75: Women's (and Men's) Communication*, p. 37.

33 Henley, "Power, Sex, and Nonverbal Communication," *Siscom '75: Women's (and Men's) Communication*, p. 37; see also Henley, *Body Politics: Power, Sex, and Nonverbal Communication*, p. 209.

34 "Any Woman with Her Own Income Ought to Know How to Protect It," New

York Life advertisement, *Time*, 26 May 1975, p. 63; "Career Education Materials Show Sex Bias," *Springfield News-Sun*, 1 August 1976.

35 Barrie Thorne and Nancy Henley, "Difference and Dominance: An Overview of Language, Gender, and Society." Reprinted with permission of Newbury House Publishers from *Language and Sex: Difference and Dominance*. Edited by Barrie Thorne and Nancy Henley (Rowley, Mass.: 1975), pp. 15–16.

36 Diana W. Warshay, "Sex Differences in Language Style," in *Toward a Sociology of Women*, ed. Constantina Safilios-Rothschild (New York: John Wiley & Sons, 1972), pp. 3–9.

37 F. Kluckhohn, "Dominant and Variant Value Orientations," *Personality in Nature, Society, and Culture*, ed. C. Kluckhohn and H. A. Murray, 2d ed. (New York: Alfred A. Knopf, 1955), pp. 342–357.

38 Robin Williams, *American Society*, 3d ed. (New York: Alfred A. Knopf, 1970), p. 575; Warshay, "Sex Differences in Language Style."

39 Konrad Lorenz, *On Aggression* (New York: Harcourt, Brace and World, 1963), p. 103.

40 Bernard, *The Sex Game*, p. 60.

41 Ibid., p. 62.

42 Bernard Shaw, Preface to *Saint Joan*. By permission of the Society of Authors on behalf of the Bernard Shaw Estate.

43 Robin Lakoff, "Language and Woman's Place," *Language in Society* 2 (1973): 76. By permission of Cambridge University Press.

44 Thorne and Henley, "Difference and Dominance," p. 29.

45 Nancy Henley, "Power, Sex, and Nonverbal Communication," *Berkeley Journal of Sociology* 18 (1973–74): 1–3.

2 Power, sex, and talk

1 Nancy Henley, "Power, Sex, and Nonverbal Communication," *Berkeley Journal of Sociology* 18 (1973–74), p.7. © 1973.

2 Based on: Discussion by Henley, "Power, Sex, and Nonverbal Communication," p. 7; Roger Brown, *Social Psychology* (Glencoe, Ill.: Free Press, 1965), Copyright © 1965 by The Free Press of Glencoe; Roger Brown and M. Ford, "Address in American English," *Journal of Abnormal and Social Psychology* 62 (1961): 375–385; Roger Brown and A. Gilman, "The Pronouns of Power and Solidarity," *Style in Language,* ed. T. A. Sebeok (Cambridge, Mass.: Technology Press, 1960).

3 D. I. Slobin, S. H. Miller, and L. W. Porter, "Forms of Address and Social Relations in a Business Organization," *Journal of Personality and Social Psychology* 8 (1968): 292.

4 Erving Goffman, *Interaction Ritual* (New York: Doubleday & Company, Anchor Books, 1967), p. 64.

5 Henley, "Power, Sex, and Nonverbal Communication," p. 8; see also Nancy Henley and Barrie Thorne, "Womanspeak and Manspeak: Sex Differences and Sexism in Communication, Verbal and Nonverbal," in *Beyond Sex Roles*, ed. Alice Sargent (St. Paul, Minn. : West Publishing Company, 1977), p. 209.

6 Cheris Kramer, "Sex-Related Differences in Address Systems," *Anthropological Linguistics* 17 (1975): 198–210.

7 Barbara Eakins and Gene Eakins, "Verbal Turn-Taking and Exchanges in Faculty Dialogue," *Papers in Southwest English IV: Proceedings of the Conference on the Sociology of the Languages of American Women*, ed. Betty Lou Dubois and Isabel Crouch (San Antonio, Tex.: Trinity University, 1976), pp. 53–62.

8 Marion M. Wood, "The Influence of Sex and Knowledge of Communication Effectiveness on Spontaneous Speech," *Word* 22 (1966): 117–137.

9 Marjorie Swacker, "The Sex of the Speaker as a Sociolinguistic Variable." Reprinted with permission of Newbury House Publishers from *Language and Sex: Difference and Dominance*, Edited by Barrie Thorne and Nancy Henley (Rowley, Mass., 1975), pp. 76–87.

10 Wood, "The Influence of Sex and Knowledge of Communication Effectiveness on Spontaneous Speech," p. 117.

11 David W. Johnson, *Reaching Out: Interpersonal Effectiveness and Self-Actualization* (Englewood Cliffs, N.J.: Prentice-Hall, 1972), p. 239.

12 Swacker, "The Sex of the Speaker as a Sociolinguistic Variable," p. 81.

13 Robin Lakoff, "Language and Woman's Place," *Language in Society* 2 (1973): 45–79; Otto Jespersen, "The Woman," *Language: Its Nature, Development and Origin* (London: Allen and Unwin, 1922), pp. 249–250.

14 Robin Lakoff, *Language and Woman's Place* (New York: Harper & Row Publishers, 1975), p. 54; Jesperson, "The Woman," p. 249.

15 Jespersen, "The Woman," pp. 245–247; Lakoff, *Language and Woman's Place,* pp. 54–55.

16 Shulamith Firestone, *The Dialectic of Sex* (New York: William Morrow & Company, 1970), p. 100.

17 Howard M. Rosenfeld, "Approval-Seeking and Approval-Inducing Functions of Verbal and Nonverbal Responses in the Dyad," *Journal of Personality and Social Psychology* 4 (1966): 597–605.

18 Fred L. Strodtbeck and Richard D. Mann, "Sex Role Differentiation in Jury Deliberations," *Sociometry* 19 (1956): 3–11.

19 William F. Soskin and Vera P. John, "The Study of Spontaneous Talk," *The Stream of Behavior*, ed. Roger Barker (New York: Irvington Publishers, Inc., 1963), pp. 228–281.

20 Soskin and John, "The Study of Spontaneous Talk," p. 270.

21 Cheris Kramer, "Sex Differences in Communication Behavior" (Paper presented at the Speech Communication Association Convention, Houston, Tex., December 1975).

22 Lakoff, "Language and Woman's Place," pp. 53–56.

23 Ibid., pp. 56–57.

24 Maryann Hartman, "A Descriptive Study of the Language of Men and Women Born in Maine around 1900 as It Reflects the Lakoff Hypotheses in 'Language and Woman's Place,'" *Papers in Southwest English IV: Proceedings of the Conference on the Sociology of the Languages of American Women*, ed. Betty Lou Dubois and Isabel Crouch (San Antonio, Tex.: Trinity University, 1976), pp. 81–90.

25 Betty Lou Dubois and Isabel Crouch, "The Question of Tag Questions in Women's Speech: They Don't Really Use More of Them, Do They?" *Language in Society* 4 (1974): 289–294.

26 Lynette Hirschman, "Analysis of Supportive and Assertive Behavior in Conversations" (Paper presented at meeting of Linguistic Society of America, July, 1974), abstracted in Barrie Thorne and Nancy Henley, *Language and Sex: Difference and Dominance* (Rowley, Mass.: Newbury House, 1975), p. 248.

27 Pam Moore, "You May Not Like It But . . . Here's the Truth about Disclaimers," *Psychology Today* (1975), pp. 96–99. Reprinted by permission of Psychology Today Magazine. Copyright © 1975 Ziff-Davis Publishing Company. John Hewitt and Randall Stokes, "Disclaimers," *American Sociological Review* 40 (1975): 1–11.

28 The preceding discussion and examples of the addition of particles in polite speech were based on Lakoff's section on requests in "Language and Woman's Place," pp. 56–57.

29 Lynette Hirschman, "Female-Male Differences in Conversational Interaction" (Paper presented at meeting of Linguistic Society of America, December 1973); Research conducted by Hirschman, Jill Gross, Jane Savitt, and Kathy

Sanders, abstracted by Thorne and Henley, *Language and Sex: Difference and Dominance,* p. 249.
30 Lakoff, *Language and Woman's Place*, pp. 73–74.
31 Jessie Bernard, *The Sex Game* (New York: Atheneum, 1973), p. 153.
32 Angele M. Parker, "Sex Differences in Classroom Intellectual Argumentation," (M.S. thesis, Pennsylvania State University, 1973).
33 Phyllis Chesler, *Women and Madness* (New York: Doubleday & Company, 1972), p. 268.
34 Hirschman, "Female-Male Differences in Conversational Interaction."
35 W. Edgar Vinacke, "Sex Roles in a Three-Person Game," *Sociometry* 22 (1959): 359; John R. Bond and W. Edgar Vinacke, "Coalitions in Mixed Set Trends," *Sociometry* 24 (1961): 61–75; Thomas C. Uesugi and W. Edgar Vinacke, "Strategy in a Feminine Game," *Sociometry* 26 (1963): 75–88.
36 Aileen D. Ross, "Control and Leadership in Women's Groups: An Analysis of Philanthropic Money-Raising Activity," *Social Forces* 26 (1958): 130.
37 Eileen Morley, "Women's Thinking and Talking" Case 9-477-055, International Case Clearing House, Graduate School of Business Administration, Harvard University, 1976).
38 Angele M. Parker, "Sex Differences in Classroom Intellectual Argumentation."
39 Sheila Tobias (Speaking at Worship for Faculty Women, Arizona State University, April 1975).
40 Judith Bardwick, "Psychological Conflict and the Reproductive System," *Feminine Personality and Conflict*, ed. Judith Bardwick et al. (Belmont, Cal.: Brooks Cole, 1970), p. 4.

3   Why can't a woman be more like a man? communication between the sexes

1 Jessie Bernard, *The Sex Game* (New York: Atheneum, 1973), pp. 87, 136.
2 Harold Feldman, *Development of the Husband-Wife Relationship* (New York: Cornell University, 1965), p. 28.
3 Eric Berne, *Games People Play* (New York: Grove Press, 1964), pp. 41–47.
4 Bernard, *The Sex Game*, p. 143.
5 Kurt H. Wolff, *The Sociology of Georg Simmel* (New York: The Free Press, 1950), p. 52.
6 Oliver Wendell Holmes, *The Autocrat at the Breakfast Table* (Boston: Houghton Mifflin Company, 1882), p. 52: "One man who is a little too literal can spoil the talk of a whole tableful of men of *esprit.*"
7 Bernard, *The Sex Game*, p. 153.
8 Berne, *Games People Play*, p. 15.
9 Don H. Zimmerman and Candace West, "Sex Roles, Interruptions and Silences in Conversation." Reprinted by permission of Newbury House Publishers from *Language and Sex: Difference and Dominance*, Edited by Barrie Thorne and Nancy Henley (Rowley, Mass. 1975), pp. 105–129.
10 Ibid., p. 107.
11 Ibid., pp. 107–108.
12 Emanuel Schegloff, "Sequencing in Conversational Openings," in *Directions in Sociolinguisitcs,* ed. John Gumperz and Dell Hymes (New York: Holt, Rinehart & Winston, 1972).
13 Harvey Sacks, Emanuel Schegloff, and Gail Jefferson, "A Simplest Systematics for the Organization of Turn-Taking for Conversation," *Language* 50 (1974): 696–735.
14 For example, see Mark L. Knapp, Roderick P. Hart, Gustav W. Friedrich, and

Gary M. Shulman, "The Rhetoric of Goodbye: Verbal and Nonverbal Correlates of Human Leave-taking," *Speech Monographs* 40 (1973): 182–198.
15 Sacks, Schegloff, and Jefferson, "A Simplest Systematics for the Organization of Turn-Taking for Conversation, pp. 696–735, Zimmerman and West, "Sex Roles, Interruptions and Silences in Conversation," pp. 107–111.
16 Judy Kester, report in *Parade Magazine*, 7 May 1972.
17 Lynette Hirschman, "Female-Male Differences in Conversational Interaction" (Paper presented at meeting of Linguistic Society of America, December 1973); Research conducted by Hirschman, Jill Gross, Jane Savitt, and Kathy Sanders, abstracted in Thorne and Henley, *Language and Sex: Difference and Dominance*, p. 249.
18 Phyllis Chesler, "Marriage and Psychotherapy," in the Radical Therapist Collective, eds., produced by Jerome Agel, *The Radical Therapist* (New York: Ballantine Books, 1971), pp. 175–180; Portion quoted in Thorne and Henley, *Language and Sex: Difference and Dominance*, p. 258.
19 Zimmerman and West, "Sex Roles, Interruptions and Silences in Conversation."
20 Ibid., p. 117.
21 Barbara Eakins and Gene Eakins, "Verbal Turn-Taking and Exchanges in Faculty Dialogue," *Papers in Southwest English IV: Proceedings of the Conference on the Sociology of the Languages of American Women*, ed. Betty Lou Dubois and Isabel Crouch (San Antonio, Tex.: Trinity University, 1976), pp. 53–62.
22 Harvey Sacks, "On the Analyzability of Stories by Children," in *Directions in Sociolinguistics,* ed. John Gumperz and Dell Hymes (New York: Holt, Rinehart & Winston, 1972).
23 Zimmerman and West, "Sex Roles, Interruptions and Silences in Conversation," p. 125.
24 Lynette Hirschman, "Female-Male Differences in Conversational Interaction."
25 Fred L. Strodtbeck and Richard D. Mann, "Sex Role Differentiation in Jury Deliberations," *Sociometry* 19 (1956): 3–11.
26 Fred Strodtbeck, "Husband-Wife Interaction over Revealed Differences," *American Sociological Review* 16 (1951): 141–145.
27 Eleanor Maccoby and Carol Jacklin, *The Psychology of Sex Differences* (Stanford: Stanford University Press, 1974), p. 228.
28 Morris Zelditch, "Role Differentiation in the Nuclear Family: A Comparative Study," in *Family, Socialization and Interaction Process*, ed. Talcott Parsons and Robert F. Bales (New York: The Free Press, 1955), pp. 307–352.
29 E. F. Borgatta and J. Stimson, "Sex Differences in Interaction Characteristics," *Journal of Social Psychology* 60 (1963): 89–100; Anatol Rapoport and Albert M. Chammah, *Prisoner's Dilemma, A Study in Conflict and Cooperation* (Ann Arbor: University of Michigan Press, 1965), pp. 191–192.
30 John H. Gagnon, "Sexuality and Sexual Learning in the Child," *Psychiatry* 28 (1965): 214; Bernard, *The Sex Game*, pp. 150–151.
31 Elinor Langer, "The Women of the Telephone Company," *New York Review of Books* 14 (12 March 1970 and 26 March 1970), abstracted in Thorne and Henley, *Language and Sex: Difference and Dominance*, p. 267. © 1970 by *New York Review of Books*.
32 H. T. Moore, "Further Data Concerning Sex Differences," *Journal of Abnormal and Social Psychology* 4 (1922): 81–89. Copyright 1922 by the American Psychological Association. Reprinted by permission.
33 M. H. Landis and H. E. Burtt, "A Study of Conversations," *Journal of Comparative Psychology* 4 (1924): 81–89. Copyright 1924 by the American Psychological Association. Reprinted by permission.
34 "Nobody's Perfect," *I Do, I Do* (Radio Corporation of America, 1966), side 1. Copyright © 1966 by Tom Jones and Harvey Schmidt. Portfolio Music, Inc. owner of publication and allied rights throughout the world. Chappell & Co.,

Inc., administrator. International Copyright Secured. *All rights reserved.* Used by permission.

35 Martin Grotjahn, *Beyond Laughter* (New York: McGraw-Hill Book Company, 1957), p. 52.

36 Rose Laub Coser, "Laughter among Colleagues," *Psychiatry* 23 (1960): 81–95.

37 Bernard, *The Sex Game*, p. 68.

38 Henry Wadsworth Longfellow, "The Song of Hiawatha," Part X.

39 *Phoenix Gazette*, 22 April 1975.

4 Sex patterns in sound

1 G. P. Nerbonne, "The Identification of Speaker Characteristics on the Basis of Aural Cues" (Ph.D. dissertation, Michigan State University, 1967), cited by Mark L. Knapp, *Nonverbal Communication in Human Interaction* (New York: Holt, Rinehart & Winston, 1972), pp. 155–157; L. S. Harms, "Listener Judgments of Status Cues in Speech," *Quarterly Journal of Speech* 47 (1961): 164–168; P. Fay and W. Middleton, "Judgments of Kretschmerian Body Types from the Voice as Transmitted over a Public Address System," *Journal of Social Psychology* 12 (1940): 151–162.

2 J. A. Starkweather, "The Communication Value of Content-Free Speech," *American Journal of Psychology* 69 (1956): 121–123.

3 Knapp, *Nonverbal Communication in Human Interaction*, p. 160.

4 David W. Addington, "The Relationship of Selected Vocal Characteristics to Personality Perception," *Speech Monographs* 35 (1968): 492–503.

5 Ernest Kramer, "Personality Stereotypes in Voice: A Reconsideration of the Data," *The Journal of Social Psychology* 62 (1964): 247–251.

6 Mildred Freburg Berry, Jon Eisenson, *Speech Disorders: Principles and Practices of Therapy*, © 1956, pp. 32–33. Reprinted by permission of Prentice-Hall, Inc., Englewood Cliffs, New Jersey. Louise J. Cherry, "Sex Differences in Child Speech: McCarthy Revisited," *Research Bulletin* (Princeton, N.J.: Educational Testing Service, 1975). Dorothea McCarthy, "Some Possible Explanations of Sex Differences in Language Development and Disorders," *Journal of Psychology* 35 (1953): 155–160.

7 O. C. Irwin and H. Chen, "Development of Speech during Infancy: Curve of Phonemic Types," *Journal of Experimental Psychology* 36 (1946): 431–436.

8 Mildred Templin, *Certain Language Skills in Children: Their Development and Interrelationships* (Minneapolis: University of Minnesota Press, 1957), p. 147.

9 Josef Garai and Amram Scheinfeld, "Sex Differences in Mental and Behavioral Traits," *Genetic Psychology Monographs* 77 (1968): 169–299.

10 Templin, *Certain Language Skills in Children: Their Development and Inter-relationships*, p. 147.

11 H. Winitz, "Sex Differences in Language of Kindergarten Children," *American Speech and Hearing Association* 1 (1959): 86.

12 M. Shatz and R. Gelman, "The Development of Communication: Modifications in the Speech of Young Children as a Function of Listener," *Monographs of the Society for Research in Child Development* 38 (1973), no. 5, serial no. 152, cited by Cherry in "Sex Differences in Child Speech," p. 14.

13 C. Garvey and M. Ben Debba, "Effects of Age, Sex, and Partner on Children's Dyadic Speech," *Child Development* 45 (1974): 1159–1161.

14 P. Menyuk, "Syntactic Structures in the Language of Children," *Child Development* 18 (1963): 407–422.

15 Louise Cherry, "Teacher-Child Verbal Interaction: An Approach to the Study of Sex Differences," in *Language and Sex: Difference and Dominance*, ed. Barrie Thorne and Nancy Henley (Rowley, Mass.: Newbury House, 1975), pp. 172–183.

16 Cherry, "Sex Differences in Child Speech," pp. 4–7.
17 M. Lewis and R. Freedle, "Mother-Infant Dyad: The Cradle of Meaning," in *Communication and Affect, Language and Thought*, ed. P. Pliner, L. Krames, and T. Alloyway (New York: Academic Press, 1973); Cherry, "Sex Differences in Child Speech," pp. 17–18.
18 E. B. Thoman, P. H. Leiderman, and J. P. Olson, "Neonate-Mother Interaction during Breast Feeding," *Developmental Psychology* 6 (1972): 110–118.
19 Michael Lewis, "Parents and Children: Sex-Role Development," *School Review* 80 (1972): 229–240.
20 Cherry, "Sex Differences in Child Speech," p. 18.
21 Jean Berko Gleason, "Code Switching in Children's Language," *Cognitive Development and the Acquisition of Language*, ed. Timothy Moore (New York: Academic Press, 1973), pp. 159–167.
22 Dorothea McCarthy, "Some Possible Explanations of Sex Differences in Language Development and Disorders," pp. 155–160.
23 Ibid.
24 Gleason, "Code Switching in Children's Language," pp. 159–167.
25 McCarthy, "Some Possible Explanations of Sex Differences," pp. 155–160.
26 Ibid.
27 I. G. Mattingly, "Speaker Variation and Vocal Tract Size," *Journal of Acoustical Society of America* 39 (1966): p. 1219, abstract.
28 Jacqueline Sachs, Philip Lieberman, and Donna Erickson, "Anatomical and Cultural Determinants of Male and Female Speech," *Language Attitudes: Current Trends and Prospects*, ed. Roger W. Shuy and Ralph W. Fasold (Washington, D.C.: Georgetown University Press, 1973), p. 75.
29 J. A. Kirchner, *Physiology of the Larynx* (Rochester, Minn.: American Academy of Ophthalmology and Otolaryngology, 1970).
30 G. F. Walker and C. J. Kowalski, "On the Growth of the Mandible," *American Journal Physical Anthropology* 36 (1972): 111–118.
31 Sachs, Lieberman, and Erickson, "Anatomical and Cultural Determinants of Male and Female Speech," pp. 74–84.
32 Ibid., p. 81.
33 Berry and Eisenson, *Speech Disorders*, p. 230.
34 Ibid., pp. 3–4.
35 D. E. Morley, "A Ten-Year Survey of Speech Disorders among University Students," *Journal of Speech and Hearing Disorders* 17 (1952): 25–31.
36 Jon Eisenson and Mardel Ogilvie, *Speech Correction in the Schools* (New York: The Macmillan Company, 1963), pp. 301–302; Berry and Eisenson, *Speech Disorders*, pp. 250–251; Ronald Goldman, "Cultural Influences on the Sex Ratio in the Incidence of Stuttering," reproduced by permission of the American Folklore Society from the *Journal of American Folklore* 69(1), 1967.
37 Berry and Eisenson, *Speech Disorders*, p. 4.
38 Hildred Schuell, "Sex Differences in Relation to Stuttering: Part I," *Journal of Speech Disorders* 11 (1946): 277–298.
39 O. Bloodstein and Sonja M. Smith, "A Study of the Diagnosis of Stuttering with Special Reference to the Sex Ratio," *Journal of Speech and Hearing Disorders* 19 (1954): 459–466.
40 Goldman, "Cultural Influences on the Sex Ratio in the Incidence of Stuttering," pp. 78–81.
41 Berry and Eisenson, *Speech Disorders*, pp. 250–251, 3–4.
42 I. W. Karlin, "Stuttering: Basically an Organic Disorder," *Logos* 2 (1959): 61–63, cited in Charles Van Riper, *Speech Correction: Principles and Methods* (Englewood Cliffs, N.J.: Prentice-Hall, 1972), p. 263.
43 John L. Fischer, "Social Influences on the Choice of a Linguistic Variant," *Word* 14 (April 1958): 47–56.
44 Roger Shuy, Walter Wolfram, and William Riley, *Linguistic Correlates of Social Stratification in Detroit Speech*, Final Report, Project 6-1347 (Washington, D.C.:

U.S. Office of Education, 1967), cited by Thorne and Henley, *Language and Sex*, pp. 240–241.

45 William Labov, *Sociolinguistic Patterns* (Philadelphia: University of Pennsylvania Press, 1972), pp. 242–243; Peter Trudgill, "Sex, Covert Prestige, and Linguistic Change in the Urban British English of Norwich," *Language in Society* 1 (1972): 179–195. By permission of Cambridge University Press.

46 Lewis Levine and Harry J. Crockett, Jr., "Speech Variation in a Piedmont Community: Postvocalic *r*," *Explorations in Sociolinguistics*, ed. Stanley Lieberson (The Hague: Mouton, 1966), pp. 76–98.

47 Frank Anshen, "Speech Variation among Negroes in a Small Southern Community" (Ph.D. dissertation, New York University, 1969), cited by Thorne and Henley, *Language and Sex*, p. 238.

48 Walter Wolfram, *A Sociolinguistic Description of Detroit Negro Speech* (Washington, D.C.: Center for Applied Linguistics, 1969).

49 Labov, *Sociolinguistic Patterns*, p. 243.

50 Shuy, Wolfram, and Riley, *Linguistic Correlates of Social Stratification in Detroit Speech*.

51 Trudgill, "Sex, Convert Prestige, and Linguistic Change in the Urban British English of Norwich," pp. 179–195.

52 William Labov, "Hypercorrection by the Lower Middle Class as a Factor in Linguistic Change," *Sociolinguistics*, ed. W. Bright (The Hague: Mouton, 1966).

53 Trudgill, "Sex, Covert Prestige, and Linguistic Change in the Urban British English of Norwich," pp. 179–195.

54 Eisenson and Ogilvie, *Speech Correction in the Schools*, p. 278.

55 Van Riper, *Speech Correction: Principles and Methods*, p. 150.

56 Letty Cottin Pogrebin, "Down with Sexist Upbringing," *Ms.* 1 (Spring 1972): 28. © Ms. Magazine Corp. Reprinted with permission.

57 Eisenson and Ogilvie, *Speech Correction in the Schools*, p. 278; Berry and Eisenson, *Speech Disorders*, p. 193.

58 G. Lynch, "A Phonophotographic Study of Trained and Untrained Voices Reading Factual and Dramatic Material," *Archives of Speech* 1 (1934): 9–25; E. Murray and J. Tiffin, "An Analysis of Some Basic Aspects of Effective Speech," *Archives of Speech* 1 (1934): 61–83.

59 James Carrell and William Tiffany, *Phonetics: Theory and Application to Speech Improvement* (New York: McGraw-Hill Book Company, 1960), pp. 262–263.

60 Philip Lieberman, *Intonation, Perception, and Language*, Research Monograph no. 38 (Cambridge, Mass.: The M.I.T. Press, 1967), pp. 44–45.

61 D. Crystal, "Prosodic and Paralinguistic Correlates of Social Categories," *Social Anthropology and Language*, ed. Edwin Ardener (London: Tavistock, 1971), pp. 185–206.

62 Mary Ritchie Key, *Male/Female Language* (Metuchen, N.J.: Scarecrow Press, 1975), pp. 71–72. Copyright 1975 by Mary Ritchie Key. Quoted by permission of the publisher.

63 Ibid., p. 71.

64 Ruth Brend, "Male-Female Intonation Patterns in American English," *Proceedings of the Seventh International Congress of Phonetic Sciences, 1971* (The Hague: Mouton, 1972), pp. 866–870, reprinted in Thorne and Henley, *Language and Sex,* pp. 84–87. International copyright secured.

65 Marilou Ell, "The Voice of Authority: Women's Intonation Patterns" (Paper, Department of English, Michigan State University, 1972).

66 Robin Lakoff, "Language and Woman's Place," *Language in Society* 2 (1973): 45–79.

67 Norman Markel, Layne Prebor, and John Brandt, "Bio-Social Factors in Dyadic Communication: Sex and Speaking Intensity," *Journal of Personality and Social Psychology* 23 (1972): 11–13.

68 P. J. Moses, *The Voice of Neurosis* (New York: Grune & Stratton, 1954).

69 G. Legman, *Rationale of the Dirty Joke: An Analysis of Sexual Humor* (New York: Castle Books, 1968), pp. 336–337.

70 Marya Mannes, "Women Are Equal, But—," *Current Thinking and Writing*, ed. Joseph Bachelor, Ralph Henry, and Rachel Salisbury (New York: Appleton-Century-Crofts, 1969), p. 25.

71 Judith Hennessee, "Some News Is Good News," *Ms.* 3 (1974): 25–29. Reprinted by permission of Curtis Brown Ltd., 575 Madison Avenue, New York, New York 10022. Copyright © 1974.

72 Ibid., p. 27.

73 Ben Graf Henneke and Edward Dumit, *The Announcer's Handbook* (New York: Holt, Rinehart & Winston, 1959), p. 19.

74 Hennessee, "Some News Is Good News," p. 27.

75 Many of these questions suggested by Cheris Kramer, "Women's Speech: Separate But Unequal?" *Quarterly Journal of Speech* 60 (1974): 20.

76 Maryann Hartman, "A Descriptive Study of the Language of Men and Women Born in Maine around 1900 as It Reflects the Lakoff Hypotheses in 'Language and Woman's Place,'" *Papers in Southwest English IV: Proceedings of the Conference on the Sociology of the Languages of American Women*, ed. Betty Lou Dubois and Isabel Crouch (San Antonio, Tex.: Trinity University, 1976), pp. 81–90.

77 From "I Ain't Down Yet" by Meredith Willson from *The Unsinkable Molly Brown*. © 1960, 1961, 1966 Frank Music Corp. and Rinimer Corporation. International copyright secured. All rights reserved. Used by permission.

78 *Good Morning, America* (New York: Harcourt Brace Jovanovich, Inc.) Reprinted with permission.

5 When words speak louder than people: the language of gender

1 Patterned after a similar riddle about a doctor and son as told by Casey Miller and Kate Swift, "One Small Step for Genkind," *New York Times Magazine*, 16 April 1972, p. 36.

2 Ethel Strainchamps, "Our Sexist Language," *Woman in Sexist Society*, ed. Vivian Gornick and Barbara K. Moran (New York: Basic Books, 1971), pp. 240–250; Otto Jesperson, *The Growth and Structure of the English Language* (New York: D. Appleton, 1923), p. 1.

3 Miller and Swift, "One Small Step for Genkind," p. 36.

4 Alma Graham, "The Making of a Nonsexist Dictionary," *Ms.* 2 (December 1973): 12–16. © Ms. Magazine Corp., 1973. Reprinted with permission.

5 Ibid., p. 12.

6 Julia P. Stanley, "Paradigmatic Woman: The Prostitute" (Paper presented, in brief versions, at South Atlantic Modern Language Association, 1972; American Dialect Society, 1972; and Linguistic Society of America, 1973). By permission of the University of Alabama Press.

7 Edward Sagarin, *The Anatomy of Dirty Words* (Secaucus, N.J.: Lyle Stuart, 1962), p. 122.

8 Ruth Herschberger, *Adam's Rib* (New York: Harper & Row, Publishers, 1970), pp. 11–12; Julia P. Stanley, "What's in a Label: The Politics of Naming" (Paper presented at symposium on sexism in language, Northeastern Illinois University, Chicago, April 1974, and at the South Central American Dialect Society, Houston, Tex., November 1974).

9 Mary Daly, *Beyond God the Father* (Boston: Beacon Press, 1973), pp. 7–8.

10 Julia P. Stanley, "Prescribed Passivity: The Language of Sexism," in *Views on*

Language, ed. Reza Ordoubadian and Walburga Raffler-Engel (Murfreesboro, Tenn.: Inter-University Publications, 1975).

11 Stanley, "Prescribed Passivity."

12 Cited by Jean Faust, "Words that Oppress," *Women Speaking,* April 1970, reprinted by KNOW, Inc., P.O. Box 86031, Pittsburgh, Pa. 15221.

13 Alleen Pace Nilsen, "The Correlation between Gender and Other Semantic Features in American English" (Paper presented at Linguistic Society of America, December 1973).

14 Faust, "Words that Oppress."

15 Cheris Kramer, "Sex-Related Differences in Address Systems," *Anthropological Linguistics* 17 (1975): 198–210.

16 Robin Lakoff, "Language and Woman's Place," *Language in Society* 2 (1973): 65.

17 Graham, "The Making of a Nonsexist Dictionary," p. 13.

18 Alleen Pace Nilsen, "Sexism in English: A Feminist View," *Female Studies VI,* ed. Nancy Hoffman, Cynthia Secor, and Adrian Tinsley (Old Westbury, N.Y.: The Feminist Press, 1972), pp. 102–109.

19 Patterned after similar comments by Key, *Male/Female Language* (Metuchen, N.J.: Scarecrow Press, 1975), p. 48.

20 Graham, "The Making of a Nonsexist Dictionary," p. 13.

21 Patterned after point 3 in "Guidelines for Equal Treatment of the Sexes in McGraw-Hill Book Company Publications" (New York: McGraw-Hill Book Company, n.d.), p. 4.

22 The last phrase is from Key, *Male/Female Language,* p. 43.

23 Judith Hole and Ellen Levine, "The Politics of Language," *Rebirth of Feminism* (New York: Quadrangle Books, 1971), pp. 222–225.

24 Patterned after similar discussion in Casey Miller and Kate Swift, "Is Language Sexist?" *Cosmopolitan,* September 1972, pp. 89–92, 96.

25 Janet Shuster, "Verb Forms of 'Power and Solidarity': Sex as the Basis of Power" (University of Chicago, 1974).

26 Stanley, "Paradigmatic Woman: The Prostitute."

27 Faust, "Words That Oppress."

28 *Woman–Identified Woman* (New York: Gay Flames, 1972), p. 3, cited by Stanley, "Paradigmatic Woman: The Prostitute."

29 Theodore Reik, "Men and Women Speak Different Languages," *Psychoanalysis* 2 (1954): 3–15, cited by Connie Eble in "How the Speech of Some is More Equal Than Others" (Paper presented at Southeastern Conference on Linguistics, University of North Carolina, 1972).

30 Reik, "Men and Women Speak Different Languages."

31 Stanley, "Paradigmatic Woman: The Prostitute."

32 Nilsen, "Sexism in English: A Feminist View," p. 260.

33 Ibid., p. 260.

34 Stanley, "Paradigmatic Woman: The Prostitute."

35 Nilsen, "Sexism in English: A Feminist View," p. 260.

36 Ibid., p. 264.

37 Nancy Jo Hoffman, "Sexism in Letters of Recommendation," *Modern Language Association Newsletter,* September 1972, pp. 5–6.

38 Ibid., p. 6.

39 Ibid., p. 5.

40 Ibid., p. 6.

41 Key, *Male/Female Language,* p. 97; Faust, "Words That Oppress."

42 Emily Toth, "The Politics of Linguistic Sexism" (Paper presented at Modern Language Association, 1971).

43 Faust, "Words That Oppress."

44 Nilsen, "The Correlation between Gender and Other Semantic Features in American English."

45 Graham, "The Making of a Nonsexist Dictionary," p. 16.

46 Alan Jay Lerner and Frederick Loewe, "The Simple Joys of Maidenhood,"

Camelot (Columbia Masterworks), side 1. Copyright © 1960 by Alan Jay Lerner and Frederick Loewe. Chappell & Co., Inc., owner of publication and allied rights throughout the world. International Copyright Secured. *All rights reserved*. Used by permission.

47 Kate Millett notes that Norman Mailer uses the female reference to show contempt, *Sexual Politics* (New York: Doubleday & Company, 1970), p. 316, cited by Key, *Male/Female Language*, p. 94.

48 Graham, "The Making of a Nonsexist Dictionary," pp. 13–14.

49 Key, *Male/Female Language*, p. 58.

50 Graham, "The Making of a Nonsexist Dictionary," pp. 14–16.

51 Nilsen, "Sexism in English: A Feminist View," p. 262.

52 William Morris, ed., *The American Heritage Dictionary of the English Language* (Boston: American Heritage Publishing Company and Houghton Mifflin Company, 1969).

53 Stanley, "Paradigmatic Woman: The Prostitute."

54 Nilsen, "Sexism in English: A Feminist View," pp. 263 ff.

55 Lakoff, "Language and Woman's Place," pp. 63–64.

56 Key, *Male/Female Language*, p. 57.

57 Nilsen, "Sexism in English: A Feminist View," p. 263.

58 Lakoff, "Language and Woman's Place," pp. 61–62. Some of the sentences following are patterned after Lakoff's examples in her discussion.

59 Lakoff, "Language and Woman's Place," p. 60.

60 Faust, "Words That Oppress."

61 Stanley, "Paradigmatic Woman: The Prostitute."

62 Ibid.

63 Ibid.

64 Peter Fryer, *Mrs. Grundy: Studies in English Prudery* (London: Dennis Dobson, 1963), p. 75.

65 Edward Sagarin, *The Anatomy of Dirty Words*, p. 134.

66 Ibid., p. 129.

67 Stanley, "What's in a Label: The Politics of Naming."

68 Ibid.

69 Ethel Strainchamps, "Our Sexist Language," p. 244.

70 Stanley, "Paradigmatic Woman: The Prostitute."

71 Faust, "Words That Oppress."

72 Archaeological item suggested by an example from Stanley, "Prescribed Passivity: The Language of Sexism."

73 Graham, "The Making of a Nonsexist Dictionary," p. 16.

74 Ibid., p. 12.

75 Elizabeth Burr, Susan Dunn, and Norma Farquhar, "Women and the Language of Inequality," *Social Education* 36 (1972): 841. Reprinted with permission of the National Council for the Social Studies and Elizabeth Burr, Susan Dunn, and Norma Farquhar.

76 Lakoff, "Language and Woman's Place," pp. 74–75.

77 Nilsen, "The Correlation between Gender and Other Semantic Features in American English."

78 Barrie Thorne and Nancy Henley, "Difference and Dominance: An Overview of Language, Gender, and Society," in *Language and Sex: Difference and Dominance*, ed. Thorne and Henley (Rowley, Mass.: Newbury House, 1975), pp. 29–30.

79 Carole Schulte Johnson and Inga Kromann Kelly, "'He' and 'She': Changing Language to Fit a Changing World," *Educational Leadership* 32 (1975): 527–530.

80 Ibid, p. 528.

81 V. Kidd, "A Study of the Images Produced through the Use of the Male Pronoun as the Generic," *Moments in Contemporary Rhetoric and Communication* 1 (1971): 25–29.

82 J. Schneider and S. Hacker, "Sex Role Imagery and Use of the Generic 'Man' in

Introductory Texts: A Case in the Sociology of Sociology," *American Sociologist* 8 (1973): 12–18.

83 S. L. Bem and D. J. Bem, "Does Sex-Biased Job Advertising 'Aid and Abet' Sex Discrimination?" *Journal of Applied Social Psychology* 3 (1973): 6–18.

84 Paul Gray, "The Father Tongue," *Time,* 9 August 1976, p. 72. Reprinted by permission from *Time,* The Weekly Newsmagazine; Copyright Time Inc. 1976.

6 Silent sounds and secret messages

1 "The Sound of Silence," © 1964 Paul Simon. Used by permission.

2 Ray L. Birdwhistell, *Kinesics and Context* (Philadelphia: University of Pennsylvania Press, 1970), p. 176.

3 Michael V. Salter, H. Nicholson, M. Williams, and P. Burgess, "The Communication of Inferior and Superior Attitudes by Verbal and Nonverbal Signals," *British Journal of Social and Clinical Psychology* 9 (1970): 222–231.

4 Sigmund Freud, "Fragment of an Analysis of a Case of Hysteria (1905)," *Collected Papers Volume 3* (New York: Basic Books, 1959), cited by Mark Knapp, *Nonverbal Communication in Human Interaction* (New York: Holt, Rinehart & Winston, 1972), p. 103.

5 Nancy Henley, "Power, Sex, and Nonverbal Communication," *Berkeley Journal of Sociology* 18 (1973–74): 1–26.

6 Birdwhistell, *Kinesics and Context,* p. 54.

7 W. E. Galt, "The Male-Female Dichotomy in Human Behavior," *Psychiatry* 6 (1943): 9, cited by Henley, "Power, Sex, and Nonverbal Communication."

8 Michael Argyle, V. Salter, H. Nicholson, M. Williams, and P. Burgess, "The Communication of Inferior and Superior Attitudes by Verbal and Non-Verbal Signals," *British Journal of Social and Clinical Psychology* 9 (1970): 222–231.

9 Robert Rosenthal, Dane Archer, Judith Koivumaki, M. Robin DiMatteo, and Peter Rogers, "Assessing Sensitivity to Nonverbal Communication: The PONS Test," *Division 8 Newsletter* (Division of Personality and Social Psychology of the American Psychological Association, January, 1974), pp. 1–3. Reprinted by permission of Psychology Today Magazine. Copyright © 1974 Ziff-Davis Publishing Company.

10 Irene Hanson Frieze, "Nonverbal Aspects of Femininity and Masculinity Which Perpetuate Sex-Role Stereotypes" (Paper presented at Eastern Psychological Association, 1974), abstracted in *Language and Sex: Difference and Dominance,* ed. Barrie Thorne and Nancy Henley (Rowley, Mass.: Newbury House), pp. 290–291.

11 Robert Rosenthal et al., "Assessing Sensitivity to Nonverbal Communication: the PONS Test"; Robert Rosenthal et al., "Body Talk and Tone of Voice: The Language without Words," *Psychology Today* 8 (September 1974): 64–68.

12 Nancy Henley and Jo Freeman, "The Sexual Politics of Interpersonal Behavior," *Women: A Feminist Perspective,* ed. Jo Freeman (Palo Alto, Cal.: Mayfield Publishing Company, 1975), p. 392.

13 Michael Argyle, *The Psychology of Interpersonal Behavior* (Baltimore: Penguin Books, 1967), p. 115; William Libby, "Eye Contact and Direction of Looking as Stable Individual Differences," *Journal of Experimental Research in Personality* 4 (1970): 303–312; Ralph Exline, David Gray, and Dorothy Schuette, "Visual Behavior in a Dyad as Affected by Interview, Content, and Sex of Respondent," *Journal of Personality and Social Psychology* 1 (1965): 201–209.

14 Z. Rubin, "Measurement of Romantic Love," *Journal of Personality and Social Psychology* 16 (1970): 265–273; Exline, Gray, and Schuette, "Visual Behavior in a Dyad as Affected by Interview, Content, and Sex of Respondent," p. 207.

15 Ralph Exline, "Explorations in the Process of Person Perception: Visual Interaction in Relation to Competition, Sex, and Need for Affiliation," *Journal of Personality* 31 (1963): 18; Henley, "Power, Sex, and Nonverbal Communication," p. 14.

16 J. S. Efran and A. Broughton, "Effect of Expectancies for Social Approval on Visual Behavior," *Journal of Personality and Social Psychology* 4 (1966): 103–107.

17 Ralph Exline and L. C. Winter, "Affective Relations and Mutual Glances in Dyads," *Affect, Cognition, and Personality*, ed. S. S. Tomkins and C. E. Izard (New York: Springer Press, 1965).

18 Albert Mehrabian and John T. Friar, "Encoding of Attitude by a Seated Communicator via Posture and Position Cues," *Journal of Consulting and Clinical Psychology* 33 (1969): 330–336.

19 Carolyn M. Holstein, Joel W. Goldstein, and Daryl J. Bem, "The Importance of Expressive Behavior, Involvement, Sex, and Need-Approval in Inducing Liking," *Journal of Experimental Social Psychology* 7 (1971): 534–544.

20 Chris Kleinke, Armondo Busto, Frederick Meeker, and Richard Staneski, "Effects of Self-Attributed and Other-Attributed Gaze on Interpersonal Evaluations between Males and Females," *Journal of Experimental and Social Psychology* 9 (1973): 154–163.

21 Nancy Henley and Barrie Thorne, "Womanspeak and Manspeak: Sex Differences and Sexism in Communication, Verbal and Nonverbal," *Beyond Sex Roles*, ed. Alice Sargent (St. Paul, Minn.: West Publishing Company, 1977), p. 214; Lynn O'Connor, "Male Dominance: The Nitty Gritty of Oppression," *It Ain't Me Babe* 1 (1970): 9–11.

22 Exline, "Explorations in the Process of Person Perception," p. 3.

23 Henley, "Power, Sex, and Nonverbal Communication," p. 14.

24 Jane van Lawick-Goodall, *In the Shadow of Man* (Boston: Houghton Mifflin Company, 1971), pp. 244–247, 284–286.

25 P. C. Ellsworth, J. M. Carlsmith, and A. Henson, "The Stare as a Stimulus to Flight in Human Subjects: A Series of Field Experiments," *Journal of Personality and Social Psychology* 21 (1972): 302–311.

26 C. Hutt and C. Ounsted, "The Biological Significance of Gaze Aversion with Particular Reference to the Syndrome of Infantile Autism," *Behavioral Science* 11 (1966): 346–356; suggested by Henley, "Power, Sex, and Nonverbal Communication," as support for averted gaze as submissive.

27 Nancy Henley, *Body Politics: Power, Sex, and Nonverbal Communication* (Englewood Cliffs, N.J.: Prentice-Hall, 1977), pp. 163–166.

28 O'Connor, "Male Dominance: The Nitty-Gritty of Oppression," p. 9.

29 "Survey Finds Men Prefer Bosoms," *Dear Abby,* Abigail Van Buren, *The Arizona Republic*, 23 February 1976; "Women Notice Male Bodies Poll Shows," *Dear Abby,* Abigail Van Buren, *The Arizona Republic*, 1 March 1976.

30 "Women's Faces Show Emotions: Men Hide Theirs," *Phoenix Gazette,* 13 December 1974.

31 "Women Remember High School Classmates Better Than Men, Tests Show," *Phoenix Gazette*, 28 November 1974.

32 Goodall, *In the Shadow of Man*, p. 247.

33 R. J. Andrew, "The Origins of Facial Expressions," *Scientific American* 213 (1965): 88–94.

34 Jeanette Silveira, "Thoughts on the Politics of Touch," *Women's Press* 1 (Eugene, Oreg.: February 1972), p. 13.

35 Susan J. Beekman, "Sex Differences in Nonverbal Behavior" (Paper, Michigan State University, 1973).

36 Howard Rosenfeld, "Approval-Seeking and Approval-Inducing Functions of Verbal and Nonverbal Responses in the Dyad," *Journal of Personality and Social Psychology* 4 (1966): 597–605.

37 Daphne Bugental, J. W. Kaswan, L. R. Love, and M. N. Fox, "Child versus Adult Perception of Evaluation Messages in Verbal, Vocal, and Visual Channels," *Developmental Psychology* 2 (1970): 367–375.

38 Daphne Bugental, J. W. Kaswan, and L. R. Love, "Perception of Contradictory Meanings Conveyed by Verbal and Nonverbal Channels," *Journal of Personality and Social Psychology* 16 (1970): 647–655.

39 Daphne Bugental, L. R. Love, and R. M. Gianetto, "Perfidious Feminine Faces," *Journal of Personality and Social Psychology* 17 (1971): 314–318.

40 Phyllis Chesler, *Women and Madness* (New York: Doubleday & Company, 1972), pp. 278–279.

41 Henley, *Body Politics: Power, Sex, and Nonverbal Communication*, pp. 176–177.

42 Shulamith Firestone, *The Dialectic of Sex* (New York: William Morrow, 1970), p. 90.

43 Erving Goffman, "The Nature of Deference and Demeanor," *American Anthropologist* 58 (1956): 473–502; Erving Goffman, *Interaction Ritual* (New York: Doubleday & Co., Anchor Books, 1967), p. 78.

44 Birdwhistell, *Kinesics and Context*, p. 45.

45 Albert Mehrabian, "Significance of Posture and Position in the Communication of Attitude and Status Relationships," *Psychological Bulletin* 71 (1969): 359–372.

46 Albert Mehrabian, *Nonverbal Communication* (Chicago: Aldine Atherton, 1972), pp. 69–70.

47 Mehrabian and Friar, "Encoding of Attitude by a Seated Communicator via Posture and Position Cues," pp. 330–336.

48 Henley and Freeman, "The Sexual Politics of Interpersonal Behavior," p. 394.

49 Anonymous, "Exercises for Men," *Radical Therapist* 1 (1971): 15, reprinted in Thorne and Henley, *Language and Sex*, p. 297.

50 Henley and Freeman, "The Sexual Politics of Interpersonal Behavior," p. 400.

51 Irma Galejs, "Social Interaction of Preschool Children," *Home Economics Research Journal* 2 (1974): 153–159.

52 Rosenfeld, "Approval-Seeking and Approval-Inducing Functions of Verbal and Nonverbal Responses in the Dyad," p. 600.

53 Amram Scheinfeld, *Men and Women* (New York: Harcourt, Brace and Company, 1943), p. 200.

54 Paulette Peterson, "An Investigation of Sex Differences in Regard to Nonverbal Body Gestures," *Siscom '75: Women's (and Men's) Communication*, ed. Barbara Eakins, Gene Eakins, and Barbara Lieb-Brilhart (Falls Church, Va.: Speech Communication Association, 1976), pp. 20–27.

55 J. E. Singer, "The Use of Manipulative Strategies: Machiavellianism and Attractiveness," *Sociometry* 27 (1964): 128–151.

56 J. Mills and E. Aronson, "Opinion Change as a Function of the Communicator's Attractiveness and Desire to Influence," *Journal of Personality and Social Psychology* 1 (1965): 73–77.

57 R. N. Widgery and B. Webster, "The Effects of Physical Attractiveness upon Perceived Initial Credibility," *Michigan Speech Journal* 4 (1969): 9–15.

58 "Women Notice Male Bodies Poll Shows," *Dear Abby*, Abigail Van Buren, *The Arizona Republic*, 1 March 1976; "Survey Finds Men Prefer Bosoms," *Dear Abby*, Abigail Van Buren, *The Arizona Republic*, 23 February 1976.

59 "Self-Appointed Judges Rate Coeds; Lose Signs After Police Hassle," *State Press* (Arizona State University), 2 May 1975.

60 "Male Actors More Modest?" *Phoenix Gazette*, 1 May 1976.

61 Ellie Schultz, "Author Believes Pant Fashions Liberate Women," *Arizona Republic*, 10 November 1974.

62 W. L. O'Neill, *Everyone Was Brave: The Rise and Fall of Feminism* (Chicago: Quadrangle Books, 1969), p. 270, cited by Henley and Freeman, "The Sexual Politics of Interpersonal Behavior," p. 394.

63 Schultz, "Author Believes Pant Fashions Liberate Women."

64 Robert Sommer, *Personal Space* (Englewood Cliffs, N.J.: Prentice-Hall, 1969); Robert Sommer, "Studies in Personal Space," *Sociometry* 22 (1959): 247–260.

65 Frank N. Willis, Jr., "Initial Speaking Distance as a Function of the Speakers' Relationship," *Psychonomic Science* 5 (1966): 221–222; see also Darhl Pederson and Anne Heaston, "The Effects of Sex of Subject, Sex of Approaching Person, and Angle of Approach upon Personal Space," *Journal of Psychology* 82 (1972): 277–286; and Stanley Heshka and Yona Nelson, "Interpersonal Speaking Distance as a Function of Age, Sex, and Relationship," *Sociometry* 35 (1974): 92–104.

66 Teresa J. Rosegrant and James C. McCroskey, "The Effect of Race and Sex on Proxemics Behavior in an Interview Setting," *Southern Speech Communication Journal* 40 (Summer 1975): 408–420.

67 Julian J. Edney and Nancy Jordon-Edney, "Territorial Spacing on a Beach," *Sociometry* 37 (1974): 89–104.

68 Herbert Petri, Richard Huggins, Carol Mills, and Linda Barry, "Variables Influencing the Shape of Personal Space" (Paper delivered at the American Psychological Association Convention, August 1974, New Orleans).

69 J. L. Freedman, "The Crowd: Maybe Not So Madding After All," *Psychology Today* 4 (1971): 58–61, 86.

70 Frieze, "Nonverbal Aspects of Femininity and Masculinity Which Perpetuate Sex-Role Stereotypes."

71 Dale Lott and Robert Sommer, "Seating Arrangements and Status," *Journal of Personality and Social Psychology* 7 (1967): 90–95.

72 Silveira, "Thoughts on the Politics of Touch," p. 13.

73 Marge Piercy, *Small Changes* (New York: Doubleday & Company, 1973), p. 438, cited and quoted by Thorne and Henley, *Language and Sex: Difference and Dominance*, p. 296.

74 V. S. Clay, "The Effect of Culture on Mother-Child Tactile Communication," *Family Coordinator* 17 (1968): 204–210; S. Goldberg and M. Lewis, "Play Behavior in the Year-Old Infant: Early Sex Differences," *Child Development* 40 (1969): 21–31.

75 Sidney Jourard, "An Exploratory Study of Body Accessibility," *British Journal of Social and Clinical Psychology* 5 (1966): 221–231.

76 Signey Jourard and J. E. Rubin, "Self-Disclosure and Touching: A Study of Two Modes of Interpersonal Encounter and Their Inter-Relation," *Journal of Humanistic Psychology* 8 (1968): 39–48.

77 Henley, "Power, Sex, and Nonverbal Communication," pp. 10–11.

78 Goffman, *Interaction Ritual*, pp. 47–95; Goffman, "The Nature of Deference and Demeanor," pp. 473–502.

79 Nancy Henley, "Status and Sex: Some Touching Observations," *Bulletin of the Psychonomic Society* 2 (1973): 91–93.

80 Goodall, *In the Shadow of Man*, p. 244.

81 Nancy Henley, "The Politics of Touch," *Radical Psychology*, ed. P. Brown (New York: Harper and Row, Publishers, 1973), pp. 421–433.

82 Henley and Thorne, "Womanspeak and Manspeak: Sex Differences and Sexism in Communication, Verbal and Nonverbal," p. 215.

83 Henley, "The Politics of Touch."

84 O'Connor, "Male Dominance: The Nitty-Gritty of Oppression."

7   Speaking up: communicating with confidence

1 J. B. Priestley, "Journey down the Rainbow," *Saturday Review*, 18 August 1956, p. 35, cited by Carolyn G. Heilbrun, *Toward a Recognition of Androgyny* (New York: Alfred A. Knopf, 1973).

2 Nancy Faires Conklin, "Toward a Feminist Analysis of Linguistic Behavior," *The University of Michigan Papers in Women's Studies* 1 (1974): 51–73.

3 Ibid., pp. 51–73.

4 Elizabeth Burr, Susan Dunn, and Norma Farquhar, "Women and the Language of Inequality," *Social Education* 36 (1972): 842; "Guidelines for Equal Treatment of the Sexes in McGraw-Hill Book Company Publications" (New York: McGraw-Hill Book Company, n.d.)

5 Casey Miller and Kate Swift, "One Small Step for Genkind," *New York Times Magazine,* 16 April 1972, p. 36 (reprinted from *New York* Magazine, December 20, 1971); Dana Densmore, "Speech is the Form of Thought (KNOW, Inc., P.O. Box 86031, Pittsburgh, Pa. 15221, March 1970).

6 Alleen Pace Nilsen, "The Correlation between Gender and Other Semantic Features in American English" (Paper presented at Linguistic Society of America, December 1973).

7 Paul Gray, "The Father Tongue," *Time*, 9 August 1976, p. 72.

8 Alma Graham, "The Making of a Nonsexist Dictionary," *Ms.* 2 (December 1973): 13.

9 Many of these suggestions were taken from the following: Nancy Henley and Barrie Thorne, "Womanspeak and Manspeak: Sex Differences and Sexism in Communication, Verbal and Nonverbal," *Beyond Sex Roles*, ed. Alice Sargent (St. Paul, Minn.: West Publishing Company, 1977), p. 216; Nancy Henley, "Nonverbal Interaction and Personal Growth," *Siscom '75: Women's (and Men's) Communication*, ed. Barbara Eakins, Gene Eakins, and Barbara Lieb-Brilhart (Falls Church, Va.: Speech Communication Association, 1976), pp. 144–145; Nancy Henley, "Sounds of Silence," *Womankind* Television Series, Program 6, KAET-TV Channel 8, Arizona State University, 17 March 1976).

10 Henley, "Nonverbal Interaction and Personal Growth," pp. 144–145.

11 Henley, "Sounds of Silence."

12 Henley, "Nonverbal Interaction and Personal Growth," p. 145.

Index